50 Queer Lives

To my father for becoming a compassionate queer ally in his later years, and to my mother for her inspiring passion for life. To Yi Zhang for his unfaltering optimism, love and power to lift my spirits, and to Bain Duigan, instrumental in the conception of this book but no longer with us. And in memory of my dear friend, Sam Dunningham.

30 Queer Lives

Conversations with LGBTQIA+ New Zealanders

Matt McEvoy

MASSEY UNIVERSITY PRESS

Contents

Introduction

Before I began writing this book, I thought I had some understanding of the queer people of Aotearoa, having counted myself among them for decades.

As a gay Kiwi kid growing up through Auckland Catholic schools, books about All Blacks, Sir Edmund Hillary or wealthy businessmen were ubiquitous in the school library or bookshops, while stories about other New Zealanders were rarely, if ever, seen. My motley crew of friends and I wanted to read about New Zealanders we could relate to, but the singular elevation of the sports hero genre led to a sense of isolation, making us feel that perhaps we weren't 'real New Zealanders'.

The people you'll meet inside this book hail from a wide range of backgrounds of sexuality, gender, ethnicity and privilege, and they stretch the length of the country, from Panguru to Invercargill. Travelling across Aotearoa to bring their 30 stories together, meeting them and listening carefully to their life stories cut through landscapes of hardship and tragedy, love and triumph. As they opened a window to their interior worlds, each person I met expanded my own horizons and my understanding of the diversity of human experience.

Most of these people don't see themselves as role models, but to me they certainly are. The stories of what drives them to forge ahead in the face of numerous obstacles are told with honesty and generosity. They show us how to live with integrity, optimism, hope, determination and compassion. They refuse to fade into the background, or to maintain a self-defeating façade. Instead, they channel their energies into creating lives of meaning, creativity and authenticity.

The conversations that form the base of the stories in this book took place between 2018 and 2021. The pandemic meant that the intimacy of face-to-face was sometimes replaced by technology, but even then I found that the willingness of people to share their lives far outweighed an occasional lagging internet connection.

I wanted to provide a platform for people to tell their stories without interpretation or commentary. The first-person conversational style was the most intimate and direct way to achieve this, so that readers could feel as though they were sitting in the room with us, witnessing the conversation unfold. Before we began, I took care to make it clear to each person that it was fine to discuss only the parts of their lives that they felt comfortable talking about, and I also invited them to ask me anything at any time. If my interviewees were prepared to be open about personal, emotional aspects of their lives, then it was only fair that I should offer the same candour.

Our conversations were rich with insight and hard-won wisdom. Often there was laughter and sometimes tears, and always it was an immense privilege. I hope I've done justice to the trust they've placed in me.

Some of the older people interviewed for this book told me that they've been astonished to see the progress that's been achieved over their lifetimes. As the saying goes, we see further when we stand on the shoulders of giants. In Aotearoa we remember people of mana such as Ngahuia Te Awekotuku, who created one of our first gay liberation groups in the 1970s, when her travel visa was suspended on grounds of 'sexual deviance'; Carmen Rupe and Georgina Beyer, the groundbreaking transgender icons and activists; and Fran Wilde for her promotion of the Homosexual Law Reform Bill in 1986, which precipitated a more confident LGBTQIA+ community, one in which Rainbow Youth could be founded in 1989 and the hugely popular Hero parades, often attended by prime ministers of the day, could run throughout the 1990s. Louisa Wall's Civil Union Bill in 2004 led to the celebration of full marriage equality in 2013. As I write, New Zealand has the queerest parliament in the world, and the gay conversion therapy ban has passed its first reading.

But for all there is to celebrate, there remains much to fight for. Queer people are more likely to suffer from isolation, we are over-represented in mental health and suicide numbers, and some of us are still pushed away from our families as we simply attempt to live authentic lives.

We do not exist in separate silos, and our identities are not limited to one facet or aspect. Our experience of the world is shaped by myriad intersections — of race, gender, sexuality, disability, culture, age and economic status. In this book Takunda Muzondiwa talks about her Zimbabwean Christian family, Grant Robertson tells of life as a queer man and rugby fan at the highest levels of public service and scrutiny, Nathan Joe discusses being Asian and gay in Christchurch, Henrietta Bollinger recounts life at the intersection of disability and queerness, Leilani Tominiko relates being a transgender Samoan Kiwi in the world of wresting, and Ariki Brightwell considers the impacts of colonisation on Māori attitudes to queerness.

The book has revealed acceptance in unexpected places. Rural Southland and the New Zealand military upend their image as conservative bastions while the Royal New Zealand Ballet, despite being welcoming of queer dancers and choreographers, still finds the telling of queer stories a challenge.

I hope this book encourages empathy and understanding, challenges stereotypes of what a queer life can be, and offers courage and hope to people struggling in their own lives. Although this book is now complete, I've come to see that learning from each other is a lifelong project. Everyone has a story, everyone's life has something to teach us, if only we have the sensitivity to ask the right questions and take the time to listen.

Most of all, writing this book has taught me that despite all our uniqueness, what we have in common is much stronger than our differences. I hope the stories in this book help you find the courage and inspiration to show your own true colors.

Matt McEvoy
Auckland
October 2021

Grant Robertson

Grant Robertson is New Zealand's Deputy Prime Minister, the MP for Wellington Central, the Minister of Finance, and Minister for Infrastructure, Racing, and Sport and Recreation. He was first elected to Parliament in 2008.

D ad decided in his mid-thirties that he wanted to get out of banking and become a minister — a Presbyterian minister not a government minister — so we moved to Dunedin from Palmerston North for his religious training. I was about six years old. Our social life consisted of church families and kids at the youth group. Dad was also a rugby referee and, for me, going to Carisbrook, the stadium not far from where we lived, was the non-church part of my weekend. I'm the youngest of three boys, so I'd tag along with my brothers to sit and watch games all day. I was obsessed with it and could name all the players. Rugby was a big thing; my eldest brother never played but my middle brother and I did. The blokey stereotypes of New Zealand men were all around me in the seventies and eighties, and I certainly sensed this, although I never felt that I couldn't be myself; I wasn't put in a box by my parents, never told what I had to be, and I still love rugby.

It was quite a traditional religious upbringing, but not evangelical — Mum was more concerned with social justice than Christian doctrine. A group of families sponsored a Polish refugee family to come and live in New Zealand, however I certainly saw the other side of the church during the Homosexual Law Reform debate. I have a vivid memory of being at a church rafting picnic when a petition *against* the reform was being handed around for signatures. Yes, most people signed it; it was enthusiastically received. That was the mid-eighties, and I was about 14 years old. I respect the social values I grew up with, but the realisation that a large group within my own community was so conservative and unwilling to support the rights of gay people struck me very hard.

At home, Mum and Dad were on opposite sides of the homosexual law reform issue. I remember some vigorous dinner table debates that caused friction. Dad was more traditional than Mum and he was against the law reform, and yet later in life he was enormously supportive of me. When I was moving out of home years later, and going through all these boxes of things I'd kept, I found some old newspaper clippings showing which way Parliament members had voted. I don't remember keeping them, but clearly it was important to me and it shows the whole issue was very live in my mind even as a teenager. I stopped going to church soon after. The church has struggled over the years with gay issues and ordaining gay ministers; to this day they still haven't sorted it out. My mother was an archivist for them for 25 years, so I was kept abreast of the ongoing debates.

Although the church was difficult, I owe a lot to those values of social justice that were taught. In my maiden speech in Parliament in 2008, I referenced some of what my mother instilled in my brothers and me: that we should treat others as we'd wish to be treated; we are our brothers' and sisters' keepers; work hard and you'll do well — that Calvinist tradition creeping in. At the same time, I was certainly aware of the church being a negative force in terms of human rights.

King's High School in Dunedin was a lower-income working-class school. I do have to sometimes clarify to people that it was quite the opposite of King's College, Auckland. Through those years, I was becoming aware of my sexuality, which was difficult in a conservative, boys-only environment. The reform bill being such a prominent news story pushed me to wonder if it was me they were talking about on TV and the radio, but most of the gay stereotypes I was seeing didn't feel like me at all. I went through phases of feeling different, but then thinking that maybe everyone feels like this and eventually I'll like girls.

That waxed and waned until I was about 16. By then I was quite sure I was gay and eventually I told one or two close friends, which led to a particularly unfortunate incident. There was a big house party and I wasn't invited, which was unusual. I decided to go anyway and in a reckless moment of self-indulgence, I bought a bottle of gin and proceeded to drink the whole thing on the way there. By the time I arrived, I was completely off my face. On the front door of the house was a note saying 'no fags'. I don't remember much after that, but apparently I let fly at a few people. The host called my parents to come and get me. I got home and was violently ill.

I probably should have come out to my parents then, but I didn't because I was just so embarrassed about the whole thing. The rest of that year was a struggle with worrying about who knew and who didn't, and I withdrew deeply into myself. I tried to put all those anxieties in a box, and focus on study and not think about it. When I became head boy at King's, I took girls to the formal balls.

At Otago University I did a politics degree. It was good because I met other gay people living normal lives and learnt more about it. In my second year I moved into a flat and everyone in my circle knew. So I thought, I have to come out to my parents now. I organised to come home for dinner on a Sunday night to tell them. Events did not go according to plan. I got a call from Mum the day before the dinner saying she was upset and needed to come and see me. I immediately thought someone had told her, but actually it was much worse. My father had been arrested for theft as a public servant. As an accountant, he'd been stealing clients' money for a long time. It was a complete shock to the family — and also meant I parked the coming out till a little later.

Dad went to prison. While he was in there, I finally told Mum. She obviously knew, as mothers do. Some of her first words were 'don't get AIDS', which I suppose was understandable in 1992. I told Dad when he was released from prison. He was a bit annoyed because he'd heard rumours through people he knew at university and thought I should have told him, but he was incredibly supportive after that. So, I didn't get to come out in quite the manner I'd planned.

I became president of the Otago University Students' Association in my third year, and then president of the New Zealand Union of Students. Jim Bolger was prime minister at the time; he referred to me as a fulltime paid-troublemaker. That was definitely a career highlight. How radical was I? Well, the International Socialists criticised me for not being radical enough while the Young Nats thought I was the harbinger of all evil, so it felt like I was getting the balance about right. I've always been on the left, always believed in the power of institutions to make change. Our focus was on student welfare: fees had increased sharply while allowances were being cut back. We led occupations at every university in the country in 1996, and kept student issues on the agenda until the Clark government came in and made some of those changes we'd fought for.

After graduating, I was recruited by the Ministry of Foreign Affairs. Being a National government, I was a little surprised they hired me, but to their credit they wanted more diversity in the diplomatic ranks and so I was posted off to Sāmoa to manage New Zealand's aid programme, and to see that it was used effectively for basic education, women's empowerment and healthcare.

My next posting was to the United Nations in New York. It was spectacular for both my career and my queer life. I'd only been to a few gay places before, like Casper's Bar in Wellington and the Staircase and

Legend clubs on Karangahape Road. In New York I enjoyed the huge dance parties but felt more comfortable in slightly grungier bars in the East Village, with their jukeboxes playing the alternative music I liked. And by then I'd met Alf. In 1998, a friend, Dean Knight, was assembling a rugby team called the Krazy Knights to play a match against the Ponsonby Heroes, the world's first inter-gay rugby match. Dean's a law lecturer at Victoria University now and still active in gay issues, but I wasn't easy to recruit; it took a lot of persuading. I loved rugby but my previous experience of rugby culture wasn't great and I'd stopped playing because of the distasteful, homophobic macho culture — and I was older and didn't want to get hurt.

But Dean persisted, agreeing to let me play number 8, so I finally caved and said yes. It was brilliant fun. It allowed me to finish my rugby career in an enjoyable setting, while other guys got to exorcise emotional demons they still felt from being excluded from rugby all through school. Alf was the halfback; 10 years later we had our civil union in front of a Presbyterian minister, and now I'm the Minister for Sport it feels like parts of my life have come full circle.

One of the proudest achievements of my career was at the UN in New York. Alf joined me there about a year later. I was often invited to diplomatic dinners and most people would bring their spouse. I asked around and discovered there was something called the 'blue book', which named every diplomat at the United Nations, their nationality and the name of their spouse, and was used to help organise official UN events and dinner invitations. Alf was not listed alongside my name as my spouse.

When it was time for the new year's blue book to be produced, I asked them to list Alf Kawai, but they said that's not possible because the United States doesn't recognise same-sex relationships. I challenged them on this discrimination; it took stubborn persistence, but I won. They finally relented, changing UN diplomatic protocol and listing Alf's name with mine. As soon as it happened, there was a wave of congratulatory phone calls and meeting requests from diplomats across the UN.

As finance minister, there's not usually a partner invited to meetings, but attending sporting events, I'm often expected to bring a partner. People have always been fantastic about making Alf feel welcome; he is a private person so he doesn't chase opportunities to attend events, but where there's a good case for it we're not shy. I do realise I'm a white male in a position of status and so our experiences would seem effortless compared to others in the queer community.

Was I worried about people's reaction to a minister of sport being gay? No, I asked for the job. I said to Jacinda, I really want the sports portfolio. I believe there's an overemphasis on sport in New Zealand. We don't have a good balance; we should value our arts and culture much more, particularly in boys' schools like the one I went to. The government is trying to address this in the way we diversify the honours system to be not only sport and business, so people such as Annie Crummer, the Topp Twins and Joy Cowley have been honoured in recent years. Theatres and performing arts venues are vitally important creative places where non-conforming people of all varieties can be themselves and explore their talents.

I don't think sport is the only driver of the aggressive macho culture in New Zealand, but it's certainly wrapped up in the same cultural fabric. The whole idea of the archetypal Kiwi bloke being a fearless stoic is slowly changing with the likes of John Kirwan's openness about mental health and depression, but the stereotype remains and it does make it hard for young men to talk about problems and emotions. It's still seen as unmanly to ask for help, an admission of vulnerability. There were times when I wasn't able to articulate my own feelings, which probably led to a period of drinking too much at university. We can't separate sport from politics because they're both part of our country's identity.

A problem occurs when a public clash of beliefs results in hurtful rhetoric, such as when Israel Folau made those comments ['God's plan for homosexuals is HELL . . . unless they repent of their sins']. This was an important moment for New Zealand rugby and I was encouraged by the many sportspeople who stood up and said they didn't agree with such damaging comments. Some of the All Blacks wore rainbow-coloured laces in solidarity with queer people, and it was uplifting to have those guys say 'its OK to be you'. TJ Perenara, the All Blacks halfback at the time, said Polynesian sexuality had always traditionally been diverse and I think he donated some money to gay rugby teams.

Music has been a big part of my life; my mother played guitar and piano and there was always music around the house. Unfortunately, I myself am tone-deaf and can't play an instrument or sing, but at uni in Dunedin I'd be out watching bands every weekend: The Chills, The Bats, The Clean, Straitjacket Fits. Brilliant times. And if you can't actually play music, one way into the music scene is to carry around the sound gear, so that's what I did. Then I learnt to do the lighting, and from there I started managing bands, such as a band Matt Heath was in called Kid Eternity, and a novelty band that accidentally became quite popular called Too Many Daves. There's some truly dreadful footage of me on YouTube where I'm bouncing around the Empire Tavern with them, singing a song called 'Bollocks to the Real World'.

I think being queer inclines people towards the liberal, progressive end of the political spectrum, which has been the strongest supporter of minorities and social progress. But as barriers are broken, some within the community often move to more conservative positions. The gay male community has always had a strong libertarian streak and since decriminalisation in 1986, this has become more apparent. The lesbian community has remained champions of social equality and maintained strong links to the left and activist groups. Labour has traditionally been good at embracing social causes and equality as an objective. I would still ask gay men, having achieved a number of milestones that make life easier for themselves, to have a sense of responsibility to their community and please not to forget others who are struggling.

We definitely still need places that represent queer culture, whether it's a bar or in films or books; equally, people should feel comfortable walking down the street holding hands — that shouldn't have to be only in a queer space. While we've made great progress in my lifetime, as a white homosexual male many obstacles have been removed for me that still exist for others in the queer community. For some people it still hasn't got better, I'm very aware of that. We have to keep supporting them.

Occasionally, I do have a moment where I step back and consider where I am — budget days, for example; billions of dollars that is not just dollars and cents but people's lives. At those times, I realise the privilege and responsibility of the job. We all have moments of self-doubt, we shouldn't deny that. Every time we're faced with a new challenge, we should expect some uncertainty, and not pretend we're superheroes but realise that we're humans with frailties and anxieties.

I feel optimistic about the future of New Zealand and its queer people, but we can't pat ourselves on the back now that we have marriage equality and say we're done. It's a long path before everyone in society is accepted and has the freedom to be themselves, but I have confidence. I see us on a journey from tolerance to acceptance, and then to the embracing of queer people. The further we travel down that path, the better the world we'll be living in.

Takunda Muzondiwa

Takunda Muzondiwa is a performance artist and poet from Zimbabwe. She is best known for her speech at the 2019 Race and Unity Speech Awards, the video of which made global headlines and has been viewed over one million times.

My name, Takunda, translates as 'we have overcome', meaning a victory which is communal. My Zimbabwean culture is rooted in traditions of cooperation and kinship over individual aspiration and success. Sixteen languages are spoken in Zimbabwe; someone who only speaks one would be seen as unusual. I grew up speaking Shona, Ndebele and English, and later I learnt French and now te reo Māori. African languages are some of the most beautiful in the world; sonically they are so rich and captivating. It's a shame we don't often hear them in Aotearoa.

I had the best time as a kid in Zim. It was so carefree with a big family and close friendships. The sun was always out so I would play late into the evenings with friends, and thankfully there was no social media. The Zimbabwean economy was a mess when I was at primary school. I remember how at the end of class each day, our teachers would start selling us chewing gum, bags of chips and ice-blocks, undercutting the tuckshop prices to make some extra money. The school only found out what the teachers were up to when they noticed no one was buying snacks at the tuckshop anymore.

In the evenings our family gathered at home to cook together, then we would clean up together and sit around a fire and discuss the day's events. To me, my mother's sisters were on the same level as my mum — we don't have the Western concept of two parents having ownership over a child, and care of children is distributed throughout the wider family. Our language has words that reflect that shared care: Little Mum (Mainini) for a mother's younger sisters, and Big Mum (Maiguru) for her older sisters. It is very common to have big families. My mother has 12 siblings and my father is the youngest of 15. In Western culture, with its small nuclear families, there are fewer people to lean on and learn from. I often wonder if that could be one reason for the mental health problems in Western countries.

Church was where the community gathered to worship and socialise. It held extra weight for my family because my father was the pastor. Seeing him standing in front of the congregation from as early as I can remember must have inspired me towards the poetry and speeches I do today. Music and dance were always threaded through our church services, and at any time we could be chosen to stand up to perform a solo song or dance in front of everyone. There was no standing quietly in the back — if we were chosen we had to do it. That was quite harrowing for young Takunda, but it gave me confidence in front of a crowd that has been useful in my life many times since.

My family life in Zimbabwe was stable and happy, but outside of my childhood world, the country was becoming increasingly difficult. There were international sanctions because of Mugabe's corrupt elections, political violence and growing food shortages. My parents could see it wasn't a place which could provide opportunities for their children to flourish. I was five when they made the difficult and painful decision to emigrate, leaving Zimbabwe and all our family behind. Mum left first and I didn't see her again for nearly two years. In the mid-2000s New Zealand was suffering from a severe shortage of hospital nurses. My mother, who was a trained nurse, was granted a work visa and left Zimbabwe from Harare Airport, bound for New Zealand.

It was a lonely grind for Mum; she didn't know a single person in her new country. I always thought her English was perfect but New Zealanders thought it was broken English. Mum found a tiny room in a boarding house and took four jobs. Everything was about saving money to get my father, my older sister and me to New Zealand. She finished working well after the buses had stopped running and so she would walk home for a few hours' sleep before getting up to go to work again. She had three outfits that she wore on rotation until they began to disintegrate.

People from church helped her, and they would have helped her much earlier but she didn't feel comfortable to ask. It must have been so euphoric for her when she'd finally saved the money to get us here. I was seven when I arrived in Auckland with my dad and older sister, nearly two years after Mum. I've only recently come to understand what she went through to lay down the foundations of our new life. I don't know if I'd have had the strength to do what she did.

My big sister was thrilled about moving to New Zealand, but I was dreading it, crying and screaming every day. I was excited to see my mother, but I was so anxious about leaving Zimbabwe. At our first school in Manurewa my sister was a social butterfly. Making new friends was a breeze for her, and all the teachers loved her. I was shy and awkward, and being one of the only two black kids in the whole school made me feel vulnerable, like all eyes were on me. I didn't complain though. We were getting a better education and were living the life our parents wanted for us. Also, our fridge was full of food.

Immigrant families place a high value on attaining material wellbeing in their new country. My family poured our energies into work and education to achieve a stable life with houses and careers, but I think our emotional and mental wellbeing were neglected. Being pulled away from family and severing connections to our culture put us in a perpetual state of longing. This has weighed on me over time, and I could see that my parents were often lonely.

After a few years in Manurewa, we moved to the tiny town of Inglewood in Taranaki, where Dad was to become the new Methodist pastor. Inglewood had a population of only about 3000 people, and we were the only black family in town. One girl at Inglewood was so lovely to me. She's still my best friend now, and we go to the same university in Auckland. She would go home and learn little bits of Shona and surprise me the next day. It was really cute. Her family welcomed my whole family and helped us feel at home. My parents had friends for the first time outside Zimbabwe. My experiences in Inglewood meant that when I moved back to Auckland to start high school, it still wasn't easy, but I was in a better place to stand up for myself.

Mount Albert Grammar is one of the biggest schools in New Zealand; it has about as many students as Inglewood has people. I wasn't the only black person in the school this time — there were a few kids who looked like me — but I still felt very foreign. The presence of African people in this country is very recent so we're still building a familiarity. Racist comments were thrown at me and, as in Inglewood, teachers didn't know how to deal with it, but I had a tight group of friends and I stood stronger and more true in myself, which was an armour against ignorant people.

I was known for being an arty theatre kid at MAGs. I would dive into anything to do with the arts, and I signed up for every play or acting competition. I learnt French, and I went to France for an exchange trip, staying with a family in a wealthy area just outside Paris. They simply refused to speak to me in English; if I did, they just wouldn't respond. It was frustrating for a few weeks, but by the end of the trip I was thinking and dreaming in French. I'd love to go back and live there one day.

As a student I was an anxious overachiever. I think that's common among immigrant children who feel the weight of parental expectations. We don't want their hard work to be wasted. Being one of the only black kids at school I felt like everything I did was amplified to represent the whole community of black people in Auckland, so I was desperate not to fail at anything.

One day when I was on summer holiday before my final year at Grammar, the phone rang. My sister picked it up and told me that the headmaster wanted to speak to me. I thought, 'Oh my God, this must be serious. What have I done?' All the scenarios were spinning around in my head. He said, 'Hello Takunda. I'm calling to offer you the position of Head Girl for 2017.'

I was silent for what felt like an age, absorbing the shock. Finally I gathered my emotions enough to get a few words out. 'Yes, I'd be glad to accept,' I told him. I hung up the phone and fell to the floor crying. Dad came down to see what had happened, and when I told him the news that was the first time I'd ever seen him cry. (I did many things that made him proud that year so I became more used to seeing him cry.) When Mum came home from work Dad said, 'Takunda has some news.' After I told her we all cried and hugged each other. Seeing my parents' reactions that day is one of the fondest memories of my life.

I first became aware of sexuality at primary school. I was what people call a tomboy and I got teased for being a lesbian. I only had one good friend. We would hold hands and kiss on the cheek which felt like what a friendship should be. I feel that it's natural to be in deep infatuation with our friends, and it doesn't mean there is a repressed sexual longing. I've never felt that a sexual relationship has to be the highest, most sacred form of relationship.

My reaction to being called a lesbian was volatile. I got upset and said, no, I'm straight. My upbringing in Zimbabwe was socially conservative.

Christianity, which was imported through colonisation, has turned people away from their original traditions. Before Europeans arrived in Zimbabwe, gender and sexual fluidity was a natural part of life. Christianity stripped all that away and made it seem that homophobia is an intrinsic part of African culture, which is not correct at all. When I was younger I suffered from negative beliefs towards queer people.

At high school many of my friends were queer, and as I watched them come out to their families and receive love and acceptance, I was happy for them but also a bit resentful. I felt like I deserved that too, but I knew it wasn't going to be like that for me. Being queer became a charged and pervasive issue for me. I was becoming very anxious about it; living freely and holistically coming out was something I had to do.

My diary was filled with screeds of thoughts and worries about coming out. I decided to set myself a series of dates to tell people, starting with my friends. I noted the dates in my diary to make them concrete and binding. All my friends were wonderful and happy for me; they made me feel safe. I chose to identify with the term queer. I'd rather not have any label, but that seemed the best one. For a lot of non-queer people, their limited understanding of bisexuality within a heteronormative society confines bisexuality to a gender binary. I do not think this myself, but I know it to be the understanding held by many others and I did not want to have to explain every time I came out that I was capable of loving all genders or non-gender conforming. Queer feels like a broad all-encompassing term so I hope people will just think she likes what she likes, and not get too hung-up on the details.

The next diary date was with my sister. I'd told my friends the date so it couldn't be escaped. Every waking hour leading up to the day I was thinking about it. I didn't want her to see me differently; I still wanted to be her little sister. When I called her, bawling my eyes out, she was worried something terrible had happened. I said, 'I'm so scared, I think God hates me, please be OK with this, I think I'm queer.' My sister said,

'Oh Takunda, don't worry, I've known that for years, I still love you and God still loves you. You're perfect the way you are.' My sister is the most kind-hearted person you'd ever meet. I look up to her in so many ways. She gave me peace and set me at ease, and her fiancé was also lovely.

In the middle of all this, I entered a speech competition for Race Unity, and the video of my speech about racism in Aotearoa was picked up by *The Guardian* and went viral, quickly getting over a million views. The speech had nothing to do with queer issues at all, but the comments section was flooded with horrible comments about my sexuality, things like: 'Lesbians should burn in hell', 'She needs a man to set her straight.' I didn't understand where that came from; it was scary.

I was terrified my parents and relatives would see the comments and start questioning me; I spent literally hours every day reporting the comments to get them removed.

In time, the frenzy surrounding the video subsided. I had so many opportunities from it. There were jobs I did for Google, I was invited to Parliament, and went to Zimbabwe on a speaking tour of schools. My parents were overjoyed. Dad would ask me to write poems for him. I was super close to them at that time, but all the while there was a constant underlying anxiety about my sexuality. I worried that if I told them it would rob them of their happiness and sour our relationship.

A few years ago, I moved to a new home where it felt like I could finally breathe and live my truth, unapologetically. I've had to relearn what family means to me. My sister says that friends can become my new family, and they do tell me I'm their family, which is beautiful, but it's not the same. I can't speak Shona with them, and they don't really understand my culture and foundational experiences. Immigrant queer people with religious families often still have to sever these links when they come out.

I've been building relationships with a small group of queer people of colour. We have a shared story in common which gives us a powerful connection. There is a vitality to people like me coming out. It's a kind of exposure therapy for African people, and it shows them that queer people do come from African communities.

I'm a hopeful, optimistic person. Although colonisation erased our old enlightened beliefs about queer people, we lived without prejudice before and so we can do so again. We can heal the deep scar left by colonisation through reconnecting with our old knowledge. For example, Zimbabwean languages do not separate genders: everyone is 'they'. That alone speaks volumes about our authentic culture.

My mother and father love me very deeply, I have no doubt about that. I'm not angry with them. I've learnt to understand them, which has brought me peace. I don't hold myself in higher regard to them. If I was born at the same time, raised by the same people, socialised in the same environment, it's very likely I would hold the same beliefs. Time will heal these wounds, but I'm impatient, and I miss them so much.

I feel I'm living an authentic life now. It started with being honest with myself, then with those around me. Being honest about my passions without limitations, that's what opened my heart and freed me. There's nothing anyone can say about me that I haven't been honest and open about myself.

At my core I'm an artist, and the reason I study law and Māori studies is because I think people themselves are complex and fascinating, like works of art. With law and Māori, I want to gain an understanding of Aotearoa's culture and the institutions we live under so I can work with people in an empathetic way. I'm leaning towards child and family law. I love children; they deserve all the protection society can give them. With my acting and poetry, I'll continue to interpret and illustrate the human experience in ways which I hope can touch people's hearts. That's what feels authentic and helps me create a fulfilling, meaningful life.

Leilani Tominiko

Leilani Tominiko, aka Candy Lee, is New Zealand's first transgender professional wrestler. She made her wrestling debut in 2016, and in 2017 she became the first transgender woman to win a major indie women's title, with the Impact Pro Wrestling Women's Championship.

Wrestling is a mix of athletics and soap opera. You have to be fit and strong and a confident performer. My wrestling character is Candy Lee; her signature moves are the Candy Crush and the Gobstopper. I save the Candy Crush for right at the end of a match when I'm ready to win and need a dramatic finale. I grab my opponent, lift them up and slam them down on their backs while I trap their legs.

When I first saw wrestling on TV as a kid I just loved the showy drama. It was all men's matches back then, until I found out women could also compete. To me, the women were like warrior princesses with all the pageantry and glamour. I told myself I would grow up to be a wrestler one day.

My parents moved to New Zealand when I was five to find a better future for the family and for educational opportunities that didn't exist in Sāmoa. I'm one of nine kids — seven brothers and one sister. I'm in the middle. We moved straight to West Auckland, and I've lived there ever since. I'm close to my sister, probably since she's the only girl, and also to my little brother. I was a shy kid. I didn't really talk, and I always gravitated to groups of girls. Growing up, people would ask my mum or me if I was a boy or a girl — even when I had short hair and dressed like a boy. It was very awkward. Dad would cut our hair all at the same time, all in the same style, which I didn't like.

My parents wanted us to go to a religious school, so I went to Liston College, a Catholic boys' college. I hated it. The boys were really mean. I wasn't out as trans, but I still got picked on straightaway — 'faggot, fa'afafine, afro' — I'd get these taunts all the time. I desperately wanted to leave Liston but my parents wouldn't let me. One day, school was so bad I just decided to walk out and not go back. I ran away to a friend's house, but that lasted only two weeks because I missed my family.

> I'd gone through life being confused about my own situation but then to find other people with similar experiences gave me comfort and confidence.

I'd always felt different, but I couldn't explain it. I didn't know anything about trans people or transitioning. A neighbour went to Kelston Girls' College, which was known for having quite a few trans and fa'afafine kids, and after she had introduced me to some, I began to learn more. Finally, my parents let me change schools. This was a turning point because I met a good trans friend there. Together we went to see the school nurse, who was so great. She told us about hormone therapy and how to start the transition process if we decided to. We were referred to a clinic for youth and trans kids, and we both started on hormones at the same time. It helps so much to have someone to go through the process with you. I'd gone through life being confused about my own situation but then to find other people with similar experiences gave me comfort and confidence.

Throughout those years, I'd never stopped loving wrestling, watching my favourite characters and hoping I'd be part of it one day. After high school, I worked in a jewellery shop, and one slow afternoon I remember I researched wrestling in New Zealand on the internet. That was when I realised that I didn't have to move to America to get into the sport; there were trainers right here in Auckland. I visited a training gym close to our house and they welcomed me in straightaway.

When you start out in wrestling, you have to decide if you want to be a goodie or a baddie. Obviously, Candy Lee is a goodie; she's so sweet. Then you create your character's personality: how they walk and talk, their own special signature moves, like my Candy Crush. I wish I could make my own outfits, but I can't sew; luckily, I have friends who draw up cool designs and then I send them to a costume maker who works with spandex. The promoters work on a story for each of their wrestlers. When I prepare for a match, I fully become my character and act out her storyline. The year builds up to the big Nightmare Before Christmas show, where either there is a conclusion or it's a cliff-hanger, like the final *Shortland Street* episode of the year.

My debut as a wrestler was scary. I wasn't ready. I'd been training for about a year but I still didn't feel confident enough to get in the ring in front of a crowd, my outfit and character weren't fully created, and it was all rushed and I was anxious. Being in front of a live, noisy crowd is a vulnerable place to be, and there were ignorant guys in the audience calling me names. People are sometimes nasty to me — that's just life as a trans person, it's happened all my life so it's not surprising that it also takes place in the sport I'm passionate about — but after I'd had a few matches, people could see the pride I have in my identity and that I wasn't going to quit over some stupid name-calling. I've had the last laugh because now I'm the New Zealand women's champion — also my outfits are a hundred per cent better.

Being a wrestler is like having two personalities: you have this alter ego, a creative, healthy way to express another side of yourself. I find it quite easy to channel Candy, and when it comes time to switch her on, I turn up the personality and attitude; sassy but sweet.

People often ask me whether trans women have an unfair advantage in sport. In wrestling the winner is predetermined so it isn't an issue; perhaps it depends on the sport. There's an assumption that being male is always an advantage, which isn't true. Some sports require you to take a test for testosterone to 'catch out' trans women, but studies show that men don't always have more testosterone than women, so I feel it's a tricky subject.

I'm proud of my trans identity and my Samoan heritage, but before I identify as fa'afafine or trans, I just identify as a young woman.

Worrying about my outside not reflecting how I feel on the inside adds a lot of anxiety to my life and it's why I decided to transition. Not appearing feminine enough is one of my biggest concerns. I live my life as a girl and I'm in the wrestling ring as a woman, so I want to fit in. I spent a long time talking to doctors about it, so I'm quite OK about discussing it now, although it's not something

I bring up immediately on first dates. It can be awkward to explain it all to new people. The perception of trans people can be very narrow and basic — for example, they think that if one trans person is a sex worker, we're all sex workers. It's just ridiculous. We're all individuals, the same as everyone else.

My dad and brothers didn't like me being effeminate when I was young, but Mum was always supportive and she turned the family around. Now they accept me for who I am, and my brothers defend me when people throw hate at me. I'm proud of my trans identity and my Samoan heritage, but before I identify as fa'afafine or trans, I just identify as a young woman.

The transitioning process is a long journey, it's not as easy as just taking a few pills that will turn you into a woman overnight. I think some young people don't understand that. It's a long process, it takes time, but it's definitely been worth it for me. People can still be nasty but I've grown a thick skin over the years. It happens less often now, and that can make it more upsetting because suddenly I'm taken right back to those horrible high-school bullying days. Those ignorant people never have anything new to say; I've heard it all before.

I guess I'm happy now. In the back of my mind I know that for a trans girl finding love isn't going to be the same as for other girls, so that upsets me sometimes. I try not to dwell on dating and that stuff, instead I focus on my wrestling. That's what makes me happy so I want to do it as much as I can. Making a career out of wrestling would be amazing. I'd love to give back to my parents for all their support. I had to cancel plans to wrestle at events in Australia and Chicago because of Covid, but I've been invited back again so it's an exciting time.

My hope is that people chase what they're passionate about in life. Don't let your queer identity hold you back. Don't think that you can't do this or that because you're queer — get that out of your head. You're as good as anyone else. Just go for it.

Nathan Joe

Nathan Joe is an Ōtautahi Christchurch-based award-winning Chinese-Kiwi playwright and performance poet. He also works as a dramaturge.

Theatre helped me discover my authentic self; it drew out my exuberance and uncovered my voice. That's the beautiful thing about writing and performing — it allows us to show our eccentricities and queerness. The parts of ourselves we dampen down in 'normal' society for fear of seeming weird suddenly become valuable creative gifts in the world of performing arts. As I learnt more about writing and the stage, experimented with inhabiting different characters and often amplified or heightened aspects of myself, I discovered my extroversion and the confidence that my voice was worthy of being heard. But, you know, I think everyone has a story worth telling if you dig deep enough — you just have to ask the right questions.

The impulse to write wells up from things I'm not brave enough to say offstage, uncomfortable themes that insist on being explored, anxieties I'm desperate to cast loose into the world. Then I listen for the missing voices, where I feel there's a gap in the stories being told and characters who get to speak. Often, I find it's my own voice that is missing — the queer or Asian voice — so that guides the stories I write.

Asian artists and theatre producers are still new in non-Asian countries. There are very few Asian actors, especially Asian male actors, and even fewer Asian queer actors, not enough to write for. So, there are not many stories that get written, and the ones that do lack depth. They're usually narrow, immigrant-assimilation narratives where being Asian is always underlined exhaustively. I want to create a body of Asian work where Asian-ness comes second and we move past Chinese food, interracial dynamics and intergenerational conflict. I've settled on calling myself a Chinese-Kiwi playwright and performance poet; that feels comfortable. I shy away from calling myself a writer. Novelists and print poets get to be called writers; perhaps I've internalised some negative bias towards playwriting because, traditionally, novelists are held in higher esteem.

The beauty of the queer movement is its deconstruction of feminine and masculine polarities.

If I'm talking about my sexuality in terms of art and performing, I say I'm queer, because I'm interested in the queer movement and how that's opening new paths to explore in art; but for me as a person with my romantic and dating history, I just say I'm gay. You could say my art is more open-minded than my sexuality. Healthy Asian masculinity on stage and screen was completely missing when I was growing up and is still virtually absent today, although I'm cautious about falling into blind worship, making masculine the ideal, the most worthy and attractive. The beauty of the queer movement is its deconstruction of feminine and masculine polarities — a queer view would look beyond those tired binaries.

I never think of myself as just gay, or just Asian, but always as both gay and Asian. If you ask me to consider them separately, being Asian has given me more grief than being gay; being gay has caused me more internal conflict, but being Asian has caused me widespread problems in the world, dealing with people and their prejudices. 'Gaysian' is a fun abbreviation, has a vibrancy to it; perhaps it helps the gay Asian demographic feel accessible and light-hearted. But if a straight white person casually called me a gaysian, I'd be taken aback, and I wouldn't use it to describe myself or say I'm a 'gaysian writer', but it's a term I'm fond of.

Gay dating apps have had racism issues; guys writing 'no Asians or Indians' on their profiles, or the slightly more self-reflective but still nasty 'I'm not racist, I'm just not attracted to Asians or Indians' comments. That doesn't seem so common recently. Is that progress? Even if people are just more covert with their racism, we could call that progress. It stops it filtering down and being absorbed by the next generation.

I used to think the bedroom was the only place free from these issues but now the bedroom's not safe either. I can't help analysing the situation that exists when I'm in bed with someone. I'm hyper-conscious of things like race, age and different power dynamics. If I'm with another Asian, part of me sees it as a political act, a kind of protest against the status quo; 'two Asians doing it, yeah'.

In my early twenties I wanted to believe romance and sex were free of my personal issues about race or age or family. I wanted the solace of being accepted without worrying about all of that. I do have romantic notions, but a commitment such as marriage feels like such a foreign concept; I need every inch of space I can get because the act of creating work is all-consuming — at least for now.

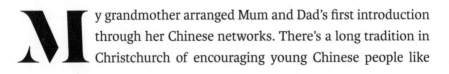

My grandmother arranged Mum and Dad's first introduction through her Chinese networks. There's a long tradition in Christchurch of encouraging young Chinese people like this. My grandfather moved here when he was young and was raised as a Kiwi, so we haven't been in New Zealand as long as the oldest Chinese families, but still a lot longer than many of my European friends' families. My grandmother lives in a Taoist spiritual world. A lot of my childhood was spent with her because my parents were so busy working. Taoism was fascinating to me as a kid; I practised it in fragments at her house. When you're young you want to join in, and I was definitely curious. The rest of the family was quite wary of her religion; they thought she took it too seriously. Our family does retain some traditional superstition and rituals, and a Chinese spiritual base emerges when it comes to events like weddings and funerals or New Year celebrations.

I grew up in Upper Riccarton, the one area of Christchurch which is known for having some small version of a Chinatown; the mythology of Christchurch being very white erases the pockets of diversity that actually exist here.

At intermediate school, a bunch of us had a cutesy phase where my friends and another group of girls all matched up into boyfriend–girlfriend couples. It was very innocent, and none of us went any further than kissing. It's so funny to remember that now. I was becoming attracted to guys around that time but with all those crazy hormones I wasn't capable of the introspection required to really think about sexuality. I had more space to reflect on it by the time I got to Riccarton High, a middle-of-the-road public co-ed school. It had a healthy balance of school ingredients although it wasn't well funded; the arts and media departments survived on meagre provisions. My friend group was liberal and progressive so I mostly had a good time. It wasn't hugely ethnically diverse, but enough that I didn't feel like the only Asian in the village.

Through those years, I'd occasionally kiss girls in a boozy party setting, for the frivolity of it; actually, come to think of it I could still be tempted by a boozy girl-kiss now, why not, right? So yes, there were some cursory experiments in heterosexuality early on, and who's to say it won't happen again. I don't know, the world is a crazy place. It was the last few years of high school when the question of being gay became hard to ignore. My friends knew I was gay or queer or bisexual or something; it was seeded through those late-night conversations that become intimate and confessional. By the time of university, I'd accepted my sexuality as a fact and would bring it up early when I met new people to let that part of myself be known, like dropping a stone in a pond and allowing the ripples to subside.

At university I did have some trouble with being gay, mainly from people from smaller towns who had come to Christchurch to study; their experience with queer culture was so limited I was sometimes their first exposure to an openly gay person. Ignorance breeds fear, fear builds walls. But mostly my sexuality struggle was more internal and existential — I was wrestling with what it meant for me and my place within my family. It's been much more stressful to deal with how my sexuality sits within my familial culture than how it exists in the wider culture.

> Ignorance breeds fear, fear builds walls. But mostly my sexuality struggle was more internal and existential — I was wrestling with what it meant for me and my place within my family.

I 'd promised myself I would come out to either my mum or dad before leaving Christchurch for Auckland. Dad is a native English speaker but Mum isn't. My Chinese is pretty good, but it lacked the nuance to express what I needed to say, so when Dad offered to drive me and all my stuff up to Auckland, I psyched myself up to tell him after our overnight stop in Wellington. That would be good timing, I thought — about halfway, enough time to talk it over.

Here's what actually happened: I couldn't bring myself to tell him until the last five minutes of the two-day car trip. It was, 'OK, here we are in Auckland, by the way, I'm gay.' We got the luggage out of the car, said goodbye and that was it. On the drive back to Christchurch, he told me he cried a lot; it was a shock to his system. When we did finally talk about it, they wanted to know if anything could be done to fix it. Could I just ignore it? Was it permanent? These were reasonable questions for people with a limited understanding of different sexualities, so I don't blame them, but I didn't really want to have these conversations so I just shut it down.

I wanted to explain to them that sexuality is complex, that I'm attracted to men and yet people can evolve, but that depth of discussion is only possible with friends and peers who share a similar understanding and language of love, gender and sexuality. I decided it's better to simply tell Mum and Dad I'm gay rather than anything more nuanced or blurry that hints at ending up with a girl. Truthfully, when sexuality comes up in family discussions now, I still feel uncomfortable talking about it.

I was only able to feel at ease with my sexuality after I left Christchurch. Auckland has a diversity of cultural arts, ethnicities and sexualities, which allows for a more open flow of ideas and creativity. It didn't even feel like there was a queer culture growing up in Christchurch, it was so invisible. Now it's a city with a quiet queer identity — it exists but is very subtle. Showing affection with a guy in public will still get you stares and comments; people aren't used to it. Being queer is OK but displaying that queerness is a problem. The first gay bar I went to was in Christchurch. It was always dead quiet in there, which made it really uncomfortable; it reflected the queer culture of the city at the time. I was about 18 then and longing for queer visibility, and so not seeing it at such a venue came as a shock. There were a few queer university groups, but no wild hedonism — just nice people, good discussions.

Being seen as an effeminate guy is a problem in Christchurch. There's an ingrained misogyny to the homophobia down here. I'm not really 'straight passing' so when I'm in an environment that could be homophobic, I adopt a toned-down personality to flatten out any campness for my own safety — not necessarily physical safety, it could be to avoid awkward social tension. A line in one of my poems says, 'There's something about a certain breed of Christchurch boy that makes me act all butch'. It's sad to create a shell persona but it avoids questions like 'Oh, so you like sucking dick?', which is obviously a provocation, not a genuine curiosity about my sexuality.

Poetry performance to me is an act of confession, literally standing on a stage describing personal tribulations of life to a room of complete strangers. The paradox of performance is that baring your soul to hundreds of people is much easier than telling just one person. Satire in poetry allows me to explore some difficult personal themes such as being mainly attracted to Pākehā guys; 'When he says he loves me, what I hear is, you're one of us now, turns out I have a fetish for colonisers.'

The unspoken convention is to be attracted to what's dominant, powerful or popular. My journey as an Asian person, and probably for all people of colour, is to ask myself why that is the case, to consider why I might follow that norm.

It seems there are at least three elements woven together which reinforce the convention: culture, numbers and love. Our culture teaches us what is worth valuing about ourselves and others; for example, that some faces are more media-worthy than others. Then there are simply more European guys in New Zealand; and also there's love, just the simple coincidence of attraction. It's tricky to unpick these threads and consider them individually, but, to extend the Socrates quote 'the unexamined love isn't worth loving'. If we don't think deeply about why we love someone, how can that love have a solid foundation? So, for me, it's wrestling with my tastes, biases, everything I'm attracted to and repulsed by, and trying to figure out why. Much of it is beyond our control, but an understanding of where these powerful forces flow from is enlightening.

Mum and Dad run a fish and chip shop in Christchurch. It's been the family business since I can remember. When I was old enough, I worked there on the busy days, but all the while I'd cringe about it in that self-conscious teenage way. If you yearn to be the alternative arty kid, different from all the other Asian kids, the worst thing that can happen is to have parents with a chip shop, at which you work. I felt like I had 'fish and chip shop' written on my back everywhere I went.

When I got past that, as I grew up, I understood the fish shop in a wider context; how it represented the struggle of providing for our family, what that hard work had won, what was made possible with a stable upbringing and good education. It actually represents the heroic journey of people traversing the world, arriving in a foreign land and putting down roots in a new community.

I wonder if we're running out of time, it feels like Earth's on the brink; is capitalism crumbling? If that's all true, then what is the most important story to tell? It must be something urgent and essential, not just an entertaining distraction from the turmoil.

Sexuality, gender and race will gradually become inherently part of the culture and public consciousness and less central to stories. One day the token gay friend will be simply the friend, and we'll think nothing of it.

Eliana Rubashkyn

Eliana Rubashkyn is a scientist and consultant for the United Nations Gender Identity, Gender Expression and Sex Characteristics Program. After arriving in New Zealand as a stateless person, she has campaigned for LGBTQIA+ asylum seekers, refugees and intersex people.

My Mother is Jewish Ukrainian. She was born a few years after the Second World War, the first generation born to Holocaust survivors. After the defeat of the Nazis, Ukraine came under Soviet influence, which was still very bad for Jewish people — they weren't allowed to live in the cities, only in remote places where no one else wanted to live. My mother's dream was to study medicine but by law only 1 per cent of students at Ukrainian universities could be Jewish; they wanted to keep Jewish people down. It was difficult under that regime. She looked for any way to leave and managed to escape to Colombia, arriving in Bogota City in the 1960s. She settled there, married a Colombian man, and I came along soon after.

When I was born, everyone knew I was different, but they tried to ignore it and hide it. I had a different arrangement of genitals that was outside medical expectations for male or female anatomical sexes. The doctor and my family agreed I should be raised as a boy. Throughout my childhood I naturally displayed very feminine behaviour, but I was encouraged by everyone around me to embrace a masculine identity. Despite that, I recall a good childhood, at least in my memory. Gender identity for a child isn't such an important thing — you're just a kid who wants to play and discover the world. The complexity comes later.

We say Colombia has a 'machismo' culture. It's the Spanish word for aggressive masculine values; there are traditional roles for men and women, with women being treated badly. It's even worse for transgender women. Many LGBTQIA+ people are murdered every year, and no one gets arrested because often police are part of the violence. Colombian people are not open to differences or diversity, especially when that diversity is visibly obvious. It's a homogeneous society and very Catholic. I was considered strange in many ways, for being foreign in a country with little migration, having an unmarried mother, and behaving differently to my supposed gender. I had a strong sense of being different in every aspect and couldn't develop genuine friendships.

At puberty, my body changed in socially uncomfortable ways; there was no body hair or deeper voice, but I developed breasts. My mother wanted me to hide my breasts with binders, to correct my body. It's a painful memory, as are those of the different interactions we had with doctors who suggested different treatments or surgical options to 'normalise' my sex characteristics. I became introverted, and spent those teenage years deep in books and studies, especially science and chemistry, and I realised I was good at learning languages.

After high school I was accepted to the National University of Colombia to do a chemistry degree. It's probably the best university in Colombia. I started to experiment with makeup and feminine clothes, wanting to make sense of the other side of my identity as a woman. I began cross-dressing at home, putting lipstick on in my bedroom. I was glad my body was complicit in that journey, and I never regret that I developed large breasts when I was 12. I grew up understanding that I was a pseudo-hermaphrodite, and I was told not to ever tell that to anyone. Eventually, when I decided to try dressing as a woman on the streets, I was attacked, first stabbed several times in the back and another time shot at from a car.

I knew I wanted to escape Colombia, just as my mother had escaped from the Ukraine in the 1960s. I realised that if I stayed, no one would allow me to be the person I wanted to be — not my family, or my community, my country or my university. I decided to go as far away as possible. I wanted to be born again, to start a new life. I applied for as many overseas scholarships as possible and was lucky enough to be accepted to Taipei Medical University, a place where I could also begin to transition to a woman. All my family knew was that I was going away to study.

Soon after settling in Taipei, I came out as a woman to my family. I didn't get the support I'd hoped for, but still, life in my new city was better, and the Taiwanese medical system helped me understand better the particularities of my intersex variation: Partial Androgen Insensitivity Syndrome (PAIS). I started taking oestrogen, while working hard on my studies in chemistry, infectious diseases and public health. A year went by quickly, but the rule is that international students must reapply for their visa. Hong Kong was supposed to be the easiest place, so I bought a ticket and packed an overnight bag.

At customs in Hong Kong, the immigration officer stared at me for a long time, looking from my passport to my face. While I was transitioning to a woman, I'd never given a thought to my passport; I never realised it could be a problem, I was so focused on studying and my new life in Taiwan. The officer called his supervisor over, then they became hostile. They thought I was faking my identity. The hormones had changed my face dramatically and I'd grown my hair long, so I didn't look anything like my photo. The situation became nasty. They confiscated my passport and took me to a room where I was forced to strip naked. I was refused entry to Hong Kong and detained in an airport cell awaiting deportation to Colombia, the place I'd worked so hard to escape.

I still had my phone, so I appealed for help on social media. Amnesty

International heard about me and got me released from the airport prison, but without a passport I was stateless and stranded on the streets of Hong Kong. I didn't know anyone and I couldn't access my Taiwanese scholarship funds, so for eight months I lived in horrible refugee slums, slept rough on the streets or in shipping containers. For a while I slept on the floor of an HIV testing clinic. In one of the refugee shelters I was raped by a group of men. It was extremely painful; they took everything that made me human, and my inner peace was destroyed.

My situation seemed so hopeless until the United Nations did something very unusual: they used a mechanism within the Refugee Convention to recognise my gender status as female. Then, with my new gender recognised, the UN helped me appeal for asylum to many countries — France, Sweden, Canada, the United States, Australia and New Zealand — all of which refused to help me except New Zealand. New Zealand was the only country to allow me to resettle as a woman without requiring genital surgery or modification to recognise my identity; it would welcome me with no conditions.

It was extremely painful; they took everything that made me human, and my inner peace was destroyed.

The New Zealand embassy in Hong Kong gave me a pamphlet written in Spanish, which gave me a warm hopeful feeling, explaining how they help refugees to resettle. I felt it could be a place where I wouldn't need to be afraid. Before I finally left the nightmare of Hong Kong, I gave a live interview for CNN. They were calling me the world's first refugee to gain asylum due to changing gender, which I suppose was true. However, they did not make a clear mention of my variation of sex characteristics, as at the time the UN was unable to provide protections for intersex people under the provisions of the Refugee Convention. I landed at Auckland airport in May 2014, to start my new life as a woman.

I understand gender issues can be confusing. It's new to many people and I don't mind explaining: I was raised as a boy but later I had a deep feeling this wasn't my real identity. Intersex is a matter of physiology and anatomy, where the body doesn't match medically normative male or female types. Intersex is our hardware and being trans our software. I was born with a hardware that is special and unique, and my software did not match medical or social expectations.

Being intersex is something I have embraced more and more with time. I've stopped feeling shame in having a body that is different, and since 2020 I stopped identifying as a transgender woman and started embracing a non-binary gender identity. Today I identify as a non-binary person, rather than trans, and I embrace the physical variations of my sex characteristics.

Except for my mother, my family doesn't support me, but I don't blame them; I can't demand their acceptance. I talk to my mother regularly, though I haven't seen her in more than 12 years. So many thing have changed. The only part of me that hasn't changed since growing up in Bogota is my Jewishness, my religion that I use as a way to give meaning to my suffering and to understand that I am valid, despite the close-minded notions of some.

I married a Jewish man named Itamar in 2015. We had a small ceremony in Auckland. I met him on a dating website when he was finishing military service in the Israeli army. He wasn't afraid of loving me, even though he sacrificed everything to be with me. His parents are very traditional Yemeni and Iranian and his whole family has ostracised him; they don't accept anything about him or us. They wanted to put him in a psychiatric hospital when they found out about our relationship.

After years of fighting and struggling, I'm at a peaceful place in my life. I can help advocate for the many intersex and gender-diverse people who still seek to escape persecution around the world. You never see a trans or intersex person trying to run across a border because they aren't given food and support to help them even reach the border. When I lived in refugee camps it was nearly all endosex, straight, fully able men. The real vulnerable and powerless people are not represented there, they're left behind, still being persecuted in their home countries. I want New Zealand to adopt a quota for LGBTQIA+ people as part of the total quota of refugees that come here, to ensure the most vulnerable of all are not overlooked.

The United Nations High Commissioner for Refugees is not providing effective protection for intersex people. There is a lack of understanding of our unique realities, which are a combination of both medical and social issues and are poorly understood, and of our particular needs in the international protection systems for refugees.

Itamar and I gave up everything to come to New Zealand but now it feels like a good ending. I'm respected, loved, safe, and peace has returned to my life. I live in a place where I'm protected. There have been a few more trans refugees coming here since I did, which makes me happy, although I would like intersex and non-binary identities to be recognised as well; there is a shift happening. Sometimes they've heard about me and contact me for advice when they first arrive.

Scott Mathieson

Scott Mathieson runs a family farm near Aparima Riverton, in Southland. A former chef, he travelled widely before returning home to take over the farm.

Ardoyne Farm has been in our family for four generations. It's a 640-hectare dairy farm sitting above Colac Bay, a tiny town about 40 minutes from Invercargill. We look down onto Foveaux Strait and right across to Stewart Island. It's beautiful here but also rugged and blustery, with some of the worst weather in New Zealand — and I've lived in Wellington. In summer it stays light until after 10 at night, but if we get a rare hot summer evening, I don't get to relax in the garden because I have to get up at four in the morning for milking.

It might sound a hard life to a city person, but it's in my blood and I love living and working on the land, especially now my partner Daegan has moved here with me. We have honeybees, vegetable gardens and goats for making cheese. Daegan is an artist who often works with weaving so we have special sheep and alpacas to produce fibres for his projects.

The house has a few rooms set aside for homestay guests, usually city people and tourists who want to experience New Zealand farm life. It's a great way to meet new people and have some company. We don't really have nights out. The only entertainment option in Colac Bay is a little pub, which has a great $10 burger night on Thursdays and a pool table we've never used. Slowly, more gay people are moving here from urban centres so we sometimes host a Sunday gay lunch at our farm. That's our rural gay scene.

As a kid I wasn't much good on the farm. I was a bit chubby and liked playing video games in my room rather than hunting and fishing. It was an idyllic childhood, though; very happy with lots of friends and family coming to stay with us. At Christmas the whole farming community would get together at the town hall where Santa would give out gifts that the parents had bought for their kids. Usually the boys got toy guns and ran around shooting each other. One year Santa gave me a Spice Girls sticker book; I don't think Mum thought I was queer, she just thought I was different. Luckily there wasn't much pressure to stay on the farm, and Mum encouraged me to have urban career aspirations.

Slowly, more gay people are moving here from urban centres so we sometimes host a Sunday gay lunch at our farm.

It took a long time to come out. I was completely closeted and in denial until I moved overseas. Even at university I didn't come out; looking back I regret that — it would have been so much easier. The problem was I'd never known any out queer people; not friends, school teachers or anyone connected to my family. I was scared of the reaction I'd get in Southland. Everyone in our town was traditional and quite conservative.

Country schools are so small; at Aparima College there were only 20 in our senior year. We'd known each other all our lives so it was peaceful, and I never experienced any bullying. I already knew I wasn't attracted to girls — you find porn so you know what gets you excited — but I'd fooled myself into thinking it was a choice and so I could choose to deny being gay if I wanted to. After high school, I headed north to Massey University. I thought I was moving to a big, diverse city but Palmerston North turned out to be the Southland of the North Island. I wanted to be a vet but it was extremely competitive so I did a degree in zoology and ecology instead. I had fake girlfriends through those university years. Although I wasn't physically attracted to them we were always good friends and loved hanging out together.

When some German friends from Massey invited me to stay with them in Berlin, after graduation, it turned out to be the perfect place for a closeted queer kid from the country. It's one of the coolest cities and I fell in love with it. Gay culture is a huge part of Berlin life; in fact, the closet doesn't really exist there, and the freedom was incredible. Away from all the stale expectations of my old life I could finally figure out how to be myself. The nightlife was an important part of that exploration, but I didn't just suddenly burst onto the gay scene. I took my time to meet people, seeing how they lived and getting comfortable with what was right for me; my first experiences with men were in Berlin.

I was doing bar work and odd jobs until I settled into an au pair job with a lovely German-American family with quadruplet four-year-olds, where the girls were identical and the boys were identical, but the boys and girls didn't look alike. They became my new family in Berlin, and I travelled to New York and all around Europe with them. I lived in their beautiful old apartment in Zehlendorf, in south Berlin. The family had moved to be close to JFK, the American international school where the quads were preparing to start. Luckily for me, this area was full of au pairs and I ended up meeting some of my closest German friends.

Berlin is also where I came out to my parents. They were coming to visit while on holiday in Europe and I decided it was time to tell them. I was happy in Berlin, so if they didn't accept me, I was prepared to stay. They planned their trip well ahead, so I had months to torment myself over it. I broke out in hives. These little bite-looking pimples covered my body, and the doctor said it was caused by stress. I was constantly running over in my mind what to say, where to do it, planning for their different reactions. I was an anxious mess. I was convinced that Dad would take it badly but Mum would be alright.

It was actually the reverse. Dad said, 'Son, we'll always love you.' Southern men don't say the word 'love', so this was overwhelming. Mum was supportive but needed a bit of time. She thought it could be 'just a phase' because I was in Europe and it must be what trendy Europeans did. Then they returned to New Zealand and gradually got used to the idea of having a gay son. They told the wider family and the community. Mum even joined some gay pride groups on Facebook and started chatting with them online.

Dad said, 'Son, we'll always love you.' Southern men don't say the word 'love', so this was overwhelming.

I then moved to Wuhan in China — before Wuhan became famous. Gay culture is odd in China. People aren't harassed and there's no threat of physical violence, which you can get in some conservative Western places, however, queer concepts are seen as foreign, not really part of Chinese culture, so it's not discussed but it's acceptable in the shadows. I fell in love for the first time and had my first proper boyfriend in Wuhan.

His mother was of an older generation and had no awareness of queer people, but I can confirm that there are definitely a lot of gay guys in China.

Returning to New Zealand, I chose Wellington to study hospitality and cooking. After Europe and China, it was hard to adjust to Kiwi life. Then, to get a job, I headed to Auckland and cooked at the Hilton Hotel. The culture in restaurant kitchens is not healthy. It's a constant rush, everything is urgent and noisy, with long hours and big egos; drinking and drugs were common ways of coping, and I soon realised that I don't really belong in big cities.

The daily battle to earn enough money to rent a tiny shoebox started to seem pointless and I reminisced about country life, living on the land, growing my own food. To be honest, the reason I stayed in Auckland so long was to meet someone. I thought if I moved back home to Southland I'd be single forever and die alone. I remember telling my sister that with so many nieces and nephews, I'd be OK as an old maid. Accepting my fate, I moved back to the farm.

I was a different person when I returned. There's nothing that opens the mind like travel and being immersed in different cultures, especially for a rural farm boy. It was wonderful to be back but seeing old friends was strange. Many of them had stayed in Southland so our life experiences had been quite different. I wanted to talk about the music in Berlin or some crazy food I ate in China, but that didn't seem interesting to them. I often wonder about who I would have been if I'd stayed in Southland; that potentially closed, repressed person is so frightening to me.

Soon after I returned, I was interviewed by *The Southland Times* about urban young people moving back to the country. I expressly told the interviewer I wanted the article to state that I'm gay, but when the paper version was published, I couldn't believe that it had been cut out. They said that older readers wouldn't like it, and only the online version kept it in. I think it's important to point out this homophobia in the media.

Still, it is getting better for queer people in the provinces; queer culture is becoming more prominent in New Zealand society, and more people are understanding and comfortable with it. The people it angers have become the minority, so they rarely speak out. The only place I don't feel comfortable is in rural pubs late at night. Straight guys full of beer can get stupid, but I've never had any discrimination to my face.

> # It is getting better for queer people in the provinces; queer culture is becoming more prominent in New Zealand society, and more people are understanding and comfortable with it.

There are so many closeted gay men in Southland. If you see a dating app with a blank profile, it's probably a married man who wants to hook up in their sleep-out while their wife is at a school meeting. It's usually a long drive to meet anyone so I would try to get them to send clear, recent photos. A few times I drove to a meet-up and found the pictures they'd sent must have been from decades earlier and taken in very flattering light, but by then you've made the effort so you may as well go through with it. I understand why men try to lead a straight life — it's still very traditional down here with all the pressure to get married and have kids — but I'm glad I haven't taken that path.

I'd been adding and deleting dating apps for months in depressing cycles of hope and despair when one day Daegan popped up. He was doing an art project in Manapouri, about an hour and a half away. We chatted online for a while, then organised a date in Dunedin. It was an amazing first date. There's a place called Tunnel Beach in Otago where, in the 1870s, some Victorians dug a tunnel down through the stone cliff onto a secluded beach. We spent hours there talking and kissing, swept up in the moment. At one point we realised some bewildered tourists were watching and taking photos of us. I couldn't stay late because I had to drive three hours back to the farm for 4 a.m. milking, but we were really attracted to each other and we planned to meet again. After we'd caught up a few times I invited him to stay on the farm for the summer, to see if he liked it. We had an amazing time together and he's never left.

Daegan is a very caring, warm, supportive person. Although I am the trained chef, he's the one who does all the cooking; I grow the vegetables and herbs and he cooks them. I'm so happy and relieved I met him. My countryside life would be bland and monotonous if he wasn't here. Also my home wouldn't be as attractive — we have his beautiful art and some of his collected pieces displayed around the house.

I don't see a bright future for these huge dairy farms. They're not sustainable, and people are eating less meat and worrying more about the ecosystem. Regenerative agriculture has the potential to solve our problems by lowering carbon emissions and water run-off, so I've started the process of converting our farm to regenerative practices. It means fewer chemicals, fewer inputs and a more holistic approach, which is better for the water, soil, animals and biodiversity. Transitioning to regenerative agriculture will be better for the planet and set the farm up for the future generations of our family.

We do miss the simple spontaneity of the city, going to an art gallery or meeting friends at a restaurant. I love it when our friends come down to stay with us. We cook them food we've grown ourselves and they enjoy the beauty of the place. Occasionally we take a trip up to Wellington or Auckland, so it's the best of both worlds, but I'll never get used to the early morning starts on the farm.

Humans love to classify and label, so we're still known as 'the gay farmers', but we're accepted in our community and being the gay farmers is fine with us.

Henrietta Bollinger

Henrietta (Etta) Bollinger is a writer and disability rights advocate who has had work published in *Starling*, *Mimicry* and *Scum* magazines and plays performed in New Zealand, Australia and England.

C reativity is a consistent thread through our family. Mum is an actor and director and now a documentarian, Dad is a writer and musician, my sisters are both film-makers, and I have always been drawn to poetry and the written word. Dad says that when he read to us when we were kids, my sister Sally would be intently focused on the pictures while I was fascinated by the sounds of the words. The arts have always been valued in our family, and the creative impulse nurtured and understood.

In the same way, my parents didn't seem to have anxiety about who I was. They created a safe and open home where the opinions of all their kids were valued and we were encouraged to express ourselves. Being a teenager is hard but I was given the space to be myself. Having a family who accepts and supports you and stable, suitable housing shouldn't be a privilege, but it is. I know many people in my disabled and queer communities who live without those things.

I'm two minutes younger than my twin sister, Sally. We were born early and I was born with cerebral palsy. The world places high value on a non-disabled way of being, which influences the picture parents have of their future children. When they're confronted with a different reality, like disability, it can be hard to accept. I feel lucky that my parents took it in their stride. Being twins meant our parents simply had the same expectations of what education we'd receive and what opportunities we'd have. Sally was used to being around me so her natural instinct was to include me in everything; the other kids followed her lead. Our little sister, Elsie, was the same. Inclusion came naturally — it does if kids are taught not to be fearful.

I live in a Wellington flat with two other queer disabled people and a ginger cat. Disabled people are often confronted by an inaccessible world and there are demands to explain ourselves and our body, so the solidarity of having disability, queerness and friendship in our home is a lucky combination. This is particularly true given that accessible housing is so hard to find.

Our lives come up against systems that limit our freedom and connections with the communities we live in.

For me, disability advocacy isn't as much a choice as it's borne out of necessity: if we're not vocal we don't get what we need. Our lives come up against systems that limit our freedom and connections with the communities we live in. When we get to the stage where disabled people are an active part, then I will enjoy feeling as if I have made a valuable contribution to the fight for accessibility, but I'd prefer to live in a world that has already considered my existence and my need to access the world.

cademic learning suited me. In high school, particularly, the teachers encouraged me as a writer and there was a little community of queer kids, which was really affirming. History fascinated me as a kind of storytelling. I became interested in Germany when I was 10 years old and began learning German from that age.

This was also when I learnt that my Jewish grandmother escaped from Germany in 1938, just before Britain declared war. When I was a bit older, I discovered that my grandmother's brother, Arthur Kronfeld, was a psychiatrist who worked at the renowned Institute of Sex Research in Berlin in the 1920s; Sir Ian McKellen played him in the film *Zina*.

The institute was famous for its pioneering research on same-sex love and transgender people and used their work to promote understanding and public acceptance of these groups. When the Nazis came to power they deemed the institute 'unGerman', destroying it in 1933, with thousands of books and stories about queer and trans people hauled into the street and burnt. I was proud to learn of my lineage to that queer history.

Young disabled people shouldn't sit in sex education classes feeling like it doesn't apply to them.

Sexuality has also interested me as an area of research. At university, I interviewed a number of disabled people about their experiences of sex education because I hadn't felt it had been aimed at me as a disabled young person. I wanted to find out if that was an individual experience or a collective one. The disabled people I spoke to felt that their schools' sex education courses were not made relevant to them, and they didn't see themselves reflected. Nothing resonated. Others said they found it hard to picture themselves in relationships.

This exclusion left me desiring alternative conversations about disabled sexuality, where we give ourselves permission to explore our desire and sensuality, whether that happens alone, in relationships or through seeing sex workers. Young disabled people shouldn't sit in sex education classes feeling like it doesn't apply to them. It's a fundamental, legitimate part of everyone's lives.

As a disabled person you grow up in a medical system that gives you lots of practice talking about your body, but not what you like or enjoy about it. There's nothing about sensuality. Touch and physical closeness often serve only a practical purpose, such as when support workers are with us. We get many invasive questions about how a disabled person's life and body works.

People have been amazed that I have friends who aren't paid support workers, and others can't believe I have a university degree or a job. Then there are the more boundary-crossing questions about sex and sexuality, which are perhaps similar to the questions queer people get asked about sexuality and how they have sex. Complete strangers have come up to me and said, 'If I was in your situation, I wouldn't be able to live.' I know that if someone were faced with a disability, they would find a way to adapt their life; it wouldn't be as impossible as they think.

Disabled queer people exist, we are a part of the community. If events, ideas and experiences aren't accessible for us, people think that we're just not interested. The queer community is still learning about how to include disabled people, and disability is often not seen as an identity in the same way as queerness is, which is frustrating. I would love it if we could get to a point where queer people automatically consider the presence of disabled people in their spaces and vice versa.

These are meaningful issues for us living at the intersection of a queer-disabled identity. If we designed the world so that disabled people

could be fully present and fully themselves, that would be a world that would work for everyone.

When I was younger I thought the world of disability was mundane and that anything else was much more interesting, but now I see it as a world with so much nuance to explore. It's been important for me to create something that comes from our own culture, so I'm writing a lot about queer-disabled themes for the teenage version of myself — writing that didn't exist when I needed it most. Reading about other people's experiences that echo my own can be significant; you get a bolt of recognition that someone else in the world knows just what that feeling is like. The first theatre piece I wrote was in response to the invasive questions I get as a disabled person; having a wheelchair draws a lot of attention and reactions.

People see my writing as vulnerable, and perhaps it is, but it's also crafted that way — experiences distilled into words. What's special is when I hear people's raw, uncrafted responses to what I've written, when they tell me what it has meant to them. Whatever state the world is in, whatever is happening in people's lives, we all need storytelling. The beautiful thing about writing is that my words can do the travelling for me. I've had plays performed in Australia, London and Cambridge. People around the world can see and hear my work, and my ideas can travel.

Andy Davies

Andy Davies is a highly successful Tāmaki Makaurau Auckland businessman who is best known for his property development in Ponsonby, including the retail and restaurant spot Ponsonby Central and the new Auckland boutique hotel The Convent.

My Baptist parents ran a Christian bookshop in the centre of Nottingham. Dad loved books but I never saw Mum read anything other than the Bible. She'd had a tough upbringing as one of 11 kids from a small village in the Lake District called Cockermouth. Mum was looking for a fresh start in a new country, but while she was ready to leave, Dad kept wavering. The destination was to be either California, where they knew no one, or New Zealand, where they knew one person. When the landlord doubled the rent on the bookshop, that was the last straw for Mum. She marched into the P & O shipping company with my sister and me in tow and bought four tickets to Auckland. When Dad asked where we'd been, she gave him his ticket and said, 'We leave in a month; come with us or stay here. Either way, the kids and I are getting on that ship.' He decided to come with us. The shop and the house were quickly sold, and we departed England on the four-week journey to New Zealand.

For a six-year-old kid travelling around the world on a ship, the *Canberra*, was an amazing adventure. The staff were all friendly and I was allowed to help the stewards in the restaurant. We sailed through the Mediterranean, through the Suez Canal and out into the Arabian Sea.

After grey, post-war Nottingham, it was just magical.

We arrived in Auckland in 1964 with £100 and the address of my parents' one contact. Mum and Dad were real grafters, and Dad soon had a job at the hospital and Mum found work in the laundry there. For the first few years they were working so much that I hardly saw them, other than each Sunday when we went to church twice. My sister is six years older so she looked after me. I started at Kohimarama School and despite my strong Nottingham accent, I fitted in easily and gathered a bunch of friends. Even though it was tough getting started in a new country, we all felt it was a better life than we'd had in England.

They were strict but loving parents and I remember it as a wonderful childhood. Mum had a good head for business and a sharp eye for an opportunity. She'd always been a skilled baker and as she became acquainted with 1960s Auckland, she could see the city was littered with rundown cafés serving terrible food. With her trademark self-confidence, she began a new career of buying dilapidated cafés, working 14-hour days to renovate them, changing the menu and hiring new staff. Once each kitchen was turning out good food and the café was full of happy customers, she'd sell it and repeat the process at another location. There were a couple on Vulcan Lane, and she started Verona on Karangahape Road, which is still going today. The biggest was called Peppers on Queen Street, which had an ice-cream parlour and café on the ground floor and a restaurant upstairs. Mum had opened 26 cafés around the city by the time she finished.

As soon as I could count, I'd help Dad balance the books and tally the day's takings. In time, with all the cafés, the family was doing well and they could afford to send me to Saint Kentigern College, which was an expensive school even then. In the afternoons, I'd finish school at St Kent's and get straight on the bus into town to work. This was an expectation, not a choice, but I still loved it. Verona is the one I remember best. All sorts of colourful people came in — business guys, prostitutes, artists. Mum had a big heart, and everyone was welcome, but she didn't miss an opportunity to get the Bible out and give a quick sermon to whomever she thought needed it.

The first transgender person I met worked in the Verona kitchen; some days Margaret would wear a dress, some days not. One day a fight broke out in the kitchen between a staff member and another transgender person. Margaret whacked them on the head with a baking spoon and covered them in cake batter. Mum jumped in to break it up. Occasionally, Margaret would come into work with a black eye, courtesy of her boyfriend, and Mum was always sympathetic to that and tried to help where she could.

The streets and lanes of the city were where I spent most of my teenage years. No one warned me to be careful or not to talk to strangers. I knew the shop owners and the city workers who were regulars in our cafés. I loved it, but I didn't have the usual social life of a teenager — everything was school or work, with church on Sundays — and my schooling always took a back seat to Mum's business ventures. Once, before a new café was opening, it was nearly midnight and I was still painting the walls even though I had a big exam the next day. I told Mum I really needed to study. 'Ah, don't worry, you'll pass,' she said. I finished the painting and went home for a few hours' sleep before the exam. She was wrong. I didn't pass.

I started to get into trouble with some of the teachers — having had a taste of the world outside the school gates, I preferred it to sitting in a classroom. School now seemed tedious compared to the life of business and banks and property. The final chapter at school was around the time my newly acquired facial hair meant I could get away with buying booze and cigarettes at some of the less scrupulous liquor shops. I bought to order for other students, adding a decent mark up, obviously. Saint Kentigern's didn't see the advantages to this. 'You're wasting your money at this school, perhaps you'd like to go elsewhere', they advised. So I left. I was 15. There were a few years of drifting through farming jobs, and starting a fashion design course I wasn't really interested in, until gradually it sank in that it was time to fly the nest. I saved some money and bought a plane ticket back to England.

London was an exciting place to be in the seventies. Bowie and Boney M were all over the radio, cocaine was just arriving and I was a teenager finally free of his conservative parents. My first job was in a menswear shop, which I hated, and I moved on to pouring pints in a pub near Wembley Stadium. It was a real den of thieves and villains, and I was much more at home there. Trucks would load and unload round the back of the pub and suddenly we'd only be selling one brand of cigarettes, that sort of thing.

I had girlfriends in London, but there were occasional dalliances with blokes. I always dismissed those as something that might happen at a party after a few drinks, nothing to take seriously, until a sense emerged that it might be more than that. Any gay life was still undercover then; because it was illegal, the police would send young men into public toilets to try and trick men into sex and then arrest them. There were gay pubs in London, but it was still years before the dance-club culture took off. Mum had tricked me into returning to New Zealand by then.

It was always a complicated relationship with Mum and me. She knew I was having a good time in London, and I started getting letters and calls asking when I was coming home and saying 'your father's getting older' and other guilt trips. One morning I got a call saying Dad had had a heart attack and it wasn't looking good. Mum bought me a ticket to collect at Pan Am Airlines and said I better come home straightaway. When my sister met me at Auckland airport, I was prepared to go straight to the hospital to see Dad on death's door, but she said he was at home. They'd only kept him in hospital for two days. We arrived at the house to find Dad happily sitting in his La-Z-Boy chair, with a cup of tea and an Eccles cake. I was furious. I understand it's natural for mothers to want to have their kids around, but her methods were more extreme than most.

During my absence Mum and Dad had done well. Now they gave me a car and encouraged me to set up a business, so I made a range of t-shirts and sold them at the Cook Street Market. Everyone brought them back complaining they'd shrunk to half the size — I didn't know I had to prewash the fabric.

I found my attraction to guys harder to ignore. In London, I had always brushed it off, telling myself it was because I was on holiday or it couldn't be anything serious because I was high as a kite and anyway, I always had a girlfriend. But Auckland was home and it felt more real, like there was more at stake; I wasn't just playing around overseas anymore. There was a gay pub called the Empire, and I decided to go there for a beer one night, only it wasn't just going for a beer, it was going for a beer at a gay bar. I drove around in anxious circles for about an hour before I finally got the courage to go in. I met some nice guys in there; we became friends and had some fun.

Everything changed when I met Chris, the handsome boy around town. We fell for each other and moved into a crumbling old villa in Grey Lynn. It was a great area, lots of Pacific Island people, music playing and drunks talking to themselves. It wasn't chic but it was colourful and friendly. We kept two bedrooms fully made up to maintain for my family the fiction that we were just friends and certainly weren't sleeping together. Of course, Mum suspected something was going on. She'd barge in and demand to know which bed Chris was sleeping in.

One night she came around and started forcing the windows open at one in the morning. We tried to barricade ourselves in, then Chris ran out the back to escape and tumbled down the hill into the next property. She was mad, you have no idea. We renovated that Grey Lynn house, sold it and doubled our money. That didn't seem hard, I thought, and so began my career in real estate. Chris and I broke up soon after and he left for

Los Angeles. Anyone's first break-up is tough, but we got through it and I'm grateful that we've remained best friends to this day.

I didn't have to come out to my family because my sister Joan did it for me without being asked. She'd got so fed up with Mum constantly asking about my private life — 'Has Andy met any nice girls lately? When is he going to settle down?' — that finally she said, 'When are you going to stop lying to yourself, Mum? Andy is gay. Who on earth did you think Chris was?'

> # I didn't have to come out to my family because my sister Joan did it for me without being asked.

I received a phone call from Joan saying, 'Hi Andy, Mum's just leapt up from the table and is on her way over to see you, and by the way, I've told her you're gay.' Mum marches up to my front door bawling her eyes out and demanding I tell her the truth. I'd always avoided the issue of girlfriends by saying I was too busy or I hadn't met the right girl, and now, face to face with Mum asking me the direct question, 'Are you gay?', I cowardly did the same thing.

She left angry and distraught, saying I was lying to her. I stewed on it for a while until eventually I called and asked them to come over to talk. I could hear Mum crying before she'd even knocked on the door. Yes, I was gay and, yes, Chris had been my boyfriend, I told them. It was the first time I'd ever seen my father cry. He was usually very stoic but that day he was amazing, although Mum was a nightmare. Dad said, 'I just want you to be happy.' Mum said, 'I'm disowning you, you're out of the will.'

Two weeks later, she was on my doorstep again, this time brandishing tickets to Sydney. She'd booked me in for a month of gay conversion therapy with a Christian church group. 'If one month's not enough, we'll pay for more. You can beat this,' she said. There was no way I was doing conversion therapy; people who do that end up killing themselves with the guilt and trauma. I was 28 years old, happy with myself, and I wasn't changing. After a while Mum calmed down and we began to talk every day, like we used to.

In the early eighties, we kept hearing about an illness called AIDS. Not much was known about it except that young men in big American cities were disproportionally affected. When Chris returned to Auckland from Los Angeles in 1985, he wasn't well. A few months later he was diagnosed with HIV, just as the severity of the illness was becoming clear. It wasn't a disease that people recovered from. He told Mum and me about it and Mum was so strong. She said, 'We'll fight it together, we can get you better.' Chris changed his life, focusing on health, vitamins and wellness. He started working at one of Mum's cafés so she could keep an eye on him. Against massive odds he stayed alive, and to this day he is one of the longest-surviving people with the virus I know. So many of my friends died of AIDS in the eighties — I really dodged a bullet; it probably helped that I was in a relationship through the worst years of the disease, but honestly it was also just luck. I was going to a funeral a week.

I was buying and selling houses through this period, and I also started a cleaning company called Busy Bees. Then things really took off when I started a company developing and investing in commercial real estate. Even though money was extremely tight in those early deals, I had the ability to walk confidently into a room, sign the contracts and go home for a good night's sleep. The finance always seemed to fall into place; I didn't see the need to carry a load of anxiety around. It was a lot of work running the company but life was great. Then the weekend of my fortieth birthday: the love of my life chose to leave me — a wonderful birthday present. I moved out of the house we shared into Mantells in Mount Eden, a Mediterranean-style events venue that I was renovating. No sooner had I moved in than a torrential downpour completely flooded the place; someone had poured concrete into the drains. The universe was telling me it was time for a change. I sold out of the real estate company and flew off to spend some loot and have some fun.

Mardi Gras, Sleaze Ball, Harbour Party . . . I was at them all. Then I started on the international circuit parties, a series of huge events that move around the world: the White Party in Miami, the beach parties in Mykonos, London Pride. I met so many people and had a mad amount of fun. Often the same crew would be at the next city on the gay party circuit. With most of my twenties and thirties spent building up my property business, this was a delayed phase that lasted for two years and we burnt through hundreds of thousands of dollars. I'd been to Paris five times before I saw the Eiffel Tower. We would land in these great cities and all we'd see were hotel rooms and sweaty dance floors. We'd leave the party a bit worse for wear and have to walk around London or Berlin in the middle of the day dressed as cowboys, as we tried to find our hotel. After a while the fun wore off. I suppose that was inevitable. The dance floors, hotels and pools all blurred into one and it started to feel vacuous and repetitive.

When you shut the door on partying, however, it creates a vacuum that can be scary. Because I came to it all later in life, perhaps it was easier to step away, but still, it left a space that needed to be filled. After those self-indulgent days, the need for a more balanced, healthy, fulfilling life led me down two main paths: the first, to a local SPCA, where I began to volunteer once a week, and the second, to try to have a child with a lesbian friend. Sadly, children didn't come along and it's my biggest regret — I would have loved lots of kids running around on the farm with the dogs. It was very disappointing. But I became more and more involved with the SPCA until I decided to build my own dog shelter on the farm I owned. I hired staff, the shelter grew bigger, and Last Lamppost Dog & Animal Rescue has now found new homes for hundreds of abandoned dogs.

Commercial real estate and construction may seem like straight, macho industries but everyone knows I'm gay and I've never had any discrimination.

With my property company, I've tried to create some elegant new buildings and rejuvenate dilapidated old ones. Not everyone will like them, but I can honestly say that my heart and soul have gone into each. The Convent Hotel in Grey Lynn was a derelict halfway house, best known for 24-hour drinking and fighting when I bought it and now it's fully restored in its original Spanish Mission style, complete with Catholic paintings and artefacts. I sourced the furniture and fabrics from a trip to India.

When we built the Haka Lodge on Karangahape Road, I installed colour-changing neon lights that are visible from the city. They cost a hundred grand, but it adds a little sparkle to the environment. I like to be proud of what I do; I couldn't just throw up cheap apartment buildings. I have my offices above Ponsonby Central, which is an ongoing development project, and I've become good friends with some of the people who run their businesses there.

Commercial real estate and construction may seem like straight, macho industries but everyone knows I'm gay and I've never had any discrimination or homophobic attitudes on the building sites. We should try to be ourselves, not apologise for who we are, and I think people respect that. The only person who's ever had a real problem with me being gay was my mother.

I'm 62 now, and I'm not feeling old but I do think more about what I'll leave behind, my legacy, what people will say at my funeral. I hope they say 'He was a good person, a kind, fun person.' I have not been scholarly and academic but they might say he did a bit to make the city a better place. At one time I controlled most of the pokie machines on Karangahape Road — they were inside buildings I owned that were leased to bars and strip clubs. I pulled them all out. People sitting there all day feeding their family's money into those horrible machines is just wrong. They paid us big money for those little machines, but money's not that important.

I had always thought I'd die on a dance floor. If you'd said to me back in my twenties that I'd end up living on a farm with rescued dogs and puppies, I'd have said you were mad, yet here I am. I'm glad I got over that flashy phase of fancy houses, Porsches and fake tan; I can hardly get in and out of a Porsche these days and I'm much more content on my farm with friends and the dogs. I don't dwell on the past too much. It can't be changed, and I don't have too many regrets, and when there are times when I say, 'Andy, that wasn't your finest moment', I try to learn and improve.

The Last Lamppost is becoming a charitable trust. I want this work to continue long after I'm gone. Those dogs give me so much joy. When I see them leave with their new family, it feels as if we're making a small difference in the world. I firmly believe in karma, not in the tit-for-tat way, but in the sense that doing something good for others is also doing something good for yourself.

Sawyer Hawker

Sawyer Hawker joined the military at 24 and is now a Lance Corporal who works as a logistics supply technician at the Burnham military base, near Ōtautahi Christchurch.

Mum always told us, 'I don't care who you bring home for dinner as long as they treat you with respect.' She's the matriarch of the family so whatever she says goes. Mum has been an immense help in my life, smoothing out the difficult times and celebrating the good times.

I was born and mostly raised in Invercargill, a cool, sleepy little town. I was the eldest of four daughters. A lot of the time it was just Mum and us sisters at home. Dad was away a lot; he started his working life as an apprentice baker and moved up to managing food exports. I was a typical tomboy, always out in the sandpit with my trucks or running around with the dog. In photos when I was younger, I look like a little boy with my collared shirts and shorts. Getting me into a dress or anything pink or frilly was a nightmare, so Mum just didn't bother. I was about five when I came home from school and told her I wanted short hair. All four of us sisters had lush long hair at the time, but she took me down to the hairdresser and I had it chopped off. As long as we were happy, healthy and not causing a fuss, Mum let us be ourselves. She never pushed me into anything. It was an awesome childhood, really.

James Hargest College is the biggest school in Southland, and although going to high school interfered with important teenage activities like sleeping and socialising, I didn't mind it. History, classical studies and English were my favourite subjects, and I always gave sports a go, despite not being spectacularly good at them. My friends and I struggled through puberty together and I never thought my feelings were more uncomfortable than anyone else's — puberty is never a fun time for anyone. My attraction was always to women, and I knew that from my early teens. I thought, I'm a girl who likes girls, so I must be lesbian. Everyone I talked to about it was accepting, so for a long time that was my identity, the space where I belonged.

My first girlfriend was someone from high school. The school culture was open-minded and inclusive and so we were totally open about it. Some students took their same-sex partners to the ball and that was accepted. I know other pockets of New Zealand society are trapped in the conservative past, but James Hargest College was awesome. In my last year of high school, 2007, I was made deputy head girl. I look back with pride on that; it was a great honor.

For kids from Southland, enrolling at Otago University is the well-trodden rite of passage, but after high school I had no idea what I wanted to do next. Wasting a bunch of money figuring it out at university wasn't an option, so I took jobs at Rebel Sport, then Briscoes. I'd always wanted to work serving the community, perhaps in the ambulance service, fire service or the police. At 21, I went to Auckland to study paramedicine, but halfway through Mum became unwell and needed surgery, so I moved home to help out.

I refer to this period as my quarter-life crisis. I was lacking direction and craving a challenge. One evening I was at Mum's house for dinner because I'd run out of food at my flat, when a recruitment ad for the army came on television. Mum suggested the defence force could be worth looking into. The more I thought about it, the more it seemed like a good idea; being part of a meaningful mission of service appealed to me. I applied and was accepted as a trainee medic, and I was able to finish the diploma in paramedic science that I started in Auckland.

Being a lesbian in the army was no big deal. New recruits are thrown together from different races, religions, sexuality and genders. To succeed as a soldier requires focus and teamwork. We're up at sunrise and flat out all day, and there's no time to worry about anything but the next instruction. I'd always thought I was a reasonably fit person, but that illusion was shattered on day one of training. I was up at five to go running, without coffee, and I'm not a morning person. The first months were a real challenge and my body was in shock, but I got used to it and even started to enjoy being pushed to my limits. The tough training created a tight, supportive unit with strong bonds. When people talked about their partners at home, I'd mention my girlfriend. I'm always open any time the topic of sexuality or gender comes up because it removes barriers and creates understanding and connection. Years later, I'm still good friends with my new-recruit group.

> I'm always open any time the topic of sexuality or gender comes up because it removes barriers and creates understanding and connection.

When I signed up for the armed forces, I did consider the possibility of being deployed to a combat zone — it's naive to think it would never happen. If duty calls, then I will fulfill the service I'm committed to provide. I'm absolutely prepared to do that, but I hope I won't have to. There are those in the army with a personality that welcomes the chance to test their training on active deployment, and the armed forces need those people. My role now is logistics; the old-fashioned term is 'quartermaster'. On operations and in garrison at Burnham, I manage the supply chain of weapons, ammunition, rations, uniforms — anything the frontline troops require. Although my role isn't in the direct firing line, warfare is unpredictable. I've had full combat training and would be able to engage if required.

As new recruits, we had many different groups come to talk to us. One of them was Overwatch, a support and networking group for LGBTQIA+ soldiers who might be questioning their identity or sexuality or just need a friendly person to talk to. Commanding officers also seek advice from Overwatch on how to support their troops. We meet regularly, usually around Pride events to organise our uniformed presence in the parades. Having the support of Overwatch gave me a lot of confidence that I was in the right place. NZDF has had the rainbow tick since 2019, which acknowledges inclusion of lesbian, gay and transgender troops.

After about five years in the army, however, I began reflecting on life and the future. I was 27, and my mind was turning to thoughts of marriage and having a family. I'd love to be a dad, I thought. Wait, a father? Not a mother? My subconscious served up the masculine word; it gave me a shock and triggered a period of soul searching. I had no idea where thoughts of being a dad came from but it felt natural. It resonated with me, while being a mother just didn't feel right.

Although I was part of the LGBTQIA+ community, I knew very little about transgender people and had never met anyone who I knew was trans, so those concepts were foreign to me. I did some research and found that, yes, some people do feel that their body isn't in harmony with how they feel inside. The more I learnt about other people's gender-identity experiences the more I came to understand that I could be transgender.

Mum was the first person I told. That was hard — not because I worried about her reaction but because saying it out loud made it real; it meant admitting it to myself. The true blessing of my journey is that I look back and don't hate any part of my life before transitioning. I was given freedom by everyone around me to just be myself no matter what that was. Having no negative experiences or pressure to conform to female norms meant I never really self-analysed very much — I just lived life. Perhaps that means I came to the full realisation about my identity later than some people. Once again Mum was a superstar. It didn't matter if no one else supported me because my mum did, and having her as my safe place gave me courage.

Armed with the research, I visited the base doctor to discuss my situation. Transitioning to a new gender isn't something that routinely comes up in military medical situations, so the doctor was surprised but supportive. She consulted with her colleagues in civilian practice, and presented me with information, options and medical contacts. I was granted two weeks' discretionary leave by the doctor and set about preparing to transition. I changed my name and underwent an evaluation by a psychologist.

Two weeks later, I returned to the base ready to tell my commanding officer why I'd been away. I knew there had been others before me in the armed forces in similar situations who had paved the way, but I was still nervous about the reaction and the effect on my career. On a Friday afternoon, I sat down for a coffee with Major Payton. He told me an explanation wasn't necessary, that a soldier's private business is their own.

I said, 'Well, sir, this is something I really do need to tell you. I identify as someone who is different from the body I've been given. With medical and family support, and hopefully the army's support, I'm going to transition and start afresh.'

He immediately gave me his full support, while admitting to not knowing much about being transgender. 'We'll ride this new waka together,' he promised, and asked me to write down what I wanted to say to the other soldiers so he could read it to them on my behalf. He said everyone should know that their commanding officer was behind me 100 per cent. I have enormous respect for him — it was a wonderful example of leading from the front. The brilliant thing about being a soldier is that if you meet the standards of performance and have the right attitude, the army is a very inclusive, easy place to be.

The American military has a real polarising political issue with LGBTQIA+ soldiers. There *has* been discrimination in our army's past, just as there has been in wider New Zealand society, but things are different now. Today in the defence force we're free to love who we choose and have the right to serve our country as our authentic selves.

If you meet the standards of performance and have the right attitude, the army is a very inclusive, easy place to be.

When it came time to choose my name, I wanted a sense of continuity and respect for the original names my parents gave me. Sarah had existed for 27 years and was still part of me; also it was easier to keep the same initials and therefore my signature. As a kid, I'd loved the Tom Sawyer character in the Mark Twain book, and it felt like a smooth evolution to go from Sarah to Sawyer. My middle name, Ellen, after my grandmother, I masculinised to Allen. From Sarah Ellen I became Sawyer Allen.

As part of my transition I had a bilateral mastectomy, often referred to as top surgery. It's a fairly routine procedure, similar to a breast-reduction operation for a woman, with the added cosmetic aspect for me of creating a masculine look to the chest. The public health system does offer this procedure but it's not high priority and you can be bumped up and down the long wait-list at any time, but with crowdfunding and the generosity of family and friends, which was overwhelming, and the addition of savings, it was possible to choose a private surgeon. I met Dr Chris Porter in Christchurch. He's a lovely man and an accomplished plastic surgeon and he was totally affirming throughout the process. I'm hugely grateful to him and his team for the gift they gave me. The quintessential guy thing is to take your shirt off at the beach, and now I can do that with confidence.

Transitioning felt like coming home, a peaceful feeling of contentment. Now I set even higher standards for myself; I don't want special treatment from anyone. Diversity helps us become better soldiers, it makes us stronger not weaker. In the community and on operations we are constantly dealing with people from many different backgrounds, so we need to be open and approachable to break down barriers. People can be afraid of what's unfamiliar, but what unites us is much greater than what divides us — our similarities far outweigh our differences. New recruits need to be New Zealand residents for five years and have a clean security clearance, then they can join the defence force. Black, white, Muslim, Chinese, gay or straight — we all have to meet the same military standards.

Penelope and I were married in the summer of 2021 in a small ceremony. She is an amazing woman and so supportive and loving in every way. We'll have a larger celebration when friends and family can join us from overseas. She is a massage therapist at a clinic close to the army base, and she now also shoulders the weighty job of being an army wife. We have a husky dog named Kacela that we love taking on long walks. If there's theatre, ballet or just a movie happening in Christchurch, we sometimes drive up. I do a lot of reading — I love learning new things so I'll pick up any reading material that's not nailed down. Hopefully children are in our future. We'd love to create a family together and we're flexible about how. We're on the fertility clinic wait-list for sperm, but adopting or a long-term foster child would be awesome too.

Penelope and I live in army housing next to the Burnham military base, in a strong, stable community. Soldiers are often away on exercises or posted to emergencies throughout the country and there's always the possibility of overseas deployment, so it's important that our army spouses and children have others around them who understand the experience of being an army family.

I feel as if I've found my calling in the army. I'm planning to be here until I retire. The army has given me training, and a home, but it's also nurtured me and kept me employed through my transition. Without them, that could have been a much tougher time in my life. I want to give back by reaching higher-ranking positions so I can be there to support new people coming through, just like I was supported.

For young people figuring out their path in life, the defence force is within your reach if you're prepared to be challenged. We sometimes do our best growing and learning when we're outside of our comfort zone, and I've found the NZDF has always pushed me towards my potential.

There's no such thing as failure in my book — it's all learning. Take courage, and don't be afraid.

James Dobson

James Dobson, one of New Zealand's best-known designers, established the fashion label Jimmy D in 2004, and won the prestigious Mercedes-Benz Start Up Award with his first collection.

In the nineties, I had a huge crush on my Japanese teacher at high school. It was such a crush that I lived in a delusional world in which he asked me to move to Japan with him, and it was so real in my mind that I told all my friends about it. One afternoon I stayed late to declare my undying love to him but there was a girl in the classroom struggling with her homework. I waited and waited until I *had* to get home and missed saying anything to him. I still think about how that girl saved me from potentially one of the most awkward conversations of my life. The strange thing is, I never equated my obsession with the Japanese teacher with being gay or being attracted to guys — I completely compartmentalised it in my mind.

My two brothers are about 10 years younger than me and so I basically grew up as an only child, completely overindulged and showing early signs of precocious, bratty behaviour. One Christmas, my uncle gave me a Matchbox car. I unwrapped it and said, 'Is that all?' I remember this vividly because suddenly all the oxygen was sucked out of the room and my parents were so embarrassed. My uncle explained that he didn't have a lot of money and that it was the best he could do. Soon after, my little brothers arrived, and I had to leave my private school because the fees were too expensive and I quickly learnt that I wasn't the centre of the universe. Thank God for siblings.

At Heretaunga College I had a small group of misfit friends. We sat in the same place every lunchtime. I suppose we were the geeks, but we didn't get bullied. Sex and sexuality weren't really burning issues for any of us. I lived in blissful ignorance, but probably mostly denial. I asked my friend Emma to go to the school ball with me. I guess I thought I had a crush on her but at the time I remember it didn't feel quite right, it felt a bit performative, but I feel like I never even knew what gay was. I didn't know anyone gay so it wasn't part of my world.

I was quite academic at school, and when I won first prize at a science fair I was pretty sure I would go down that path, while lots of my friends were artistic, spending all lunchtime in the darkroom developing photos. I remember thinking how boring that seemed until one day I picked up a camera and I was *obsessed*. I flipped to studying mostly creative subjects.

Up until that point I never really thought about fashion; clothing was more about assimilating. I remember buying the exact same coloured turtleneck to go under the exact same shirt as one of my friends. As I discovered my creative side and started hanging out with more of the 'alternative' gang, clothes became about self-expression and I began trawling op shops for cardigans, loud op-art printed polyester shirts and patterned pants. I wanted to be noticed, to indicate that I was different, but I also was super shy and didn't want to stand out. I guess I was just trying to find my authentic self.

I studied a Bachelor of Design in photography at Massey University and did one pattern-making paper in my final year when I decided photography might not be for me. At parties, people would often ask me if I was gay. They'd say 'It's totally fine if you are', but I still didn't think I was. I remember being really exasperated on many occasions, even telling one of my friends to 'stop being so supportive!' When I hear about people coming out later in life or taking a while, I empathise. Everyone claims their identity when they're ready.

I realised I was gay when my high school best friend Jason returned from an overseas exchange trip and told me he was gay, which came as a total surprise. He invited me to a party with some of his friends, and before the night was out I was pashing one of them, and then I just kind of thought, 'Oh, that makes sense, I'm gay.'

That guy gave me this huge hickey on my neck. It was the middle of summer and I had to have lunch with my family the next day. I wore a black polar-fleece turtleneck sweater, by Starfish, and spent the whole afternoon refusing to take it off, despite the cascade of sweat rolling down my back.

When I hear about people coming out later in life or taking a while, I empathise. Everyone claims their identity when they're ready.

I never related to the glitzy, glamorous side of fashion. There was a *Pavement* magazine photo shoot in the nineties of a grungy girl in front of a suburban garage; she had braces on her teeth and wore New Zealand labels. It was the first time I saw fashion in a way I could relate to and that it didn't have to be flashy or elitist. When I started going to bars and clubs in Wellington there was a clique of good-looking young 'it' gays. I was walking around town one day and waiting to cross the road when one of them came up behind me and whispered in my ear, 'You're so ugly'. It cemented my feelings of being an outsider, but also made me realise there can be power in that too.

Through my newfound passion for fashion magazines and Fashion TV, I discovered a love for British designer Alexander McQueen and his concept-first approach to design and the theatricality of his shows. I finished my degree and moved to London with pretty much the sole desire to work for him. I remember arriving in London, going to the incredible McQueen store and being greeted by a swarthy Italian male model and thinking, 'Hmmm . . . this might not be my destiny after all.' I don't think I even left my CV.

Instead, I found a job at a store called The Library, which stocked my favourite brands. It was in South Kensington, a wealthy part of London. It was more low-key than the high-voltage Bond Street fashion strip, but we had loads of famous people coming in — Gwyneth Paltrow, all the footballers and their wives, Mick Jagger was dancing around the store one morning. Seal was a regular. He would park his Ferrari on the footpath right outside. Once he came in, spent £14,000, then asked us if we wanted to hear his new song. He got a guitar out of his car and sang it to us. That was my first week in London. It was so surreal and I couldn't help but think, I'm just a kid from Upper Hutt, this is *crazy*.

There was an amazing club scene in London. I would dress up and go to electro clash nights like NagNagNag. It was just a really exciting, liberating time. I was a pretty tenacious early-20-something at this point and I worked with a few older guys who partied a lot. For some reason I freaked out that I might kind of blank out, come to after 10 years of partying and still be working at the same place. I was too ambitious for that.

It's inspiring living in a city like London, at the edge of design, fashion and music, but it's also ridiculously fast and competitive. I knew that I wanted to either start my own label or become a stylist but both of these felt so overwhelming to do in London, with this constant stream of Central Saint Martins' graduates. So I returned home in 2003 and my label Jimmy D was born a year later.

Soon after Jimmy D launched, I entered a competition with my first collection. Part of the prize was a show at Sydney Fashion Week in the 'New Generation' section. My parents were living in the UK at that time, and my mum was so proud. She said that if I won she'd come to my show in Sydney — and I won. Mum planned to meet me there. I arrived a few days early and went out partying at the clubs, where I met a guy named Roger and had a crazy debauched time. I must have told him why I was in town as he wrote a message on my website saying I'd left my Nom*D cuff at his house, and he'd love to meet up again.

The problem was, my website was built by my much-younger brother who was somewhat of a technological savant, so the message went to him, which then got passed on to my mum. It was pretty awkward when Mum arrived in Sydney, saying, 'You have a message from Roger. He said he had a great time and that you left your cuff at his house.' I felt kind of outed and ambushed. I think Mum wanted some kind of big coming out, which was maybe fair enough, but also I thought, why should this change anything? I never felt any pressing need to tell the rest of my family. I didn't think it was something that required discussion. But, over the years, Mum has remained the conduit between the family and me for any personal information about partners and such.

In recent years, collections have become more genderless. When I first heard about people identifying as non-binary, I'm ashamed to say I was kind of confused, but now I see that these binaries are enforced on us at such a young age it can be hard to unravel them and find your own unbiased truth. Initially, genderless Jimmy D collections were borne out of both creative and practical impulses rather than any conscious political statement. After I'd designed a 'women's collection', and the final pieces were hanging on the racks, I wondered, what's in there that I can wear? For photo shoots I began casting the people around me who represented my wider Jimmy D family, regardless of their gender.

I've always been super greedy with fabric, I love billowing shapes, but also bias cutting that gives woven fabrics almost a natural stretch — both techniques allow us to create designs that can work on many different bodies and ages. Even a dark collection needs to have a playful aspect, a subtle undercurrent of subversive humour. I love fashion, but the idea of taking it too seriously kind of grosses me out. I'm often seen blasting music in my studio and catwalking around the cutting table in the new season's samples.

Fashion has a unique ability to provoke and pose questions without words. Why are pink and silk linked to femininity, for example? Why do we imbue fabric and colour with a gender? Why are we comfortable showing a man's chest but not a woman's? Can we put lace trim on men's shorts? I try to play with these ideas and loosen the restraints. Every season is a tightrope walk. Being a label that sells predominantly in New Zealand, I don't want to be too commercial, but I also can't be too crazy. It's a mind-fuck every time, but that's the challenge. I never wanted to be a super-commercial brand so playing it safe is not going to happen. I often ask myself, can we make a garment feel like it's had a life before someone buys it? Modelling agencies can be quite limited in the range of faces they have on their books, so trying to find older models or gender-diverse models for our shoots is also difficult.

I've always loved being a bit of a cultural voyeur. I love witnessing different subcultures from the sidelines, and even if I don't immerse myself fully, I have so much respect for people who commit to a scene, whether it be punk, emo, fetish and so on. It takes guts to live outside the beige norm. I work in contrasts; I like to imagine a collision of worlds. I think newness can only really come from mixing disparate things, things that haven't been previously put together, and I'm also not afraid to provoke. I think most fashion in New Zealand is boring and sex-less. I met a woman in a shop who was wearing one of my garments from the collection we did with the artist George Hajian. He'd collaged fragments from old books, some of which are vintage pornos; the print has the occasional male bum. This woman works in the corporate world and loves walking into the office with it on. It gives her a subversive sense of individuality and the power to retain her personality in a hyper-conformist environment.

My partner Dan is an artist, and he also works at the Basement sex club, which has been the subject of some of his work. A series of items he swept off the floor of the club after the patrons had gone home was the material for one of his art shows. He sandwiched the sweepings between glass. One is a used condom, which we have in our living room. Dan has sculpted papier-mâché likenesses of some of the characters who visit the club. They sit around our house naked and pierced, keeping us company.

I couldn't be in a relationship with another fashion designer — that would be way too intense — but being with a creative person who understands my work and can discuss ideas is so valuable. In that intimate informal sense, Dan and I are constantly collaborating. I'm not the most pleasant person to be around when a collection date is looming — either freaking out about whether a collection is too commercial or not commercial enough. Dan understands what it's like to bring a creative project to life. It's a very inspiring relationship. When I was newly single I went on a date with a lawyer; it was immediately obvious that it wasn't going to work.

I honestly believe that this societal idea of masculinity needs to be completely deconstructed. The world functions so well for white heterosexual men, why would they want it to change? And to keep it this way, femininity is seen as weakness. Clothing and beauty may seem superficial but they can effect change. Recently, a friend and I were wondering why our dabbling with 'femininity' stops at just clothing and accessories. If we're wearing a crystal-emblazoned top, why not wear a swipe of eyeshadow too? This is why we started an Instagram page and YouTube account called Beauty Benders, to explore and champion people who embrace the power of makeup. Cosmetics companies could double their sales, but even with all their global power and marketing machinery, they're not willing to override society's expectation that men shouldn't wear makeup — that's how strong the gender conditioning is.

Probably once a week I glue in single, straggly hair extensions, and paint on some elaborate glittery eyes and huge cartoonish lips. Going out is simultaneously a liberating and terrifying experience. I have so much respect for the bravery of people who express their gender identity in non-conformist ways.

Clothing and beauty may seem superficial but they can effect change.

Each season in fashion is a blank slate. It's intimidating but exciting to know that I have the power to do whatever I want. Fashion is obsessed with newness and youthfulness, and so as I get older, I'm glad that I'm still the same cultural voyeur I've always been. There's some exciting new scenes and club nights in Auckland that are inspiring. I think I'll probably always be the person at the back of the club who's just taking it all in. I think that's the key to staying fresh — being inquisitive and actively hunting for new ideas.

Taupuruariki 'Ariki' Brightwell

(Rongowhakaata, Te Whānau-
a-Ruataupare, Raukawa,
Ngāti Toa, Tahiti, Rarotonga)

Taupuruariki 'Ariki' Brightwell
is an indigenous artist,
muralist and educator
who works in both digital
and traditional mediums,
combining the styles of
her heritage with those
drawn from American and
Japanese pop culture.

My name comes from my Rarotongan heritage. My grandfather's first cousin on my mother's side, Taupuruariki Cowan, was known as the first Cook Island surgeon, and was the husband of Makea Nui Teremoana Ariki, Queen of Rarotonga. When he passed, my parents asked Queen Tere permission to give his name to me, which she agreed. Taupuruariki translates to high chief; my Rarotongan family say I am the only one with the name and I've never met anyone else who has it. I feel lucky and proud to have a name representing my whakapapa and character. Today I go by Ariki, a shortened version, which translated alone is a title of royalty and leadership within the realms of Hawaiki; however anyone is welcome to address me by my full name.

I was born and raised in Tūranganui-a-Kiwa Gisborne in a large family; on my father's side my grandparents had 10 children. I also have nine siblings — three including me to my Tahitian mother. Her family, who I often visited during my youth, is very large so there were many relations from both sides of the family growing up.

I went to school in Aotearoa, starting at kōhanga reo, then Waikirikiri, a kura kaupapa Māori, and I became fluent in my native tongue, as well as picking up French from my Tahitian whānau visiting the motu.

My whānau have long been keepers and practitioners of traditional knowledge, and their greatest legacy is waka ama; bringing the world of Polynesian voyaging and waka building back into the spotlight when our double-hulled sailing canoe Hawaikinui — built by hand by my whānau — arrived in Aotearoa from Tahiti. It replanted the seed of traditional voyaging and waka ama, and the first waka ama club in New Zealand, Mareikura Canoe Club, was founded in 1985. The other side of my family legacy is art; both art and waka are intertwined, as our traditions are preserved and told through art, and it is who I am today. My father is a twenty-sixth-generation tohunga whakairo (master carver) and tohunga wakahaere (master canoe builder and navigator). One of his most popular works is the Ngātoroirangi rockface carving in Mine Bay, Taupō.

His knowledge was passed down from the leaders of my tribes during his youth, through his language, whakapapa and values. His art was passed down from the greatest tohunga whakairo of the twentieth century, who founded postmodern Māori art; he learned and assisted in the creation of Takapūwāhia Marae in Porirua. When I was little my dad would frequently take me out of school to his carving post in Whāngārā while he was building the largest waka taua ever created, *Te Aio o Nukutaimemeha*. Most of my childhood memories are from that time.

I absorbed much of the arts of our ancestors by being around the great waka, watching my dad adze day to day, shaping the many tōtara logs into a hull for his waka, a sight few people witness today. The sound, the smell of tōtara and the environment had a large impact on my upbringing and journey as an artist. From a young age, my parents encouraged me to draw anything; art has been a cornerstone of my life ever since; it defines who I am and underpins our traditions of storytelling and the preservation of knowledge.

My artistic creativity also stems from my mother's side through her father, a master waka builder and navigator considered to be one of the major pioneers of Polynesian voyaging in the twentieth century who led the first modern Polynesian voyage on the bamboo raft *Tahiti Nui*, to Chile, in 1956, during a time when the *Kon-Tiki* was considered the paramount sailing vessel. Its captain, Thor Heyerdahl, claimed no one could sail back to South America. My grandfather proved him wrong, breaking the modern myth that our people were not open-water voyagers.

In the 1980s, my dad and grandfather combined their knowledge of Aotearoa and Polynesia to build *Hawaikinui*. They used customary carving tools such as adze, and chisels to carve the hulls, and natural materials like bamboo for the masts, deck and housing, coconut-fibre ropes and flax sails; it took them years of work. Setting sail, they voyaged over 5000 nautical miles across the Pacific Ocean, without modern technology, from Tahiti to Aotearoa, following the ancient route of first voyagers from Hawaiki. My grandfather captained the waka, my father was his right-hand man. Also on board was Rodo Parau, a descendant of Tupaia, the Tahitian navigator who helped Cook's *Endeavour* reach Aotearoa in 1769, my uncle Ace and British yachtsman Alex Roper.

Sailing through sun and storms, with only the navigation of the stars, the sea and the natural world to guide them, they reached Hicks Bay on the East Coast after a month, the first traditional Polynesian voyage to arrive at Aotearoa since the time of our ancestors. *Hawaikinui* proved to the world that the ocean voyages of Māori folklore were genuine. I was born after *Hawaikinui* landed in Aotearoa; if that waka hadn't made it, I wouldn't be here today. I consider it to be the waka of my pepeha, which honours the mana of my whānau. The voyage of *Hawaikinui* represents the successful struggle of our people to keep our traditions alive.

I tell you all this in detail as for Māori our whakapapa and achievements of our ancestors define who we are; my whānau's waka legacy, my father's artistic achievements and the achievements of many before us give me the strength and vision to achieve what I have done in my lifetime, not only in art but also in the decisions I have made to celebrate who I truly am. Now it's up to the next generations to keep ascending and, like those before me, my place is to influence them.

Digging back into my upbringing and takatāpui identity, growing up I never really noticed anything out of place in my interests. I loved boys' stuff like playing in the mud, catching sea creatures and running around in nature, as well as action figures, Transformers, video games and remote-control cars. That was all fun and felt comfortable. Looking back now, I would not identify those things with being a boy, I was just a kid enjoying fun whacky stuff, but deep down inside there was always something lurking in the back of my mind that didn't make sense. I come from an eccentric family, but even among my own I stood out as being different, and even more so at school, waka training and around people in general.

At that time no one in my family was takatāpui and no one talked about it, so I wasn't exposed to these concepts, especially growing up in the nineties on the East Coast. I couldn't make sense of feelings I had about my identity. I remember a few movies would play on TV with characters who I now realise were transgender, or something in that nature, which made me curious, but they were always comedies — we laughed and enjoyed the shows but in the end they didn't help me to understand.

Later on, the internet arrived in our household, when I was around 10 years old. I began instinctively searching for stuff about gender and sex, through fantasy storytelling and erotica — all the things early internet had to offer. But without anyone to talk to about it, I was left with more questions than answers. I was too afraid to mention a word for fear of how my family and community would react. I was beginning to feel depressed and angry through a lot of my teenage years, mostly because of this confusion about my identify, however I managed to pour those feelings into my art and I escaped into the fantasy world of pop culture, heavy metal music, video games, Japanese manga, anime and graphic novels, which is where I received my artistic influence in those fields. Sadly my own culture and heritage were no longer interesting to me at the time; it was too emotional and confronting to turn to.

When I was 18, my parents moved me to Wellington to study at Victoria, and later Massey University, where I studied animation and character design, earning my Bachelor of Design in 2016. Being a small-town kid, and self-absorbed in my own fantasy world, this was a big deal and a turning point in my life, and I'm forever grateful to my parents for giving me that opportunity. Turanganui-a-Kiwa Gisborne is quite isolated and has insular small-town traits like everyone knowing your business. The Māori community at the time was also very inhospitable to takatāpui, and most weren't accepted and were bullied horrendously, so I didn't feel free to express myself there.

Wellington on the other hand opened my eyes and showed me different ways of living. I had no clue how significant the city was to LGBTQIA+ rights and figures who paved the way in Aotearoa, making it an ideal city to come out. I met a small group of amazing friends who were into the nerdy stuff like I was and influential teachers who opened my eyes to the world — especially those I met in martial arts and the art of kendo, which I practised for eight years, reaching third Dan (third-degree black belt). My sensei are a lesbian couple who are strong advocates for takatāpui and women's rights and they became one of the main pillars of support during my first steps.

As time passed by, I slowly began to reflect on my life and my identity. Even coming across other transgender individuals along the way made my heart race and many of those people are good friends to this day, although sadly some are no longer with us. In my early twenties I gradually came to understand who I really am and that my identity and wairua are wahine. I think the time in Wellington, building my own path away from my family, played a massive part in discovering my true identity and establishing my life.

In the end what really pushed me to take the leap was my older brother, who came out as gay when I was 23 and was going through a lot of internal conflict of my own. Seeing someone in my family bravely facing something similar to what I was experiencing gave me the final puff of air I needed to announce my feelings to the world on social media. There was some backlash when my family found out about my announcement; but I soon found out they were hurt I didn't trust them enough to tell them first. In fact, it took years for my parents to adjust. My mother was quicker due to the social norms in Tahiti. Dad took a little longer as he saw himself as coming from a Māori warrior culture where having a takatāpui child was a loss of mana, but he said to me that our ancestors would never turn their back on one of their own, and that aroha and whānau are the strongest elements in Māori culture. He came to accept me and understand takatāpui as part of the natural world and eventually our paths of art and identity intertwined, and our bond has been stronger than it's ever been.

My mum knew about takatāpui people from Tahitian culture, where they use the word mahu, but she still said it was like getting hit by a train when I told them I would transition to a wahine; she was worried I would fall into the stereotype of prostitution and poverty, as so many in my predicament are driven to. It was hard for all of us, but I'm lucky to have parents who worked with me to understand that I haven't really changed — physically, I've changed, of course, but I'm the same person, just much stronger, more optimistic and motivated. I've also learnt to understand and tolerate those around me who do not fully embrace who I am; although it's been very difficult at times, it's built me quite a thick skin.

When I began to transition, I felt a reawakening, a rebirth; I felt I could grow into a complete person, claiming a whole part of me that was missing my entire life, and everything started to make sense. Receiving my first hormone pills was like Christmas. My family's acceptance gave me courage to be myself as my whānau, whakapapa — my Hawaiki bloodlines — and identity are everything in life. Embracing my own identity and place in the world meant all else fell into place; my passion for the arts and my own culture returned, and I began to flourish and life improved dramatically. I accepted my culture again, re-learning parts I'd forgotten and utilising its strengths in my artform, and with these influences creating a style that's truly mine. Achieving this, my dad named me the twenty-seventh-generation artist in our art legacy, for which I'm forever proud.

At present I work at an art studio at Ōwhiro Bay, on the south coast of Wellington. It's a special place where a group of artists have rented an old 1930s garage and converted it into a space which has flourished in the last decade a home for creatives from all realms. It's called Nautilus Creative Space, and it's a beautiful place to work, with fresh salty air coming in off the sea. There are old horse stables around the back dating from the late nineteenth century.

I joined the community in 2019, and not long after I came up with an idea to create my most ambitious project yet, painting a massive mural depicting Kupe's discovery of Aotearoa in 900 AD on the front of the building. With support from Creative New Zealand, the artists and the wider community, in a year we were able to create a work of art worthy of our ancestors and their time in Wellington. There's a lot of life that's gone through our studio, and I believed the artwork I had created was what this placed needed, to uplift it and keep alive the indigenous stories of the land. I'd love to see more collective spaces like this around Aotearoa because they're essential to the creativity of our artists, who share their work and culture in our communities, and help greatly with mental health, giving creatives a place of belonging and creating a space a community is proud of.

A lot of my art has been larger-than-life murals recently. I love doing them because the of the immense time and energy it takes, and the colours and quality of the art is seen by the world, telling the indigenous history of our land. Anyone passing by sees them, so they really connect with the community rather than being stuck in a gallery somewhere. In terms of work I've done with the takatāpui community, one stands out in my mind. In 2018 I was commissioned, with the help of my father, to create a mural inside the Hawke's Bay Museum for Hui Takatāpui, the annual gathering of Aotearoa's takatāpui community. I chose to base the artwork on the spiritual power and colours of Uenuku, the Māori god of rainbows, a conduit between the realms of the celestial and the living, a gateway that passes messages between the two worlds. Uenuku also has associations with peace and harmony. The mural blended the globally recognised symbol for LGBTQIA+ people and the traditional Māori meaning to create a visual celebration of takatāpui culture; it felt like a beautiful symmetry.

Other works include creating a piece for *Poutokomanawa: The Carmen Rupe generation* at the New Zealand Portrait Gallery, and for Gender Minorities Aotearoa, who commissioned me to create a series of posters to support the transgender rights movement. They were illustrated to show real people from within our community just being themselves, with the phrase 'Trans women are women'. The posters were bold but simple, the theme being that we're just the same as everyone else and deserve the same rights and treatment. They were put up all over New Zealand. I'm so pleased when I can use my art to give back to the takatāpui community among my culture.

Before I came out and decided to transition, I hardly knew my dad, even though we'd lived in the same house all my younger years. For some of that time I didn't want to know him because he was so strict and hard. Some of that hardness was caused by the pain and anger he carried with him from living through the abuse and racism of his time and the suffering of our ancestors. Now he's become more mellow in his age and thoughtful towards me; he's seen how much I embrace our Māori-Pacific culture in my art and he's acknowledged it, which is so important to me. He's not easy to impress and will tell you straight up if your work is up to standards, practices I've adopted into my own work.

What really solidified our relationship was when in 2018, when I was painting one of our ancestors at the Gisborne skate park, the first ancestral mural I had created from the stories taught by my dad passed down from my grandmother's side, he turned up on the second day out of the blue, ready to help me work. He'd put everything else aside to come and paint with me. I was completely blown away; tears of joy filled my eyes. To have him join me on a mural was one of the best feelings I've ever had; it was a beautiful revelation to see we could have a father–daughter relationship making art together, our bond has never been stronger, and the energy we share when creating is hard to explain in words.

The confidence and energy I've gained shows itself in my art, and I see it in people's response to my work, which makes me excited for the future. I'm interested in seeing where our indigenous art goes next, and where it might have evolved if it hadn't been stunted by colonial suppression. I want to create work that is contemporary and which progresses our art while still honouring our history and the mana of our tīpuna, legends and whakapapa. Being takatāpui, I think that life experience emanates through my art in subtle ways, even when I'm not creating specific queer-themed work.

Before Europeans arrived in Aotearoa, art was the language used to communicate ideas, to visually describe our culture and history, create memory and to pass on knowledge. Carving, weaving, tukutuku and waiata, among many other expressive mediums, were all used to create a continuous flow of knowledge to the next generations. A lot of our indigenous knowledge was lost through the influence of early missionaries, who pushed repressive Christian ideals, greatly impacting our relationship with sex and gender, and introduced taboo and shame still prevalent within the Māori community today. However, learning from my takatāpui seniors who are the pillars of progress of takatāpui rights and awareness, I've learnt that many markers from early Māori times can still be seen in our culture today, despite the damage Christianity has done to our community.

In Māori culture, sexuality was a way to show mana through fertility and openness.

The cornerstone of a people is its language and in te reo Māori we have no gender distinction, no words for 'he' or 'she', just the neutral 'they' and 'them' ('ia' and 'aia'). Ancient legends are still told of men and women reversing roles due to their nature and status. Some carvings survive that celebrate sexuality; everyone's seen the prominent genitalia on Māori carvings; there's nothing shy there, and some of those housed in museums in Europe depict same-sex relations.

In Māori culture, sexuality was a way to show mana through fertility and openness — you see genitalia featured on carvings in marae all the time — and there was no shyness about it until Christianity arrived and European ideals made our people feel ashamed of their urges and emotions. People began to be punished for being open about their sexuality and their bodies, they were forced into Westernised gender roles and they realised how dangerous it was to anger the colonial masters as their power and influence spread over our lands.

Traditional, open ideas about sexuality, including takatāpui, receded into the shadows and were never talked about until eventually they became a source of shame and whakamā. I still see negative reactions to takatāpui today, especially in small towns, with terrible outcomes for those who come out, but it's much better than when I was a kid, with the strong rise of activism, increasing number of LGBTQIA+ political leaders and social media circles bringing the fight to the mainstream.

Although a lot of our takatāpui history was destroyed, the colonisers were not able to crush everything. The fragments that survive remind us of more enlightened pre-European times, when Māori lived in accordance with the natural world. Colonisation has failed to erase us from history and the surviving knowledge is used and led by our rangatahi to break new grounds, to be a great source of learning and pride for takatāpui today. I see my path in life to continue advancing my people's art and culture, and to add my own chapter to our ongoing story, like my grandfather and father before me, who went up against the world for a great cause, for the survival and celebration of our culture. That's where I see my place in the world, and the experiences my whānau went through to achieve the impossible propels me on the path I'm taking now as an artist.

My advice to those going through hard times is, if you're takatāpui and someone else has an issue with it, then that's 100 per cent their problem, not yours; who cares what they think. Those who react negatively have their own problems to deal with; don't let their troubled wairua get you down. Our ancestors, activists and politicians who paved the way for our rights, did not give a damn what others thought and aimed high no matter what the cost. Remember Carmen Rupe campaigned for mayor of Wellington in 1977!

Living a full life shows the world that you are a human being like everyone else and you deserve peace, understanding and acceptance. I've been through some hard times, as we all do, but I feel that in Aotearoa things are getting better for takatāpui and we are lucky to be in a country where we can walk the streets without the fear of persecution and violence — a regular occurrence for takatāpui in many countries, like the Middle East, Russia or China, for example, who do not have a safety net for LGBTQIA+ individuals.

Aotearoa is far from perfect, but we have a strong history of activism and working for equality, we're the first country in the world to allow women to vote and one of the few countries where a treaty exists that helps the indigenous people of the land reclaim their freedom. We had the first openly trans politician. We can continue to assert our rights and mana and that is starting to be acknowledged, with our country becoming one of the most progressive nations in the world for takatāpui rights. Access to healthcare is slowly improving and society is becoming more educated about takatāpui. Even Gisborne, my very stubborn hometown, is progressing, with support groups forming, and awareness in the public health sector growing.

Transgender and LQBTQIA+ groups have pushed the fight for our rights all the way to Parliament. We now have allies to support us and that puts a big smile on my face, and merely existing and doing what I love sends ripples through the communities I engage with. Understanding history is important: we can stand back and see there has been more progress in the last 10 years than in the previous 100 years. Now that's something to feel hopeful about.

Jonny Rudduck

Jonny Rudduck, a former
Tāmaki Makaurau Auckland
pizzeria owner, is a retired
gentleman farmer.

Mum's first inkling I might be gay was when I was six. I liked baking and playing with dolls and I was a little mummy's boy, as the youngest of five kids. I was born in Western Australia in 1967. My parents separated when I was two and because Mum was a Kiwi, we moved back to Auckland. Six years later, my father decided he wanted us back together, so Mum packed us up for the trip back to Australia; I was eight then and thrilled that my father wanted to see me again.

The family reunion lasted all of two months before my father up and left once more. We were really stranded this time with no money and, being Kiwis, there was no support from the Australian government. I had to break into my father's house to steal food so we could eat. Having the family split up a second time and being totally broke was too much for Mum; she had a breakdown. Later we realised this was an early sign of the schizophrenia that would soon take hold of her. Abandoned by my father and stuck in Australia, all we could do was wait for my poor old grandmother to put together the money to bail us out with airfares back to New Zealand. We moved into her house in Auckland. It was hard for her — young kids and a mentally ill mother all crashing around her little place. Eventually we got a state house in Massey and we restarted our life in West Auckland, with nothing but the roof over our heads.

They were tough times but I have many wonderful memories. Back then our part of Auckland was still full of farms, horses and orchards, with the Henderson Creek running through the middle. Whatever problems might be happening at home, I could always escape out into the bush with the other kids to climb trees and make huts. It was now 1976. There was no social media of course, and we didn't even have a phone for a long time. We had to walk miles to a phone box with the three two-cent pieces it cost to call someone. We got our first TV when I was 14, after my grandmother wrote in to a radio station competition and won a black and white one they were giving away to make way for the new colour TVs that were coming in. We were thrilled with it.

My first sexual experience was with the man next door, who lived there with his wife and young children. It's only looking back now that I see how deranged this situation was. He would call Mum and ask if she could send Jonny over to help with something. His wife was a shift worker so she'd often be out at night and his kids would be asleep in bed. I'd go over and we'd have sex. I was 12 or 13 when it started, I suppose. I was gay and quite adventurous — not that I had come out, even to myself, at that stage — but I went along with it and liked it. I never felt scarred by it in any way.

The neighbourhood kids would hang out at his house, tempted by cigarettes, Mr Whippy ice creams and pornography. In those days we all played around the streets and at different houses. No one questioned it, and we were too young to understand how perverse and twisted it was. I'm sure people might ask, 'Where were the parents?' Well, my mum was having a breakdown so she had no idea, other parents were working, there was a migrant family who didn't speak English. This couple had a predator mindset; they picked the vulnerable kids and lured them in. One time, he held me down in front of all the other kids and rubbed shoe polish all over my cock and balls. I ran home in tears that day. Another time I was tricked into eating a carrot that the mother had been putting inside her, while all the other kids watched and laughed at me. Those bizarre things happened to everyone who went there, so I didn't think much of it. Some of the kids were affected badly by it; I know my brother and sister were.

Meanwhile, Mum's mental health was getting worse. There were violent episodes — smashing plates and screaming as if she were possessed. Mum was a devout Pentecostal Christian and we'd always gone to church twice every Sunday, but the Christians turned their back on her during those dark times. They didn't offer any help at all. I never believed in God. What kind of God would take my father away and give my mum a mental breakdown?

One night when she was very bad, the police came. Mum resisted so they handcuffed her, and she was forced into the back of a police car and driven off to Carrington Psychiatric Hospital. The next time I saw her was through the iron grille on the door of her hospital room. She was sedated and lying on a mattress, dribbling. It was confronting as a young kid to witness her dealing with those demons. That was rock bottom, but it was also the beginning of her getting well. The doctors got her medications right, and she came home six weeks later. Mum built herself back up and got her life together; she was able to lead a wonderfully normal life for many years and created a lovely warm home for us kids — although the sexual abuse from the neighbour continued.

After only two years at the local high school, I was expelled. I wasn't really a bad kid, but being the youngest in a line of troubled older brothers and sisters I was tainted by their previous exploits. It turned out to be a good thing because I ended up doing Correspondence School at home, away from all the classroom distractions, and my grades improved.

Being a curious young man and having no teachers to stop me, I often caught the bus into the city when I'd finished my school work.

One afternoon when I was using the public toilets on Customs Street at the bottom of Queen Street, I discovered that these were places where men went for secretive sexual encounters. This was 1981, homosexuality was still illegal, I didn't know any other gay people and at 14 years old, I couldn't go to bars. The only place to meet other men was in public toilets. I'd get the bus into town and spend the day doing the rounds. I could draw you a map: the first stop was Grey Lynn — those are still there — then Howe Street, then Beresford Square off Karangahape Road. One of my primary school teachers was there one time.

A man offered me twenty dollars one morning and it dawned on me that I could make some pocket money with my dick. These encounters would go on brazenly, under people's noses almost. Once Mum took me shopping for jeans in a men's store. We found a pair that fit well so she popped to the bank to get the money. While she was gone, the shop salesman slid his hands down my pants and we went into the changing rooms and had sex. I often went back in there to try on Speedos and tight shorts, and he would put the closed sign up on the front door. I was just a horny kid having adventures, probably no different to kids these days, except now they go online or it's more discreet.

Many years later, my own son was at school nearby and needed a shirt so I took him into the same store thinking, there's no way that guy would still be working there. But he was. I bought the shirts and left quickly. It was very strange. I drove past a few weeks later and the shop was closed and cleared out. I suspect that seeing me in there as an adult with my own son gave him a scare. He was the supplier of uniforms for the local schools so there must have been other boys just like me.

It plays on my conscience that these people are still out there, maybe still doing these things with children. I think about getting them to answer for what they've done, for the sake of other kids, but the years of courts and lawyers and dragging it all up again for my own children to learn about is overwhelming. I'm surprised some of the other neighbourhood kids haven't felt compelled to confront them in court. Perhaps they just bury it all and try to forget it.

I 'd been feeling the desire to escape for a while. When I turned 17, I'd had enough of my life in West Auckland; it was time to strike out on my own. It was 1984. A friend's father suggested I join the navy, which sounded like an ideal way to escape, so I signed up as a steward in the Royal New Zealand Navy. The fitness requirements were gruelling at first but I learnt to love it and passed all the training. The camaraderie and bond created with other new recruits was powerful. I think that feeling is heightened in extreme environments like the military. The navy gave me the chance to start life with a clean slate, and I grabbed it with both hands.

When my father heard I'd joined up, he came straight back into my life. He hadn't contacted me since I was nine years old — no phone calls, no birthday cards, no Christmas cards. Suddenly, I was his golden boy. He wrote to me every week and flew over for my graduation parade. He was in the army but had always wanted to be in the navy so I think I was living his dream. Then, on my first trip, to Sydney on HMNZS *Waikato*, I was so horribly seasick I thought my naval career was over. The commanding officers convinced me to swap to a non-seagoing branch, so I learnt telecommunications and was deployed safely on land at the Waiouru and Devonport bases.

The navy was extremely straight — on the surface, anyway; closeted gay men often attach themselves to stereotypically masculine careers to try to disguise their sexuality. The Homosexual Law Reform Act was passed in 1986. I remember it well because my mother was fiercely opposed to it. The law decriminalised homosexuality and Mum was out fighting against it with the church, signing petitions and going on marches. I still wasn't out to my parents at this stage. After the law passed, the navy sent an official message to all personnel to state that while the law on homosexuality had changed for civilians, it had not changed in the navy. The message from the top brass was essentially: 'You're under military law, homosexuality is not legal. If you're in the closet, stay there.'

One night, I left the base to visit a gay sauna in the city. There was a sign on the wall advertising for escorts and I was reminded of my teenage adventures earning cash around the public toilets, so I decided to give it a try. This time the experience was more salubrious; a driver would pick me up and take me to the client's hotel or house, I'd do the business and get dropped back home again. Billy was the name I always gave in my gay life; Jonny was the straight boy. The usual pay was $100 an hour for me, and $30 for the agency; good money for the eighties. I had a rip-roaring time for a few years.

One chap paid incredibly well. He was the head of a large company, and I'd see him at home when his wife was away and children were at university. Sometimes he'd have me in his office; his secretary would wave me through. He wrote me out cheques to buy clothes, he even put me through a modelling course. This was in the heady days before the 1987 share-market crash. Everyone was out having long champagne lunches and seeing rent boys. It's amazing I managed to keep it all under cover and completely separate from navy life.

After five years, however, I felt that familiar urge for a change. I'd saved most of the money from those escort jobs and I used it to buy a ticket to London. I stopped in Australia for my twenty-first birthday with my father and sister and continued on to Europe. After years of my crazy family life and the rigid structure of the navy, the freedom was wonderful, until my sister came to join me. I love her dearly but I was trying to get away from everyone I knew, and having her around meant I had to carry on being sneaky with sexual stuff in case word got home.

While I was tripping around Europe, my future wife was pouring pints of beer at the Frog and Firkin pub in Westbourne Park, London; the same pub I'd begin working at a month later. Karen and I quickly fell in love and we decided to return to New Zealand to get married. They say the first person you come out to is yourself. When I decided to marry Karen, I still hadn't reached that stage. I hadn't admitted to myself that I was gay, even though I'd been having sex with men for years. Deep down, I didn't want to be gay, it just seemed too hard. Back then, there were no positive gay role models, and certainly no examples of gay couples leading a happy life or being accepted by their family. But despite that, I really did love Karen — we had a great sex life, we were happy, and I honestly believed I could live that life.

They say the first person you come out to is yourself.

We were soon pregnant with our first child, Zachary, who was born in 1990. Two years later our little girl Stanze arrived. Everything was wonderful for a few years but gradually marriage became a struggle. That's when I met a young farmer and became completely infatuated. He was the catalyst to make me see that I could no longer live a lie. When I left Karen for him, she was devastated; she felt our seven years of marriage were a complete fraud. She didn't deserve this and it was very sad. The kids came with me because she wasn't coping and from then on it was just the three of us.

I was working for Lion Nathan with lots of blokey beer and liquor guys. Tongues quickly started wagging at the office that Jonny had left his wife for a man. I walked into the tea rooms and said, 'OK everyone, listen up, I've got something to tell you. I'm gay. I'm no different than I was before and if you've got anything to say, say it to me now.' They sat there stunned but when they came around everyone respected me for confronting it head-on — the honesty took the sting and gossip out of it.

My father was not happy with me coming out, but he'd never been around so he didn't deserve an opinion on my sexuality. I don't even refer to him as 'Dad' — that's a term of endearment you have to earn. When he found out, he covered me up in all the family photos. Mum found out through family. I was driving with her one day when she asked me if it was true and I said it was. She said she loved me unconditionally, so this won out over her devout Christianity. She rationalised it by saying we all sin. Mum had had two abortions, which she considered murder, so the way she saw it, my sins were no different to hers. Still, she spent the rest of her life praying I wouldn't be gay so I could go to heaven.

When you're in the closet trying to hide, you don't realise how tightly strung you are; the weight that lifted off my shoulders was immense. I came flying out and made up for lost time. I got a rainbow tattoo, started to dress more flamboyantly, discovered a love of dancing and gained the nickname 'dancing daddy'. It felt as if my spirit had been freed and I was really happy. Karen did eventually recover from the shock of my leaving her. She said she never blamed me and that she understood it was family and society that put us in that position. It was so generous of her to see that.

We were living in Rotorua, and at the kids' schools it was well known that I was living with a man. Zac and Stanze had a lot of nasty comments from their classmates — it wasn't the most enlightened place. I learnt to be discreet about my sexuality when it came to the kids and their schools and friends to avoid unwanted attention for them. The farmer helped me see who I really was but our relationship didn't last long. I decided it would be better for us all to move back to Auckland.

We settled in Ponsonby, a better environment, where the schools were open and accepting. A lot of kids there had parents with gay friends, and for girls it was almost trendy to have a gay dad, so Stanze was OK. Zac has always had to deal with more narrow-minded ideas about what's acceptable for boys and men. A child needs love and it doesn't matter if that love comes from men or women. It was tough on the kids at times but it's made them more compassionate, more accepting of diversity. They don't stand aside when people are being mistreated.

For gay people, sexuality is still at the forefront of who they are. Straight people never have to define themselves by what they do in bed. Children of gay parents have to deal with the sexuality of their parents very early on, before they even understand their own sexuality, and that can be tough on them. In New Zealand, we're slowly moving from the assumption that everything straight is normal, so that's making it easier for kids of gay parents.

> # It was tough on the kids at times but it's made them more compassionate, more accepting of diversity. They don't stand aside when people are being mistreated.

In Auckland, I met a man from Rome who was also named Johnny. He swept me off my feet with his romantic Italian spirit. In the whirlwind of it all, he invited us to move to Italy to live with him. He was great with my kids so I agreed to test the water with a summer in Rome. We had a wonderful time, but I realised I couldn't uproot Zac and Stanze from their friends and family permanently. It was a lovely notion but it wasn't to be. We were sitting on Sperlonga Beach, which is halfway between Rome and Naples. I was at a crossroads, not sure what I should do when we returned to New Zealand. That day the twin towers had been destroyed in the 9/11 attack, which added to the uneasy, apprehensive feelings.

Johnny said to me, 'Why don't you open a Roman pizzeria in Auckland?' No one was doing authentic Roman pizza at the time and Auckland was in love with everything Italian with the Prada yacht in the America's Cup. I quit my well-paid corporate job and nine months later Il Buco, my little pizza shop on Ponsonby Road, was born. Il Buco translates to something like 'hole in the wall', which describes the compact size of the place: standing-room only inside and a few tables and chairs on the footpath outside.

I'd play my old vinyl records, George Benson or Duran Duran. It was hard work at the start but gradually word spread, magazines gave us food awards, and pizza started racing out the door until we were probably the highest-earning food place per square metre in the suburb. It was so rewarding seeing people enjoy my food and leave the shop smiling and satisfied.

Because it was a narrow space, people had to stand close together, and that started conversations; ideas were shared, and friendships were made. It became more than just a business, it was an institution. I became a marriage celebrant because friends from Il Buco asked me to marry them; I've since married over 80 couples. The GeorgeFM studio was upstairs and because the DJs would all come down to get their coffee and pizza, I got to know them well. A Monday night slot came up and I convinced them to let me take it and do a gay show with some friends. We called it 'One in Ten with Billy and Bob', a variety show with music, gig guides, horoscopes and interviews. We were on for a couple of years and it was a lot of fun — New Zealand's only nationwide gay radio show.

I'd had many romances over the years, but there was one man who had me particularly intrigued. Nigel ran past my shop every day as I stood behind my coffee machine, and I admired him from afar. I asked a mutual friend to introduce us and we started old-fashioned dating with dinners and movies. It turned out we both lived on Brown Street. One day, he said I could have half the bathroom cabinet, and that was it, I moved in. Nigel is a wonderful man. I've never felt so loved by anyone. He's a tightly wound high-performer, but raising two kids on my own has given me the skills I need to manage his delightfully capricious nature.

We'd reached a point where we were yearning to get out of Auckland; the pace was getting faster and it was time to jump off the treadmill. I'd had a great run with Il Buco, the kids had left home, our dancing and bar-hopping days were over, and we wanted space for dogs. We planned our escape from the city. On our long Sunday drives exploring possible towns, we came across a property called Oakridge. It was quite remote, down a rough shingle road, a simple house on 50 rolling acres with a stream running through it. We knew it was the one.

Mum had the very last slice of Il Buco pizza as my Ponsonby Road chapter came to an end and a new story of farm life began. There were fruit trees and vegetable gardens to plant, swimming holes to clear, sheep, cows and chickens to look after. Among our many animals we have a bull named Don and a ram named Henry who are best mates. They are absolutely inseparable.

I'm a grandfather now. I was 23 when I had my first child and Zac was 23 when he had his little boy, Jayden. I told him he was too young to have a baby and I was too young to be a grandad, but Jayden is a delight.

It's mysterious how life takes us down one path rather than another. If I'd been born 10 years later, when attitudes to being gay had become more tolerant, I may have come out in my teens and never got married, and then I wouldn't have had my two children and my grandchild. If I hadn't been married and focused on my family, I'd have been a gay man in my twenties and thirties during the height of the AIDS epidemic, and then I might not be sitting here now.

On the farm we have three wheaten terriers named Sparrow, Finch and Tui. They're about the same amount of work as looking after children, but they bring us a lot of joy. My daughter has bought 10 acres across the road from us. She's away overseas now but she'll return with her partner soon and we'll probably have more toddlers running around before long. Over the 12 years Nigel and I have been together, we've experienced incredible highs and lows. We've helped each other through the deaths of both of our mothers, but those hard times have only made our relationship stronger. Nigel loves my kids just as much as I do, and we want to share the wonderful life we've created at Oakridge Farm with our family and friends for as many years as we have left on this earth.

Chlöe Swarbrick

Chlöe Swarbrick is a member of the Green Party. She was elected to Parliament as a List MP at the 2017 general election and then in 2020 took back the Auckland Central seat from National.

I moved to Papua New Guinea with my father, grandmother and little sister when I was six years old. My parents had separated and Mum moved to London. It was a messy childhood. Papua New Guinea was a lawless, corrupt, violent place. Dad's job was creating finance links with the local construction industry so infrastructure could be built. We lived in a compound surrounded by barbed-wire fences, guarded by soldiers with AK47s. There were very few places we were allowed to go — school, the mall, the yacht club.

When we drove out of the gates, which wasn't very often, the poverty just hit us immediately. People stripped the flesh off dogs and left the carcasses on the streets. You don't forget something like that. My seventh birthday was cancelled because of rioting; the town was locked down so no one could get to our house.

The school was full of international kids from different backgrounds, but we all sang the Papua New Guinea national anthem at the start of every assembly. All the service jobs were done by local people; the place had that colonial segregation — barriers between people enforced by guards and guns. It fostered a fear of difference, which, even as a kid, I knew was all wrong. Living there probably stirred in me early questions about fairness and justice in the world, although I may not have realised it at the time.

Back in New Zealand a few years later, I started at Hillsborough Primary School in Auckland. It felt very foreign for a while; I had to learn a new national anthem and in Māori as well — my first experience of te reo. I was rather tomboyish, and mildly teased for being really into books. Royal Oak Intermediate was my next school. It was decile three so not a wealthy community, mostly Māori and Pasifika, with a few kids of Asian and Indian background and only a few white kids. In mixing with these different cultures, I was learning that not everyone shares the same cultural understandings.

Dad has been one of the biggest influences in my life. He has always challenged me to think in deeper ways and from different perspectives, encouraging me to be open-minded, and he entertains all my questions no matter how annoying. I was 12 when he told me he wasn't my biological father. The burden of when to tell me was weighing heavy on his shoulders — the balance of me being old enough to understand why he'd delayed it but not so late that I'd hate him. He struggled with this, but just the struggle itself, the fact that he cared so much, reaffirmed to me that he was an incredible man. We've grown together in terms of challenging each other. He'd always been a Tory, which was a reliable source of healthy friction. Now he spends a lot of time calling me up and giving me his two cents on various things and we joke that me railing against his advice all my life has been perfect training for being a member of Parliament.

It was always expected I would do well academically, and I wanted to please Dad. He'd lost everything in the 2008 global financial crisis, which turned our lives upside down, and I knew he was working hard to bounce back. That unspoken knowledge that failure at school would be a big disappointment weighed heavily on me and it made me quite introverted, but by the time I reached Epsom Girls' Grammar I was tired of living up to those expectations. I started rebelling and screwing around with a bunch of friends who also weren't interested in school. There was a lot colliding in my personal life: my sense of identity and place in the world, grappling with paternity and a strained relationship with my mother. I became anxious, depressed and started abusing alcohol, which of course doesn't help anything. I was good at hiding the drinking as most teenagers are, telling Dad I was somewhere I wasn't and all that.

I remember being attracted to girls at Epsom Girls', but I was also attracted to boys. Katy Perry's song 'I Kissed a Girl and I Liked It' was out at the time, so that performative bisexuality was very high profile, but it wasn't seen as a realistic sexuality; it was just what girls would act out to get boys to like them. The openly lesbian girls I knew at school were presenting in a more butch way, which I didn't identify with either. I pushed those feelings away assuming it must just be an admiration that I have for women, so I never properly considered that side of myself.

High school wasn't a happy time — being a curious person with no space to challenge ideas or try to achieve a depth of understanding is frustrating. I was always left with more questions than answers, always wondering why, wanting to know more; memorising enough information to pass an exam was never enough for me. The only environment that gave some respite from anxiety and depression was Year 12 drama. Mrs Druit was my brilliant teacher in that class; she encouraged us to think creatively and critically, gave us space to explore ideas. That one class really got me through high school. I went back recently to thank her.

Dad was my rock growing up, but we did drift apart for a period. There are certain things you don't want to talk about with your parents: worries about not reaching standards, about how I fit in. I dated a few boys I wasn't super attracted to; it was just about having someone as there was pressure to be in a relationship. I've been vegetarian since I was 14. That decision was founded on utilitarian principals, rather than animal rights; if I didn't have to kill something to survive, then I wouldn't. I'm sure it sounds like annoying, precocious teenage posturing. I was also interested in Nietzsche and nihilism — such a perfect manifestation of how dark and depressed I was.

The drinking was an escape. It did get very bleak, and I was suicidal for a while and thought I was a psychopath. Two simple options emerged: either I was going to die or I was going to completely change my life. At the time I didn't know what changing my life would look like, but the awful depressing backstop was, if it didn't work out I could always just end it. That's a terribly dark motivation: that the worst thing that could happen couldn't be any worse than how life already was. I had no real support.

So, first I changed my surroundings. I had no desire to continue high school, and so I dropped out, enrolled at Auckland University, left home, and moved into a flat. Actually, my first flat wasn't the best choice because it was quite a party house, but on my first day at uni, I met Alex in philosophy class. We started dating and he was my partner for six years.

Drinking hasn't been a problem since high school; having taken away the things I wanted to escape from, I replaced them with a better environment and better people, and so there became no need to block things out with alcohol. I'm the first person in our family to get a university degree, in law and philosophy.

My supposed coming out happened when a TV journalist was doing a profile piece. Not long before, I'd been in England speaking with Mhairi Black, a British member of Parliament who I hugely respect and with whom I have a few things in common. She is the youngest member in the House of Commons, is tired of hearing about her age rather than the issues, and was outed about her same-sex partner by the media. Her response at the time was brilliant. She said, 'I don't have to come out of the closet because I've never been in it.' The New Zealand media are nothing like the rabid British tabloid press. Mhairi's family was harassed, she was accused of corruption and it was all far more traumatic. I wasn't hiding my sexuality or my partner, I was just reluctant to put more of my life out there for the public to chew on. I already had my age and mental health issues on a platter, which tend to create simplistic, pigeonhole caricatures that I've struggled to break away from. We're all far more complex than a couple of things that frame you.

There's a real tension between wanting to be open and being wary of the backlash. But I do feel a responsibility to young people to be visible.

There's a real tension between wanting to be open and being wary of the backlash which occurred when I talked about my mental health issues. I got loads of emails and messages saying I was just playing for attention, trying to get sympathy votes. But I do feel a responsibility to young people to be visible. If I had known someone who was open about the fluidity of sexuality when I was younger, perhaps I wouldn't have thought it was weird and dismissed those feelings of being attracted to women as well as men. I sought Mhairi's advice because I expected that sooner or later the question would come up for me, and she said that I should do it my way. She said we don't have to be anyone's hero. It was reassuring to have her share that experience.

And, of course, a couple of months later, it did come up. I was asked to do an interview on camera. The journalist said one of his questions would be about my sexuality, so when asked, I said, 'Yes, I am in a relationship with a woman.' That was just before Christmas, so over the holiday break I was waiting for it to be released. By January, the piece still hadn't been published. I think they were waiting for everyone to return from holiday for maximum exposure. The whole thing was becoming very stressful, and I was worrying about when it would be published and how it would be portrayed. I found out from my communications team that the planned headline was 'Chlöe Swarbrick is gay'. That was annoying because I was led to believe that the interview was a general profile piece; this so-called breaking story wasn't actually news to anyone who knew me anyway.

I realised that I'd become a passive bystander in the telling of my own story and needed to regain control. I wrote a post to Instagram and Facebook saying I'd been asked the sexuality question, that I didn't think that it deserved news coverage but that it's important young people know they're not the only ones who feel different. It is OK and they are accepted. It punctured the intensity of the story; a week later the story was on the front page of the *Herald*, but on my terms and with the quote I'd borrowed from Mhairi Black: 'I don't have to come out of the closet because I've never been in it.'

Sometimes when I'm out in public holding my partner's hand I become conscious of people looking at us and I let go of her hand. It's about not wanting to be stared at, perhaps it's internalised homophobia as well, so we self-police our behaviour. The action of letting go of her hand does reinforce the problem — I get that — but it's really tiring to fight all the time. No matter how strong you are, judgement wears you down. It pervades not just your mental health but also your small freedoms. Love should be a positive thing, a celebration of our humanity. Unfortunately in our Anglo-Saxon Christian culture, love, and particularly sex, have been used to shame and control people. We still live with the remnants of those archaic, arbitrary rules about which types of love are sanctioned and which are persecuted.

Before I was an MP, I tried lots of different things. With my previous partner Alex, I ran a café — well, it was really an art gallery with coffee and doughnuts. We had a menswear line called The Lucid Collective, and I was a journalist at bFM. They're all projects woven into communities. I suppose if there's a theme to what I do, it's a search for a deeper sense of meaning by bringing people together; perhaps it's a response to having a fragmented family life. Money isn't a motivation — I've always just seen it as a tool that can solve problems. I hate that people become attached to it. Money makes people miserable at both ends of the spectrum, and I've seen that people who have the least are often the most generous.

In Parliament there's that pampered, leather-bound, wood-panelled environment. I don't need that, or the chauffeur-driven famous side of being a public person. Every time I walk into Parliament, I think to myself, is this the day we blow it up? Not literally, of course.

Being in the public eye has been a struggle. I grew up in the Britney Spears, Lindsay Lohan era, when these extremely famous people were flying off the rails, getting into all sorts of trouble; it always seemed to be from confusion about their real identity, fame messing with their heads. When people come up and say, 'You're great, thank you for doing this and that', I try to tell them I'm not special, I'm the same as you, I'm just someone who fell down a rabbit hole and ended up doing this. Then there's the nasty people, often sitting at home behind a computer.

I've also noticed a tension on Twitter if I talk about my experiences as a queer person. Some people perceive this as trying to get attention rather than me discussing a perspective that differs from the mainstream hetero experience of the world. So, I can see why some people might prefer not to come out publicly. A public persona is an illusion of a person — it's reductive, static, informed by far fewer things than the complexity of a real life. People tend to engage with that concept of a person, whether they want to put them on a pedestal or tear them down. I try to reality-check people and break down that disconnect. I say I'm just a person — I don't know what the fuck I'm doing, and neither does anyone else, and that's OK.

What might the future hold? Well, I don't want to be in politics forever, but I worry my place could be filled by someone who is happy with the status quo, someone who won't speak up for people who need a voice. I've discussed having kids in the future and I think I should definitely be allowed to have children with my same-sex partner. James Shaw, our Green co-leader, was raised by two mums. I think the best way for kids to be raised is collectively, within a community, whether they have two mums, or a mum and a dad — it doesn't matter if they have stability and love.

We can extend our understanding of what a family or whānau is beyond traditional, narrow, European definitions. Even the notion of a non-traditional family is probably frightening to some people, but we should challenge ourselves and consider new ideas of what whānau can mean. Humans and society are not concrete entities, we're in constant motion like a river. Whānau can be difficult for queer and rainbow Kiwis when they come out. If you're not feeling loved or if you feel like no one is listening, remember that love and understanding does exist for you, you just haven't found it yet.

We still have a way to go as a society, but just know that there are people fighting for you, fighting to make the world better; not just for the favoured few but better for everybody.

David Sar Shalom Abadi

Dr David Sar Shalom Abadi is a Waihōpai Invercargill general practitioner and chair of local charity CHROMA, which works to empower Southland individuals who identify with the LGBTQIA+ community.

I was born 40 years ago in the Jewish community of Caracas, Venezuela, which, back then was a thriving city of culture and commerce. My great-grandparents moved there from Europe and the Middle East with my grandparents for a peaceful life and a new start away from war in Europe and between Israel and its neighbours. Venezuela was this place of opportunity that welcomed people of all origins, and with hard work and sacrifice many created a safe and prosperous life for their families. Today, people are desperate to leave Venezuela, with its terrible inequality and corruption.

My mother's father had a small engineering firm. Dad was hired there as a young man fresh from university, and that's how my parents met. Mum was an architect, then later she created beautiful glasswork paintings and sculptures. I was a shy, nerdy kid growing up in a privileged world of private schools and piano lessons. Reading a book in the library was my favourite thing. I remember being picked last for sports teams. It always seemed as if the other kids thought I was weird and made fun of me; perhaps they weren't, but that's how it felt. I retreated into books, music and my imagination — intellectual pursuits that didn't require confidence or popularity.

My whole world was steeped in Jewish culture. At school, classes were taught in Spanish but we also learnt Hebrew and had to learn the scriptures and Psalms, while my loving maternal grandmother taught me English from when I was young, and I will always be grateful to her for that. At school and home, it was clear that being gay was not a valid lifestyle; it was something to fear or ridicule. There was the absurd notion that all gay men only wanted to dress as a woman and be promiscuous. Quotes from the Old Testament were cherry-picked to support those narrow-minded attitudes, but of course they barely mentioned the Bible quotes which condone slavery and genocide, or the sins of eating shellfish, wearing makeup or mixing fabrics.

We were taught that our main aspiration in life should be to marry a woman and have children. Only a Jewish woman would do, from a wealthy family, and she had to be intelligent but submissive and an excellent cook. Even if the marriage was miserable, all that mattered to God was the creation of a traditional family unit with children. Anyone not following these rules was assumed to have mental problems or a deficient character.

At school we had study partners, and when I was 12 I remember there was one particular boy I looked forward to studying with, until I gradually realised I liked him as more than just a friend. For a week I struggled with those feelings, wanting them to go away. The problem was I couldn't find anyone to talk to; I didn't feel safe going to my family or anyone at school and there was no internet yet. So, I put my thoughts and emotions down in a diary, writing questions to myself, ideas I was curious about. My parents found the diary when they went rummaging through my drawers. A dramatic intervention followed with much crying and yelling: 'This is not who you are, you're just young and confused, we'll fix it, we love you.' I was sent to a psychiatrist. This was the nineties. There was no queer visibility, and anything in the news was still shaded in the negative undertones of AIDS.

Thankfully, the psychiatrist was blunt with my parents; she told them that I didn't have an illness, I wasn't going through a phase and that they still had the same son. Mum and Dad were frustrated to be told that they needed to change, not me. Meeting my first queer ally at that age was important; I learnt that not everyone was going to make my life hard. For a long time, my parents harboured hopes that I'd grow out of being gay, but their frustration only grew through my teenage years as they realised I wasn't changing.

The hardest part for me was the constant fear that I'd be kicked out of home if I didn't meet their expectations. What would I do as a 15-year-old kid with no money and no home? Looking back now, I realise this likely wouldn't have happened but back then it was what I feared the most. It was something that had happened to others, and sadly still occurs even today.

A support group would have been a lifeline for my family and me. If my parents could have spoken with people to see that their fears weren't founded in reality, that most people wouldn't shun them and they wouldn't lose their jobs or social standing, things might've turned out quite differently. A few religious aunts and uncles cut me off when they were told I was gay, and communication with others is still limited; they don't understand that being a good, kind person is worth much more than blindly following religious rules. Fortunately, my parents, brother and maternal grandparents have finally been able to accept me, and for that I am immensely grateful.

From a young age I was fascinated by the human body. My aunt studied medicine, and I spent hours poring over the anatomy books she brought home, with their intricate diagrams of skeletons and cross-sections of organs and muscles. I inherited those books, and the curiosity and aspiration to learn more about that world stayed with me. However, that same aunt turned her back on science later — the illness of someone close led her to embrace religion quite fervently and facts that disagreed with her devout religious faith became labelled as propaganda and fake. Having been the inspiration for my life in medicine, this was hard to accept.

One summer in my twenties, I was visiting family in Florida and my aunt and I were driving in her car when she unexpectedly stopped in a suburban street and said, 'I want you to meet a friend of mine who lives in this house.' Slightly bewildered, I knocked on the door and was greeting by an elderly rabbi who showed me inside and proceeded to lecture me about how the perverted 'gay agenda' was trickling down from Hollywood and 'the world of fashion'. I excused myself as soon as politely possible; both the rabbi and my aunt thought they were doing the right thing.

The freedom of being thrown into the medical school environment with young people of so many different beliefs and backgrounds was thrilling. Soon after starting at university, I met the boy who has been my partner in life ever since. I was sulking in the corner of a bar one night after being snubbed by someone I particularly fancied when a friendly, attractive guy walked over, said hello, and sat down next to me. He said he wasn't in the mood for his friends that night. His name was Jesús, and we talked and danced till the bar closed, and we agreed to meet again the next day at a quiet, secluded restaurant.

Jesús won me over with his warm nature. We give each other balance; he's a practical guy, I'm more bookish and theoretical. I live in my mind a lot, overthinking and creating problems that don't really exist. I might have become quite an odd, reclusive guy without him to keep me grounded in the real world.

Our families took time to accept that two men could be together. They didn't believe it was a true relationship, or they would diminish us, saying we must be confused. It's been a tough road but, with some exceptions, most of our two families accept and celebrate us now and I'm grateful to have them in our lives.

Medical school was seven years of intensive learning. It's not a relaxed, sociable way to live. When the study and exams are finally over, Venezuelan graduates take a one-year placement in a remote part of the country. I chose Margarita Island, a breathtakingly beautiful place of gorgeous beaches, accessible only by boat and the occasional flight. I settled into a pleasant routine of seeing patients about six hours a day and then heading down to the beach for an afternoon swim before dinner; there was plenty of time to ponder my possible paths in life.

As I turned over the options in my mind — cardiology, psychology, surgery — I found I was interested in almost everything, even gynaecology. An older experienced doctor I'd befriended on the island suggested I venture into general practice because it covers so many areas of healthcare. So, at the end of that wonderful year on Isla de Margarita, Jesús and I departed for Barcelona, Spain. The city had an excellent medical post-graduate school, Jesús's mum already lived there, and who doesn't love Barcelona? For four years I studied family medicine while Jesús learnt technology at an IT school. We spent quite a few of those years living with his family; they've been a huge support to us.

As we finished our studies and were ready to find work, Spain was hit hard by the banking and real estate crisis, and employment opportunities dried up. We extended the horizon of our job search. After the chaos of Caracas and the sprawl of Barcelona we craved somewhere closer to nature, hopefully with a friendly, welcoming community. Norway almost won. I'd sat the Norwegian language exam and was preparing for Scandinavian life when I received an email about a position in Australia. I wasn't really interested so they said, 'Well, how about New Zealand?' That sounded more appealing.

The medical clinic we chose was in Invercargill, which our research showed was close to Queenstown, Fiordland and many beautiful towns and lakes. It was a city of 50,000 people, small but not tiny, and it came with an airport. A few months later, I landed with Jesús in New Zealand for a one-year contract with the Invercargill Medical Centre. We've been here six years now and have no plans to leave. Invercargill has been good to us. We've been given the warmest welcome. It's a place where people stop and chat in the street; we know our neighbours and remember events in their lives. We feel like part of the community. I'm not just an anonymous doctor here to do a job.

We feel like part of the community. I'm not just an anonymous doctor here to do a job.

I t was difficult to meet LGBTQIA+ friends in Invercargill at first. Because we're a couple, it's often assumed that if we're looking to socialise we must be looking for sex. It's that age-old stereotype that to be gay means being a promiscuous party animal. My party-till-I-drop days are mostly behind me now. Queer events and visibility in Invercargill were almost non-existent when we arrived but there was a small social group I was invited to by Pikihuia, a wonderful woman I met at the gym. At the time, it was a low-key group and not too many people knew about it so only a few would turn up, but among them were some wonderful, kind people who I still count as some of my closest friends.

Being an immigrant, and finding the balance between blending in and standing out in a new culture can be a fine art, but from that small, timid social group we founded CHROMA, a bold new organisation. We created a rainbow koru logo and began to promote ourselves. Being a doctor, I had connections and some level of mana in the community, and with that and the tireless work of the other founders — Piki, Bridget, Shauna, Wendy, Ari, Beth and Amz — we got more people on board. Our most glamorous success so far is the 'Queens Go South' drag show, where we invite queens and gender illusionists from Christchurch and Wellington down to perform. We've also featured a fashion runway by some of the Southern Institute of Technology (SIT) students with transgender clients in mind, and 'Coffee with the Queens', an all-ages gathering to encourage questions, dialogue and promote understanding.

The shows have been wildly popular and sell out in record time. The Queens Go South crowd is a real assortment of Southland life: farmers from small towns, families of young and old, and of course lots of students. Everyone likes to be entertained, and events down here aren't so frequent, so Queens Go South has become a night Southlanders very much look forward to. We're thrilled that this year we are expanding the main show to two nights, with some fabulous new events.

We often hear about Southlanders being conservative and close-minded but that's not my experience. I've never felt bullied or discriminated against because of my sexuality here. I made it clear to the clinic that I was bringing my male partner and we go to social events together and are always acknowledged and welcomed. I was aware of New Zealand's progressive image before I arrived, but it's only while living here that I discovered the courageous few, like trans women Carmen Rupe and Georgina Beyer, who pushed New Zealand forward and gave the country its enlightened reputation around the world. We should all be very proud of those queer pioneers.

CHROMA is a registered charity now, and we are proud to support the local LGBTQIA+ youth group, and when they graduate from that they are welcomed into our adult group. If people have been shunned from their natural family, we can be their chosen family who will be there for them. Both the youth and adult groups now have over 20 members each. In the beginning it was hard to get even half as many.

As a doctor I always take a gentle interest in my patients' lives and aspirations, which often leads to more open discussions. My hope is that when they're in a vulnerable situation they'll feel they can be honest with me, and when patients are honest I can offer better care. It's very rewarding when patients are comfortable enough to share their sexuality or gender identity. On a few occasions I've been the first person to know, and it's a privilege to be trusted with something so personal. It's surprising how many transgender people there are in Southland. Even in Barcelona I didn't see so many trans folk at my clinic. Many come to me through word of mouth, so my patient list is growing all the time; it feels awesome to be chosen to talk to.

When people present in a way which isn't traditionally male or female, the ambiguity can make people uncomfortable, but I find it natural that human beings reflect the diversity of life — why should we all look, dress and act the same, or try to fit into simplistic male or female categories? My hope is that in Invercargill and Southland queer people won't find that necessary. Nowadays there is more discussion about homophobia and transphobia but also about bullying, depression, suicide and racism. As these difficult areas are dragged out of the dark and into the spotlight, people understand that we all have a part to play in fixing them. Everyone deserves to feel a valued part of their community.

Healthcare for LGBTQIA+ people is grossly overlooked at medical school so there is still a lack of understanding about sexual orientation and gender identity at medical facilities. We have continuing education workshops that keep us updated with medical science and skills, and I volunteered to create and run workshops on sexuality and gender issues with a great friend and artist, Ari Edgecombe, who happens to be transgender. We called our presentation 'Let's Make It Perfectly Queer'. The two of us have been visiting towns and cities around the South Island with this initiative, where I present the more factual information, while Ari talks about his personal experience of being a trans person in the healthcare system.

One of our suggestions is to use symbols of safety such as rainbow stickers at the reception and on the doors of doctors' and nurses' rooms. They are small but invaluable indications that can have a big effect on LGBTQIA+ patients. We encourage clinics to have more options than only 'male' or 'female' on forms for patients to fill out, and to ask people their pronoun rather than making an assumption. We teach respectful ways of opening up a conversation about sexuality or gender so that people share more, rather than shutting them down. Our presentation was received with open hearts and minds, and it is something we are particularly proud of and plan to continue.

> When people present in a way which isn't traditionally male or female, the ambiguity can make people uncomfortable, but I find it natural that human beings reflect the diversity of life.

Our life in Invercargill is happy, with our small group of friends and two dogs. With apologies to Auckland, I would never want to live there, spending hours in traffic, running around rushed and grumpy. We love visiting the towns around the South Island, tramping in the mountains and walking our dogs on the beach. I've started to learn Māori and have had time to rediscover the piano and read my favourite authors, like Salman Rushdie and Stephen King. Jesús does fulfilling work with Colombian refugees, bridging cultural differences and easing their entry into New Zealand.

He is my fiancé now; I proposed to him at the Ed Sheeran concert in Dunedin. I know how corny it sounds but I thought it was very romantic at the time. Sheeran was playing the song 'Photograph', which is a special one for us, and I went down on one knee. People around us were delighted; I was thinking, Oh my God, please turn away. Eventually we'll have a wedding, and I'm working on changing the minds of some family members so that they'll attend. It would mean the world to me for them to be part of our very special day.

I want to encourage people to be kind to each other and try not to judge. Take the time to be interested in others; ask if they're OK or whether they are struggling with anything. Sometimes that's all it takes for someone to confide in you. Health outcomes are much worse for queer people by all measures, but young people only need one supportive adult who knows about them and stands by them to reduce their risk of even attempting suicide by up to 40 per cent. That shows the immense power we have to make a difference in people's lives, the difference between someone being alive or dead.

It can be hard to be your authentic self when up against the pressure of what your family or society expects of you. My experience of accompanying people as they are facing death has taught me that people regret what they *didn't* do much more than what they *did* do. While we go through this brief existence called life, let us be our authentic selves and find the unique talents that we have and share them with the world. I am convinced this is how we can find true purpose and meaning in our lives.

He aroha whakatō, he aroha puta mai.

If kindness is sown, then kindness you shall receive.

Sarah Bickerton

Sarah Bickerton is a lecturer in politics and policy at the University of Auckland. Her doctoral research focused on New Zealand women's use of Twitter for political participation construction, and she is continuing her research into social uses of technology, technology policy and gender analysis.

Dad was a big science-fiction nut, so our bookshelves were full of Isaac Asimov, the Foundation series and *Dune*. I got lost in those books as a kid, transported to other worlds; I was a nerd before being a nerd was cool, even enjoying early Dungeons & Dragons. Gradually, I noticed the lack of women characters. Women were almost invisible in these stories, as were women science-fiction writers. Then I discovered the X-Men universe. As a young queer kid, X-Men felt like it was telling my story. The X-Men characters are mutants; some look like humans so their identity and powers can be kept secret, but some are clearly not regular humans and those mutants are subject to constant scrutiny and prejudice. In the 1960s, the X-Men were interpreted as an allegory for the civil rights struggle in America. In the eighties and nineties, queer people found that stories about mutants being forced to hide and shunned just for existing resonated strongly with their own experience.

The lessons that play out in these universes are extremely powerful, and often sci-fi is way ahead of current times; *Star Trek* having a black female character and an Asian character on the bridge was radical in the 1960s. Wonder Woman standing up to evil bad guys wasn't just entertainment, it was a source of courage. I tried reading Western cowboy books, for instance, and I hated them. They had no female characters and no new ideas to ignite my imagination. After the world of mutants and superpowers, horses and spurs were just boring. I'm still captivated by all those incredible science-fiction characters and universes to this day.

My family moved from Auckland to Cromwell in 1988, just as I started high school. I didn't fit in, but the town was close to Queenstown and my parents gave me season ski passes, which I loved. By that time, I had figured out I was some variety of queer. Being a nerd, I thought, 'OK, I need to research the hell out of this.' Being pre-internet, I looked up references and did old-fashioned microfiche keyword searches at the library. There were no queer books, however, there were some clinical medical references to the 'disorders' of homosexuality or hermaphroditism, written in a horrible pathological way. I was researching all this before New Zealand's Human Rights Act had passed, and my first efforts to learn about my identity came to little fruition.

I also started to feel that something was going on with my gender. I'd been raised as a boy, but was androgynous and looked young. People usually read me as a boy, but in my late teens just by shifting my long hair into a ponytail from the back of my head to the top, a simple change of t-shirt style from crew-neck to V-neck, and I'd be gendered female. As soon as I left the house, my ponytail went up to 'girl position'.

Back in my mid-teens, I tried to express to my parents that I thought I was a girl, but we honestly just came to loggerheads. It was alienating as a 15-year-old teen to have no one to talk to and no information to guide me, and I was living in a blurry limbo state. I identified with women and was pretty sure I was a chick, but I didn't have gender dysphoria [the distress that happens when there's a mismatch between the sex you were assigned at birth and your psychological sense of your gender or any markers that could signal being transgender].

My mother's family are from the Netherlands, and I was given the opportunity to finish high school there. I jumped at the chance to leave New Zealand and spend a year there. The Netherlands was probably the most queer-friendly country in the world; it was the perfect place for me to go. I discovered gay pride parades, which we didn't have in New Zealand yet, let alone in little old Cromwell. Seeing how a society could be so accepting had a big influence on me and I returned to New Zealand a year later with a broader perspective of the world.

Of course, while I was away I hadn't changed how I felt about myself. On the contrary, I was now sure I was a chick and either lesbian or bisexual. I saw a counsellor who was queer-affirming; he said there was nothing wrong with me, and taught me some emotional techniques to deal with what I was going through, so the experience was really helpful. Things came to a head with my parents, I moved out and we stopped talking. I threw myself into study and life at Canterbury University, though it was tough, scraping by on the student allowance and part-time jobs at KFC and later pizza delivery in order to stay at university.

I fell in love with astrophysics. Along the way, I also became fascinated by sociology and feminist studies, so the result was a double degree in astrophysics and sociology. However, unless you're Stephen Hawking, your career in astrophysics will probably be limited to laboratory technician work, so I continued down the sociology path because it has more options, although I do miss the stars.

I became solidly involved with university gay and lesbian groups. We succeeded in getting the first trans-inclusive language written in the university charter and held the first national UniQ conference. I also got my first girlfriend; we were together nearly four years. I had a good network of friends and felt ready to start female hormones and change my name to Sarah. One person decided he didn't approve and ended the friendship, but having surrounded myself with a supportive queer circle, he was the only one I lost.

After finishing at Canterbury, I was accepted into a doctoral programme at the University of Illinois in Chicago. Chicago was great but again it was a tough existence, living on a small PhD stipend and a student loan that I kept as tiny as possible. I was in my mid-thirties then, working as a lowly paid university lecturer/instructor and starting to feel burnt out, when I received a call from my mother saying my father had died. It was completely unexpected. I decided to return to New Zealand and take a break. Just before he'd died, Dad had written me a letter saying he wanted to reconnect with me. It's a great regret of my life that we never had a real conversation about it, but I do know he wanted me back. I saw my mum at the funeral, and she wanted to reconcile with me. We rebuilt our relationship by letting the past be in the past. Sometimes striving for forgiveness is too much — it can reopen old wounds. Sometimes it's best to build anew.

I n New Zealand, my new doctor collated all my previous medical records, and among them were notes from a psychiatrist many years before, when I'd started hormones. In the border of a page he had written 'possible intersex', but he'd never said anything to me. That culture of doctors not discussing important things with the person who is affected is frustrating and unhealthy. Back in Chicago, I came across material about intersex conditions in the university library and as I read about the characteristics used for 'diagnosis' I thought, 'Wait, this sounds a lot like me.'

I talked to some American doctors and it became clearer that I might be intersex. There are many variations that come under the term, one of them being Partial Androgen Insensitivity Syndrome (PAIS), which is what I have. My biology doesn't react to androgens in the same way as most people. Before that I had wondered if I was trans, even though I didn't fit the traditional markers or identify with this.

I've always known I was a chick; a tomboy. I'm soft butch and not naturally girly. I'd never read anything about tomboy lesbian trans women, although I now know they do exist. So, intersex fits with how I thought about myself. I had a good, stable identity, but discovering I was intersex put the pieces together for me; it was an affirmation. Some intersex people use the word 'diagnosis' to root intersex as a medical condition, which I understand, but the medical community has been atrocious towards us so I'm not sure they can be trusted to gate-keep intersex identity.

We need to get more nuanced gender and sexuality data collected by census; intersex people have been mostly ignored and invisible. About two per cent of the world are intersex, similar to the percentage of redheads or people with green eyes. Unlike hair and eye colour, however, most societies in the world are not comfortable with intersex people because we disrupt their concept of gender and sexuality. We're starting to see transgender material in high-school sex education, and now I want to see intersex information included.

It's wonderful to meet other intersex people. I was sitting down with a few of us this year, at an informal lunch we'd organised, and we looked around the room and realised this was probably the biggest intersex gathering ever held in New Zealand. There was an amazing feeling of connection. I've always felt a person's biggest strength is from our family, whether that's our birth family or the family we find as we go through life.

Representation is important, but the number one change I want to see to progress intersex rights is a ban on sex-assignment surgery of infants and children. Even though it is not something that impacted me personally, it's an unethical practice that has uniformly harmful outcomes. Imagine finding out that as a baby you'd had a life-changing operation performed on you without your consent. It is traumatising.

Surgeons push back against the intersex community, thinking they know better. It's a regressive, paternalistic model to say all children must have genitalia that conforms to social norms. Isn't a better solution to encourage society to be more open-minded about what a human body can be? Only a few countries, like Portugal and India, have legal protection of a child's bodily autonomy. New Zealand needs to join that club.

New Zealand is mostly moving in the right direction in progressing queer rights and recognition. For example, unisex bathrooms are becoming more common. I think the fear-mongering around toilets is silly. Trans and queer people aren't attacking anyone; we're far more likely to be victims of an attack. As a soft butch lesbian, I sometimes receive a double-take in women's bathrooms, but I've never had any problems. And it's frustrating that we still can't change the sex on our birth certificates easily; we have to provide medical evidence to show our physical attributes have changed, pay a lot of money and wait a long time. It should be changeable by simple self-identification.

On a personal level, I'm part of the first generation who has been out of the closet since our teens, so our entire adult lives have been lived openly. This gives us a unique perspective; our queer-hood is something we've experienced continuously. We were able to come out because of the courage of previous generations, and now it's our turn to support and encourage the new generations.

Even though I've been living and breathing academia for a long time, I'm 47 now and still want to have a career that allows me to have real world impact. I have finished my PhD and am working as a lecturer again, this time here in New Zealand. I want my life to matter; I want to keep contributing to society. I'll always do intersex and queer work, such as queer mentorship at university as a lesbian and intersex person. I'm lucky enough to be in love with an amazing woman, and she's just silly enough to be in love with me in return, God help her.

Peter Macky

Peter Macky is a former lawyer from Tāmaki Makaurau Auckland. Now a publisher and cycle-tour operator, he splits his time between New Zealand and Germany, where he has restored an ornate historic railway station in Halbe, south of Berlin.

The world I grew up in was completely different to today's. Both my father and my mother were from families with strong Remuera connections: my father was a doctor in the days when that meant something, and my mother from a leisured background with antecedents in England. My mother today is a sprightly 93-year-old. Her father was knighted in the 1930s by a grateful New Zealand government after a distinguished career in the military, law and politics. With the knighthood (which also meant something back then) and my parents' connections, it all added up to my being part of a family of some status in what was a sheltered life in Auckland — although I didn't appreciate that until much later.

The local church, St Aidan's, was a large part of this life. It was more the social ritual than anything we really believed in; everyone went to church then, it was part of the culture. I sang in the choir and would lead the solemn processional, carrying the cross up the aisle ahead of the vicar, curate and altar boys. It meant getting dressed up on a Sunday in a surplus and cassock; I enjoyed the theatre of it. Looking back, it was very camp. I've always preferred the Catholic ceremonies, being fascinated by their opulence and bizarre elaborate doctrines; Anglicans are more pragmatic and sober. When I lived in London I attended Brompton Oratory, a Catholic church in Knightsbridge. I went for the spectacle, to hear the choir and smell the incense and be sprayed with holy water.

I had three younger sisters, and we all benefited from a loving, supportive family life which included masses of relations and friends. Looking back, it really was a charmed, idyllic childhood. My first school was Remuera Primary. I remember trotting through the gates in bare feet. Then when my father founded St Kentigern Prep in 1959 as the school's first chairman, I became a foundation pupil. I always did well enough at school without putting in any great effort, being a middling student in the top stream, and I was involved with any individual sports that were going, but mainly cross-country running, swimming, athletics. However, team sports, whether cricket or rugby, were really not my thing.

My parents decided that since I'd had plenty of exposure to girls in a household with three sisters, for balance I should go to a boys' secondary school as a boarder. St Paul's Collegiate in Hamilton was selected for its combination of being out of Auckland but not too far, and my mother had strong family connections in the Waikato which no doubt she wanted me to absorb. Boarding school has often suffered from a reputation for being strict and joyless, but I didn't find that at all; there was a strong camaraderie, and being a young, closeted gay male, it made life simpler to remove girls from the social equation.

For my last two years of college, I returned to St Kentigern's and reunited with childhood friends from the prep school. I'd become frustrated with the narrow conformity of the curriculum at St Paul's; I have an enquiring temperament, and the desire to expand my horizons was already growing. Through those school years I had crushes on boys, but that's all they ever were. I felt I would let my family down if I openly explored my sexuality, and it didn't matter much to me at the time because I was happy with school and singing and sport and all those pursuits a teenager enjoys.

As my school years drew to a close, a decision loomed: what to do next? I didn't have the grades or aptitude for medical school, and having seen the hours demanded of my father I wasn't keen on that profession anyway. Law seemed to be the choice for those of us who had no idea what they wanted to do, and I certainly fitted that description at the time.

I had very little idea what I was letting myself in for at law school, particularly given the complete lack of any vocational guidance, but happily it turned out to be the right decision for me. It is, of course, a profession, with the predictability of an annuity. At university I didn't have any boyfriends or girlfriends, but I did have plenty of wonderful friendships. We'd sail the family yacht on the harbour at weekends and enjoyed a healthy, vigorous New Zealand life.

My six closest friends from St Kent's all came out as gay soon after we'd left school; it's curious that none of us knew that about each other at the time. Those friends made it easier for me to come out later, by leading the way. The only one who didn't come out after school was Bruce — he came out much later at 50 years old. It's profoundly sad that of my group of close school friends I'm the only one left: five died of AIDS and Bruce died of a drug addiction. It's only chance that I'm still here. We all slip up and do stupid things and I'm no exception. That I survived is pure luck, nothing else.

I should emphasise that being gay wasn't talked about in my childhood, although my eldest sister says that it was always understood that I was 'different' in an undefined (but certainly not threatening or disturbing) way. I did worry about the family's reaction to my coming out for fear of what the ramifications might be, but it turned out that there were none at all, despite the fact that I had constructed this idea in my mind that it could lead to some kind of catastrophe. That it never eventuated, or was ever likely to, showed how irrational I was. But I was a member of a mid-1970s conservative household, high profile in its own sphere of Auckland society, with the potential to tarnish the family reputation. And it was not until some years later, in 1986, when I was 34, that homosexuality was legalised. Up until then it had (of course) been a criminal offence.

> My six closest friends from St Kent's all came out as gay soon after we'd left school . . . Those friends made it easier for me to come out later, by leading the way.

One of my sisters married an open-minded man named Malcolm, who I knew had gay friends, one of whom was the best man at their wedding. I asked him to do me the favour of telling my sisters and parents that I was gay, which he agreed to do. It must seem weird and convoluted now, and a process somewhat lacking in courage, but that's how it was done. After Malcolm came out on my behalf, life went on as it had before. I was immensely relieved that the family knew and had no concerns. Their attitude to me didn't change; I wasn't judged or reprimanded. My family have always welcomed my boyfriends, of whom there were a number in my younger years, and included them in our activities. I have many memories of convivial family holidays where I've brought my partner and we've never felt other than completely comfortable.

After graduating from law school I joined Russell McVeagh in Auckland before the big OE in London beckoned. The highlight of my two years there was passing an audition and joining the Bach Choir under Sir David Willcocks, the legendary conductor. Sir David was previously director of the famous King's College Choir, Cambridge. With his stellar reputation, Willcocks attracted incredible soloists from the world of opera, such as Dame Janet Baker, Alfreda Hodgson, John Shirley-Quirk, Felicity Lott and Sir Peter Pears. The choir opened up British society for me at a level that was unattainable for most Kiwis on their OE. I met the Queen. Lord Rothschild was the patron, Prince Charles and the Duchess of Kent were fellow choir members. As I was a tenor and Charles a bass, choral voice groupings meant he would often be singing right behind me.

For me, our most memorable occasion was Benjamin Britten's *War Requiem*, written for three soloists, and this performance included a Russian, an English and a German singer, to demonstrate the unity of the great powers after the Second World War. Britten wrote the English voice part for his lover and muse, the tenor Sir Peter Pears, who was one of the soloists in this performance. These and other concerts, performed in such celebrated venues as the Royal Albert Hall, St George's Chapel and Royal Festival Hall, were thrilling, life-changing experiences. How many Kiwis on their OE get to sing with such famous soloists and to perform on stage at such venues, sometimes live on BBC One?

There's an anecdote from this period which I have used, perhaps a little too often, at dinner parties. I knew Sir Hardy Amies from his work with the family company, Cambridge Clothing. He visited New Zealand annually to advise whether, for example, lapels should be narrower or wider (truly!), and was very generous to me in London. At one of his parties, I was introduced to Sir Norman Hartnell, another grand dame of the fashion world (the Queen's coronation robes were designed by him in 1952) and he was a little too interested in me. He was 74, I was 24. He asked me to dinner. What to do? I prevaricated. Later that evening, Hardy's advice was: 'Peter, Peter, Peter. Lunch perhaps; dinner never.'

I returned to Auckland in the early eighties, joined a law firm and fell into a relaxed lifestyle of enjoying dinners with friends and weekends away. The eighties glitz that consumed parts of Auckland was never part of my life. Occasionally I went to gay clubs like Backstage, where the Q Theatre is today, and of course the fabled Alfie's and Staircase, but my love of clubbing wasn't sparked until a few years later in New York and more recently in Berlin. Throughout my career I've never advertised the fact that I'm a gay man, and I've never hidden it either. I wouldn't even say I was proud of it; I just happen to be a gay man. I had lots of gay clients in the firms I've been part of and my professional partners have all known I was gay and it's never been an issue for me.

I'd always wanted to study in the UK or the US. I had friends with degrees from such famous alma maters as Harvard, Oxford and Cambridge, and I'd always felt at a disadvantage that I hadn't experienced education at these highest levels. I felt it was a personal challenge to see if I could prevail at those top institutions.

NYU in New York City is where I decided to go. It has a highly regarded law school on a beautiful campus in Greenwich Village, the vibrant gay neighbourhood of the city. On my first day, in my first class, I sat in the lecture theatre almost pinching myself: the professor in front of me was the recipient of a Nobel Prize in economics. The level of intellect in that environment was exhilarating.

Equally so were the clubs in the mid-eighties, the heyday of gay clubbing in New York. In my first few months in the city I was a regular at The Saint, Twilo and the Sound Factory, all dance clubs created from cavernous old warehouses. The Saint posters featured images by Robert Mapplethorpe and I still have some of them. I was at the closing party of Studio 54; walking through the crowds past the velvet rope into the thumping music and light shows is something I'll never forget. The freedom and creativity of nightlife in those days is an era which has gone, decimated first through HIV and then through gentrification in Manhattan, with rents going sky-high. After a few months of clubs and parties I realised I couldn't keep it up and also make a success of my studies, so I shifted focus to embrace the opportunities and brilliant minds at NYU and I did well, completing a master's degree and passing the NY State Bar Exam (in the same class as JFK Jnr).

I arrived back in Auckland, armed with the experience, knowledge and confidence to start my own law firm. A friend from St Kent's offered me a room in his office space on the first floor of the Windsor Castle Tavern building in Parnell. The firm was successful, and I expanded to take over the entire floor, hiring lawyers who specialised across many areas of our profession. I think our success was due to our collective expertise and the energy I brought, which diffused through the firm. Our phone calls always went straight to the desk of the lawyer and were never screened. The mantra I repeated to my staff was to always ask a client, 'When would suit you for an appointment?' And to never tell clients how busy you are; it's our job to appear to be available 24/7.

Alongside running my law firm, I became involved with the Ponsonby Rugby League Club. I liked the game and the people, but unfortunately its committee had no idea how to manage the finances of their club. It had been going since 1908 and its assets consisted of a single jukebox worth $500. I joined the committee and immediately found that most of the club's profits were being stolen from the bar. I instituted some simple controls to encourage honesty, and after my first year as treasurer the club made a $20,000 profit, so, together with the jukebox, the Club's assets had grown to $20,500. That was in the early 1980s when $20,000 was quite helpful. It was satisfying to help the club become a successful, stable and thriving organisation.

This interest led to my joining the board of Auckland Rugby League and then Auckland Warriors' board, which I chaired for three years until the company was sold in 1999. It was a testing period, with the News Corp-backed Super League competition dividing the game, and with

Matthew Ridge as captain there were many tempestuous moments.

My law firm continued to prosper, and after 20 years of 12-hour days, about 10 years ago I was able to retire at the age of 58 to pursue other interests. I'd always been drawn to Berlin for its history and architecture and for its reputation for being a liberal centre of gay life in Europe. My partner and I decided to move there, with the idea of living an eternal summer between Germany and New Zealand. On our travels we'd visited the historic Livadia Palace, where the Romanoff royal family holidayed. I started a publishing house, and rather pretentiously decided to name it Livadia Publishers, as a nod to my love of history.

My partner and I became a very popular couple when we were in Berlin, because all our friends wanted to join us and experience the city. It became our pleasant responsibility to take visitors on bicycle tours of the city and out to the surrounding lakes and forests. Bicycles are the easiest way to get around — Berlin is flat, the weather predictable and the traffic courteous. None of that applies to Auckland, where the traffic is more likely to aim at a cyclist than avoid them.

It occurred to me that we knew the city so well that we could turn our cycle tours into a business. We began by offering a half-day tour of Berlin, and a full-day tour to Potsdam, the royal capital. We found that many guests wanted to stay on for a longer experience so we added a four-day tour to Dresden through the Spreewald forests and on into Saxony. It's a lot of fun and these tours never feel like work. Of course, with Covid, that life was suspended for two seasons but is now revived, and the tours have started again.

It was on a cycling trip that I made a discovery that would lead to one of my life's greatest adventures. A group of us were riding our bikes out of the forest into the small town of Halbe, in what was East Germany and about 50 kilometres south of Berlin, when a set of four imposing turrets loomed out through the trees. As we got closer, the building revealed itself to be a large derelict train station covered in graffiti with trees growing out of the roof and with an old 'For Sale' sign attached. I was captivated by the building, and spent hours taking photos, absorbing the site and its landscape. Summer ended and I returned to New Zealand, where the Halbe train station kept playing on my mind, and my research only added further intrigue. For a building which I soon discovered had been created with such high purposes to have fallen into disrepair captured my imagination. Looking at the photos I'd taken I thought, I need to restore it. If I don't it will soon collapse. So I flew back to Germany and bought it.

The Halbe station is a Kaiserbahnhof, a train station built for the sole use of the Kaiser, part of a network of Kaiserbahnhofs around Germany. My station at Halbe, built in 1865, was the first and was used by the Kaiser and his hunting party as a terminus to refresh themselves on their way to the imperial hunting lodge in the forests surrounding the town. When the Kaiser abdicated in 1918 and went into exile in Holland, there was no need for a Kaiserbahnhof in Halbe or anywhere else in Germany. The station was converted into accommodation for railway workers.

In the last weeks of the Second World War, in April 1945, General Theodor Busse of the German Ninth Army found his soldiers in disarray following a series of brutal battles against the advancing Russian army. Busse ordered the survivors to meet in Halbe, where they attempted a last desperate defence against the massive Russian onslaught. The Ninth Army was encircled and destroyed by the Russian forces, with a few remnants escaping westward, where they surrendered to the more agreeable Americans on the River Elbe. My station's brick façade is still riddled with bullet holes from those final days of the war.

Since the fall of the Berlin Wall in 1989 it had been abandoned. The ornate frescoes and plasterwork were ruined, pieces of the vaulted ceiling had collapsed into the rubble and dust which covered the floors. It took 10 years to fully realise the romantic ambitions I had for the place. Now I can live in an apartment at the top level of the station, and the thrill of the place hasn't subsided — if anything, it has been enhanced by the fact that it's all complete and can now be enjoyed for the marvellous destination it is.

I still find myself quietly walking through the arched salon rooms and out into the gardens in a kind of meditative state. The bahnhof is well used for functions, conferences, art shows, weddings, concerts and other events. It has wonderful acoustics, which I regularly test as I mop the floors while singing along to Bach or Verdi. There are plans for a beer garden but I don't think I'll open the bahnhof for club nights; that could be a bit hard on the building and too much for the neighbours!

After a (northern) summer, I always love returning to New Zealand, although I do have frustrations, especially with how badly (compared to Europe) the natural environment and urban design are managed. Soon there will be no green space between Auckland and Hamilton. I contrast this desecration with German towns and cities which have strict boundaries: any building must be up or infill, so that surrounding forests and lakes are left untouched by development. I wrote the book *Coolangatta: A homage* to attempt to address the lack of appreciation New Zealand has for its history and environment. The book is named for the beautiful historic Remuera house which belonged to my great-grandmother and which was demolished without warning in 2006.

Having reached my seventh decade, I am able to reflect on my social life and the gay scene in New Zealand, which I think can be rather ageist. Anyone over the age of 40 seems outside the target market of most of our gay bars and clubs. Berlin is more civilised and varied, and I find the people have a more expansive outlook on life, so at nearly 70 I'm welcomed into gay nightlife. I go out with friends, often to the KitKat Club or Berghain. We dance and socialise till the early hours. I'm very sentimental about the Covid-decimated club scene. Although it's coming back, I doubt it will ever be the same again.

From my early days when homosexuality was a subject to avoid and hardly spoken of, and certainly to be very discreet about, I never could have imagined the visibility of queer people in society today. I'm lucky to come from a privileged background — I could have done almost anything I wanted. In my world of well-travelled, educated people, being gay had no repercussions, but many others had a very different experience. I've had friendships with people whose families had dreadful and even brutal reactions to their sexuality. Sadly that can still be the experience for some young people today.

> From my early days when homosexuality was a subject to avoid and hardly spoken of, and certainly to be very discreet about, I never could have imagined the visibility of queer people in society today.

Looking to the future, I hope to continue to live in Germany and New Zealand and do more to support charities and community groups. The friendships I've made with artists, actors and fellow patrons are wonderful and I get a lot of pleasure from working with them. Each year we hold a film screening to support a New Zealand film. We hire the theatre and pay for the drinks and canapés. It's fantastic fun and I use it as a springboard to encourage guests, including some of my well-resourced friends, to get involved with charities and community groups.

Duffy Books in Homes is one venture I support. The author Alan Duff's charity has sent over 14 million books into schools and homes.

I support his programme in 16 schools and I'm pleased to say that Alan has become a good friend. The Auckland Theatre Company is perhaps my favourite charitable association, then there is Mike Chunn's Play it Strange Foundation, which encourages young Kiwis to write and record their own songs.

I would recommend to anyone to get involved in charitable work or a sports club. Whether you give time, money or expertise, you'll get back so much more than you give. Theatre, art, books, architecture, heritage, urban design, our cities and our amenties are aspects of our culture that are for everyone to benefit from. I try to expand the reach of these into areas of New Zealand which are too often neglected. I want New Zealand to up its game and, in a small way, to add to its energy, ideas and culture; that's what spurs me on.

Carole Beu

Carole Beu MNZM, one of New Zealand literature's most active champions, has run The Women's Bookshop for over 30 years. She was a founding trustee of the Auckland Writers Festival, and in 2019 was awarded an MNZM for services to the literary industry.

My bookshelves at home are overflowing. There are piles of books everywhere, like the Manhattan skyline, someone once said. It's a challenge not to set off a domino effect of collapsing novels. Publishers send me preview copies of their new books, hoping I'll love them and give them good promotion when they arrive, but it's impossible to read everything. The back of the shop is crammed full as well. I read fiction avidly. Sometimes the characters are so vivid and the writing so exquisite that I hug a book to my heart as I finish it.

When I was awarded an MNZM in 2019, I was astounded. The citation was for services to the literary industry but also mentioned support for the gay and lesbian community. I believe the more women who are honoured the better. From my buttoned-down, 1950s middle-class upbringing in suburban Lower Hutt, I don't quite know how I ended up being who I am today. My mother would be shocked and amazed. Mum was the quintessential housewife; she sewed our clothes and was an excellent baker, and the cake tins were always full of melting moments and lamingtons.

According to Mum, I had an overdeveloped sense of righteous indignation. She was always telling me to be quiet and behave like a lady, and although she did encourage me to go to university, which was forward-thinking for the time, she'd have liked me to have been a sedate and genteel young woman. At the after-event for my MNZM award I made a toast to my mother, who died years ago, and said, 'Mum if you're listening, it turns out that being stroppy and opinionated is a good thing; they've given me a gong for it.' Everyone cracked up at that.

As a kid I worked hard and obeyed the rules. I was independent but conscientious and not a wild child at all. My mother was reserved and socially anxious; my father was the outgoing one, and I was usually more like him, a personality trait that revealed itself through my love of drama and acting. I had 'elocution lessons' as it was called in those days, and was so enamoured with it that later I became a drama teacher. I have one very kind older brother, who is a renowned palaeontologist now. My father worked for General Motors on a computer the size of a room. He'd be amazed at what we do with technology in the bookshop today. He also trained pilots during the Second World War; many of those young men never came back home.

In the 1960s, women had three career choices: teacher, nurse or secretary. But, having been encouraged to get a degree, I felt better off than many, and after Hutt Valley High School I completed a Bachelor of Arts in English and history at Victoria University, where I was also active in the drama club. None of the lectures ever included shameful events like Parihaka. It dawned on me later that I'd been taught only the white colonialist version of New Zealand history, and that all the English texts we studied were written by men. After graduating, I went to Teachers' College and then took my first job at Epsom Girls' Grammar School. I was only 21, so some of my students weren't much younger than me. I'm still friends with some of those young women today.

Teaching was wonderful but after two years I felt a growing curiosity for life outside New Zealand and an ambition to get to London. My friend Glenys and I planned an overland journey across Asia, India, Kashmir,

Afghanistan, Iran, through Europe to London. Glenys wasn't a romantic friend; relationships with women didn't even cross my mind until much later. It seems incredible now to think that two young women who'd never left New Zealand would attempt that route. This was 1969; if we hit trouble in those remote places there were no cell phones or rescue helicopters coming over the horizon. Edmund Hillary's doctor, Mike Gill, who was a medical expert in intrepid parts of the world, explained what antibiotics and emergency medicines to carry, then, with naive excitement, we boarded a ship from Auckland to Singapore.

Malaysia, Thailand and Burma were stunning, with exotic heat, colours and flavours. Then we reached Calcutta, where I experienced real culture shock. The constant noise and confusion; it was as if the city were falling down around our ears and nothing would be repaired and everyone seemed oblivious. In Kashmir, a damp, cold houseboat on a lake was our home. To reach Kabul, our only way was hitchhiking up the Khyber Pass. A truck driver took us steadily higher into the mountains on a road with a sheer drop into a ravine, miles below. The driver was unfazed; perhaps he'd been sucking on the hashish lollies everyone was trying to sell us.

In Afghanistan, in the Bamiyan Valley, old Afghani men invited us to join them on their mats to drink chai tea. It was the most beautiful place. I cried years later when the Taliban destroyed the magnificent giant Buddhas carved into the cliffs there. Iran in 1969 was a liberal, free country and Tehran was glamorous, with gorgeous women wearing makeup and heels. Nine months and thousands of miles later, we arrived in London and sent a telegram home to say we'd made it.

I studied drama in education with the pioneering teacher Dorothy Heathcote at the University of Newcastle. Dorothy's powerful methods used drama to engage children's imagination and curiosity to inspire academic and social learning. Later, I toured England and Scotland with a Theatre in Education company doing school shows and workshops.

I took those methods back to New Zealand and into the drama classes at my new teaching position at Wainuiomata College. Settling back into New Zealand life, I also started acting in plays at Downstage Theatre in Wellington and doing radio drama for Radio New Zealand. The head of science at Wainuiomata College was the man who would become my husband.

Our first child, Jared, was born in 1976, with an intellectual disability. It was a shock at first, but I'm the sort of person who gets on with what needs to be done. Over the years, any sadness has faded and been replaced with gratitude for the compassionate, exuberant person Jared is, and the richness he's added to my life. He has a kind, gentle nature and he can't fathom people mistreating each other. Years later we discovered his disability was caused by chemical spraying of gorse at a neighbouring property while I was pregnant. Many birth defects were caused in New Zealand during the 1970s because of herbicides and pesticides. Jared is 45 now and has a fantastic life, partly because he has a mother who has advocated for him all these years! He has brilliant rhythm and plays drums in a professional samba band, AK Samba. They play in the Pride Parade and he always loves that.

Two years after Jared was born, our lovely daughter Anneke arrived. We moved to a 10-acre block in Coatesville with beehives, fruit trees and milking goats. It was difficult to put my profession on hold; I had to pack away acting, drama, teaching and all the collaboration and creativity that went with it. During the first of those seven years at home alone, while I was struggling with a two-year-old disabled child and a new baby daughter, I came to understand that I was a feminist. It first came from reading *The Women's Room* by Marilyn French. That book was the catalyst; I thought, Oh my God, it's not just me. When you see the world through a feminist lens everything changes: the invisible power structures of society became clear, and I began to see the inequity caused by a world where everything revolves around men.

Once my children were ready, I began to look for a new teaching job and Charmaine Pountney gave me one. For two years, I milked my beautiful white goat Evie every morning and drove to Auckland Girls' Grammar School to teach drama. Then, a small alternative school, Metropolitan College, had a vacancy for an English teacher. With a roll of 120 students, only half of whom turned up regularly, Metro, as we called it, was located in a rambling old Mount Eden villa. Metro kids didn't fit into normal schools for all sorts of reasons; they were non-conformist or had behavioural issues and some were just too bright.

> When you see the world through a feminist lens everything changes . . . I began to see the inequity caused by a world where everything revolves around men.

I remember being interviewed by students and one teacher, each having an equal vote in the decision. One student asked: 'What would you do if a student told you to fuck off?' I answered that I'd have to decide whether it was a casual fuck off or a serious instruction to fuck off. If it was the latter, I'd have to consider what I'd done to fuck them off. That response endeared me to the student interviewers and secured me the job. I taught there for five years from 1985, using the drama techniques I'd learnt in England to engage and extend the kids.

In 1986, a group of All Blacks calling themselves the Cavaliers decided to tour racially segregated South Africa. Thousands of people marched in one of the anti-apartheid protests down Queen Street. My Metropolitan drama students created a street performance piece for the march. I carried the props in a suitcase. Throngs of people stopped to watch the performance, which ended with some students lying 'dead' across the Queen Street/Victoria Street intersection holding gravestones while others played rugby over their corpses. It was a turbulent time in New Zealand with apartheid and nuclear testing in the Pacific. The kids understood and responded to these weighty political issues through drama.

The second major chapter of my life began through my friendship with Pat Rosier, who was editor of the feminist magazine *Broadsheet*. Pat and I were part of a women's group who met socially for friendship and support; some were lesbian, some not. The *Broadsheet* collective wanted someone to run a feminist bookshop in their storefront premises on Dominion Road, and Pat informed me they'd decided it should be me. Initially I dismissed the idea, having no business experience, but Pat kept on at me: 'You're raising two children, one is intellectually disabled, you're a school teacher organising thirty kids, seven classes a day, dealing with all the parents and producing drama shows. You have more than enough skills to run a bookshop.'

Pat was very astute; she had a gift for recognising people's capabilities, even when they couldn't see it in themselves. After several months of chipping away, she had me persuaded. I decided to take the leap, thinking, if it fails I can always go back to teaching. I visited other bookshops around the country that stocked feminist, gay, lesbian and alternative literature, and held discussions with the many women in publishing companies. They were all enormously helpful in offering advice and helping select my opening stock.

We launched in April 1989 with a large party and plenty of wine. The morning after, I went back into the shop and got a shock when I saw how many books I'd sold. After all that preparation, I had to order more books to restock the shelves. Some of those original shelves are still with me in the Ponsonby shop 33 years later.

Through *Broadsheet* and opening the bookshop, I naturally became friends with women in the literary and activist spheres, many of whom were lesbian. When I opened the shop, I'd separated from my husband, but that wasn't because I'd suddenly realised I was a lesbian. It still hadn't even crossed my mind; it was very gradual. One event which inspired some self-reflection was at a party when a woman asked in a teasing way, 'How come you're the only straight woman here?' Some of these women were my friends and I knew they were lesbians but it hadn't occurred to me that I was the only straight woman in the room and I thought to myself, Well, that's interesting, isn't it?

> Love isn't about male or female, it's nothing to do with gender, it's about the person.

Separating from my husband and starting the bookshop were both significant changes and put me in a space where I was receptive to new paths. It was a time of reconsidering my life. A year later, I fell in love with a woman. When it happened it just seemed obvious — love isn't about male or female, it's nothing to do with gender, it's about the person. We bought a house in Grey Lynn and were together for seven years. I've had other relationships since, but I've never lived with anyone else.

I have two very close women friends, Glynn and Michele, whom I adore. Glynn is an old teaching colleague who has been my confidante for more than 40 years. Michele is like a member of my family. We're all independent and live separately, but we see each other frequently and rely on each other for support. Many people find that their live-in partners are not very supportive anyway. I'm happy in my apartment — just me and my books, with a phone nearby so I can ring up Michele or Glynn any time and have a rant.

Many women simply do what's expected of them: get married and have children. It's only later it occurs to them that there were other paths they could have chosen. For a long time, I didn't even know gay people existed. I was in my forties when I came out. There was no big declaration, nothing was hidden in my personal life or in the book trade, and I've always been accepted. I was comfortable with myself so I didn't have any anxiety about being outed.

Until we have the same opportunities and respect, until we feel as safe as men walking in the streets, I'll keep promoting women.

After 10 fabulous years on Dominion Road I signed the lease on the Ponsonby Road shop. Word spread round the community and on moving day my customers arrived with vans, trucks and trailers, ready to pack boxes; that's when I understood I'd built more than just a bookshop, I'd created a community. People felt an emotional stake in its future. Our focus is women's books but we have trans books and plenty of books written by men. Sometimes we have men wavering in the doorway unsure if they're allowed to enter; of course we welcome them in, with a smile.

In an ideal world, labelling a space as specifically 'women's' wouldn't be necessary, and I've thought about renaming the shop, but society still regards what men say as more important. Most of the world is designed by men, for men. Until we have the same opportunities and respect, until we feel as safe as men walking in the streets, I'll keep promoting women. Each year I hold a Ladies' Litera-Tea event in a large theatre, which sells out. We feature New Zealand women writers with recently published books and indulge in a delectable afternoon tea.

I was the Auckland coordinator of the *Listener* Women's Books Festival for the whole decade of the nineties and a founding trustee of the Auckland Writers Festival. In the shop we host book launches for women writers, and the occasional lucky gay male writer. Before everything went online, The Women's Bookshop was also the place to get tickets to Hero parties and gay events and every February we'd be inundated with people buying tickets. We did it as a service to the community.

There's a resurgence of interest in feminist literature. I have more young women coming in looking for it. Suffragettes fighting for the vote was the first wave of feminism. My shop opened during the second wave, when abortion and working rights were the battlegrounds. Young women today can't believe that if a woman schoolteacher got married she had to give up her job, or that a woman couldn't get a bank loan without a husband to sign the documents for her. The #MeToo movement is part of an exciting new third wave, and it is built on all the struggles that went before.

Women who call themselves lesbian usually have grey hair now, like me, as the term is falling out of favour. Young people don't feel the need to be pigeonholed by labels. They're more fluid; they can have relationships with whomever they like. I think that's brilliant, it's the next generation. But we grey-haired lesbians want to preserve our history and the visibility that we fought so hard for, that's why some of us will stick to the term. I deliberately leave the 'lesbian' sign up in the shop, along with the 'Gay

Street' sign (a real street in New York) and in recent years have added an LGBTQIA+ sign as well.

I've been fortunate to do something I love for so many years, discussing books with the wonderful women who come into the shop every day, spending time in the company of many fabulous writers, chairing sessions at writers' festivals, attending interesting literary dinners and reviewing on RNZ's *Nine to Noon*. The Women's Bookshop is sometimes hard work to run but I feel it's a true privilege to do what I love. There's no way I'm going to retire!

Some people know from an early age that they're gay or lesbian, others change as they go through life. For me, I found over time that I had better relationships with women than men, but I've remained good friends with my former husband. We have family dinners and birthdays together, and now two gorgeous grandchildren have arrived.

The changes I've seen in my lifetime are astonishing. From signing the petition in support of the Homosexual Law Reform Bill as a straight woman in 1986, to sitting here today as a lesbian who could marry another woman if I wanted to, I do think, my goodness, we've really made some progress.

Gareth Farr

Gareth Farr ONZM is one of New Zealand's best-known contemporary composers, also renowned for his work as a percussionist. He has been commissioned to write many high-profile orchestral works and is well known for his dynamic collaborations. He is also the drag queen Lilith LaCroix.

As a teen, I was obsessed with Boy George and Frank-N-Furter from *Rocky Horror*. I'd practise their makeup on myself at home, sitting for hours in front of my bedroom mirror. I got very good at Frank-N-Furter, which was quite prototypical drag makeup. Meanwhile, I dutifully practised my Bach preludes and Beethoven piano sonatas, going through the motions, really, because I found it all quite uninspiring at the time.

I was a shy, quiet kid and a bit effeminate — the testosterone kicked in slower for me than most boys my age. At intermediate school in Birkdale, the bullying and intimidation was relentless. The guys had sensors out for anyone different and they were merciless. I was terrified of going to school and it still affects me to this day; the bullying overrode any other aspect of life for those two years. The school had physical abuse at its core: kids in trouble would get hit with a leather strap and the headmaster seemed to take great pleasure in hitting us 11- and 12-year-old boys with it. The only remedy for misbehaviour was violence, so it's not surprising that the kids were just as maladjusted as the adults. I didn't know anything else so I thought that was just the way things were. I still feel anxious remembering it now.

I didn't have crushes on the boys at school because they were the most horrible people and I wanted nothing to do with them. I hung out with the girls, who were also pretty horrible actually. When I was about nine, I did have a crush on Björn from Abba. Looking at those pictures from the seventies now I don't know what I was thinking — those hairdos! — but at the time I thought he was super dishy. After Birkdale Intermediate, I was faced with the prospect of five more years of torment at Birkdale College by the same cast of nasty characters, but luckily a few fortuitous events prevented that, and reshaped the whole trajectory of my life.

Dad was a trade unionist and he moved us from the North Shore to Grey Lynn, a few blocks from the Trade Union Centre. Grey Lynn was much better for me, more urban and diverse than bland, white North Shore. I enrolled at Auckland Metropolitan College, which was an alternative school created in reaction against those conservative, rigid schools like Birkdale and Auckland Grammar. The school motto was 'Dare to be different', which definitely felt welcoming for an anxious, troubled kid. There was no formal hierarchy, and the teachers were more like friendly mentors than scary, violent dictators.

It wasn't until my last year of high school in Auckland that I really got excited by music. It took the arrival of a dashing young Don McGlashan to spark my interest. Although he was only my music teacher for one year, it changed everything for me. He introduced me to percussion, and we started a school band. We couldn't wait for music classes every week; I was so gripped by this new world that was opening up. Don remains a good friend to this day and I've arranged some of his songs for different instruments. So, that was my school career; I entered Metropolitan College as a nervous, shy 13-year-old and left as the noisiest 16-year-old ever. Those four years started to undo the damage of Birkdale.

I launched my university career in 1985 with a degree in German language and literature, and, the year after, I added a diploma in percussion and then a Bachelor of Music in composition. Auckland

University was an exciting new world. The music school was cloistered on the edge of campus and had a library full of scores and the graceful sound of flutes or soulful sopranos would filter down from professors' lesson rooms on the floors above. The atmosphere was very focused. It was an intense three years of work but incredible to be completely immersed in music. I was comfortable enough in that creative environment that I started to feel like myself, accept myself. I was thriving in composition classes and the energy from that helped my confidence so that I found it very easy and natural to come out.

After graduating from Auckland, I won a Fulbright scholarship to the Eastman School of Music in Rochester, New York, to continue composition and percussion. I left for New York in 1991 and absolutely worked my arse off. I assumed that I'd be near the bottom of the heap among all those high-powered, wealthy international students; after about a year I realised I was close to the top, and I could breathe easier.

Rochester is a small post-industrial town in New York State, an hour's flight from New York City. It doesn't have much in common with the brash glitz of Manhattan, but it did have a bar with regular Sunday night drag queen shows. When I discovered the drag world, I was infatuated by the outrageous spectacle of it. I thought it would be full of truckdrivers in dresses, but the performers and choreography were brilliant. The night was called 'Life's a Drag', and it was packed to the rafters every Sunday. *Priscilla, Queen of the Desert* had just come out, so my close-enough-to-be-Australian accent was very popular.

I made friends with an experienced Rochester queen called Pandora and threw myself onto the stage a few weeks later. Because I was so used to being on stage, I thought it would be quite easy, but holding the crowd in a club was surprisingly difficult, a completely different proposition to a classical concert setting. I started by copying the others, lip-syncing to Madonna and Cher, but I wanted something different so I decided to experiment with a mix of drag and drumming.

My act became a sort of Turkish belly-dancing-drumming routine, something they'd never seen before, and it brought the house down. I was so skinny and saucy back then; I actually had a waistline. In towns like Rochester, drag shows are so important for the queer community because that's all there is. Drag has been so important in my musical and performance history, but getting dressed and doing makeup in a tiny toilet? I never want to do that again; my nightclub drag days are over.

After a year at Eastman I bought a car and would often drive to New York City for the shows and the clubs, just to be at the heart of it all. Once you leave Rochester, you quickly hit the freeway, and I always felt a weight lift off my shoulders; the sky seemed brighter and all the study and work melted away. Then the Manhattan skyline rose in the distance, getting bigger and bigger — it's still my favourite place on the planet.

Then I returned to New Zealand to live in Wellington. Chamber Music New Zealand offered me its composer-in-residence position; I was still only 25 so it was quite an honour. I became intrigued by the Indonesian gamelan and was exploring Māori influences, performing with orchestras, experimenting with drag and classical music, and exploring the boundaries and possibilities.

I founded Drumdrag as a performance concept to launch Lilith LaCroix upon the world. She became my more glamorous, outrageous alter-ego, literally a drum-playing drag queen. The name Lilith was invented by a couple of gay players in the NZSO one day at rehearsals. It sounded like a pouty, catty incarnation of Gareth and it stuck. I wanted Drumdrag shows to be completely live, no lip-syncing, so I found a voice teacher and quickly had to face the harsh reality that I wasn't a natural singer. Without a great voice a singer has to really sell the song with their personality and that's what I do; if I believe it, the audience believes it.

When I first started doing Drumdrag in Wellington I became aware of two different audiences: the NZSO concert crowd who consider me a serious musician, whatever the fuck that means, and my queer audience. I've always hated that segregation. My idea of success is when I see the orchestra audience at my drag shows and vice versa; worlds colliding, yes, that's what I want. Drag can be used to connect with the audience and lighten the formality of classical convention. When I'm Lilith, I can get away with slapping a cute guy on the arse, but I can't do that when I'm Gareth. 'Entertainer' is what I had on my business card at the time. Unfortunately, that's a dirty word in classical music, but whether I'm in black tie and tails or a ballgown and pearls, my job is to entertain the crowd. Otherwise what's the point? A sense of humour and the visual elements are very important — I want an orchestral piece to have as much impact as a drag show and be multi-dimensional.

I remember once playing bass drum in an evening Gershwin concert with the NZSO. I had my drag outfit with me for a show later that night and a mischievous double bassist suggested I wear it to the rehearsal. The dress code for men in an orchestra is black tie and tails but for women it's a little more flexible — a black evening dress or trousers. I arrived at the Auckland Town Hall in a long wig, earrings, fake boobs and a black lacy top. I looked quite good, I thought. The orchestra was in an uproar when I walked in. Most of the players thought it was brilliant. The orchestra manager announced it was wonderful to see Lilith LaCroix at the rehearsal, but sadly she wouldn't be appearing for the concert that evening. Drawing attention to oneself is absolutely against orchestral practice, and I totally agreed.

I do delight in creating an impact, shaking the audience out of their complacency and their assumption of how a concert should look and sound. Once when I was playing one of my own pieces with the Chamber Orchestra, I think it was in Napier, I was wearing a black PVC corset. In the foyer after the concert I overheard two older ladies say, 'Do you know, I think that young lady may have been a boy.' Then there was the time in Japan when I was playing snare drum with the London Symphony Orchestra and the legendary Leonard Bernstein was conducting. A bunch of us had forgotten our ties. Bernstein offered to buy some for us, and I asked for one with sequins. He looked at me, poked me in the chest and lisped in his low growl, 'You'll get seeequinsss . . .' Then he walked off. It was a profound moment with the maestro.

It's strange that early in life I was harassed for being different and now I get applause for it. Given a different set of circumstances I could still be in the closet at 50 years old, which is a horrific thought. I feel like my personality is free from the chains of oppression. I'm happy with who I am now. The advice I give to composition students on the rare occasions I work with them is to value their ideas, to not let their first instinct be to diminish and find fault. People often think, How good can it be if I thought it up? Have the courage to say, yes, that *is* a good idea.

For anyone who has grown up queer, self-acceptance is linked to the acceptance you feel or don't feel from the world. If we haven't accepted ourselves, our thoughts are subconsciously clouded in negativity. It might seem easy for me to say these things from my privileged position, but I didn't always respect myself or have respect from other people. When you value yourself as a person, when you're OK with how you look, then you can value and have confidence in your ideas and creativity.

RuPaul's Drag Race is a fabulous series but it's only one way of doing drag. Drag can much broader, it doesn't have to be hours of perfect makeup and immaculate hyper-glamorous costumes. If all you want to do is throw a few fake eyebrows on and a swipe of lipstick, then that's also drag. If we can find the strength to be original, to be our real selves, then we can craft our performance and become whomever we want to be. There you have it: drag as a metaphor for life.

Shaneel Shavneel Lal

Shaneel Shavneel Lal is an activist and founder of the Conversion Therapy Action Group, which works to end conversion therapy in Aotearoa New Zealand. They are on the executive board of Rainbow Youth, Auckland Pride Festival and Adhikaar Aotearoa and received the 2020 Impact Award for Inclusion.

I was born in Fiji in the year 2000, in the year of a military coup. I am iTaukei, indigenous Fijian, and Girmitiya, the descendant of slaves brought by the British colonisers from India to work on sugar cane plantations in Fiji. I lived in an extended family. My family were mainly Hindu at home, but I went to a Christian school and read the Bible every day. I may have believed in it when I was younger, but I also was never the conventional boy. Unlike other boys, rugby and soccer did not interest me. I spent most of my time befriending my English teachers.

My grandparents were well-respected elders in our Fijian community. As I grew older, my queerness became damaging to their reputation. People in my village would weaponise my queerness against my family in disputes. Soon enough, people in my community would try to pray my gay away. Elders would pray over me to release the evil spirits. They would make me wear enchanted bracelets around my wrist and waist at all times.

I was kept away from the boys to stop the spread of my queerness, as if it were a virus. I was kept away from the girls to stop me from becoming queerer. The hatred for queer people eroded the love my community had for me. My conversion therapy aimed to break me psychologically and spiritually, but my power was ancestral. The colonial forces could not break me. The collective nature of my community hid my conversion therapy from my parents.

What's considered healthy and robust discipline in the islands is illegal in New Zealand. There was a lot of violence, not only from the elders but from young people too. I carry deep trauma from my childhood as a young queer person. I remember very vividly being beaten for simply existing. It may take me the rest of my life to undo the internalised transphobia that anti-queer violence beat into me, but being who I truly am in a world that isn't cool with my existence is a revolutionary act.

I was an overtly queer kid; others knew I was queer before I did so I became an easy target for homophobic and transphobic bullying. Men perpetuated the majority of the abuse I received. It was difficult to accept I was meant to love the very people who'd orchestrated my violence. A lot of adult life has been about undoing my childhood trauma. I am healing through intimate, warm and loving friendships with men.

Gradually my family started moving to Aotearoa, and our home in Fiji became lonely. My great-grandmother still lives in Fiji. She was a source of strength and support. She knew I was different from the other kids, but she also knew that I was worthy and deserving of love and celebration. My great-grandmother is iTaukei and one of the last remaining people who understand Fiji's indigenous genders and sexualities. That knowledge of our ancestors is nearly lost. She unreservedly accepts and celebrates vakasalewalewa (third gender or two-spirit person) and veilasami vakatangane (homosexuality). Words that encapsulate queer iTaukei identities lose cultural context and important shades of meaning when translated into English.

Colonialism dismantled and uprooted indigenous queer identities. The Western queer identities often captured by LGBTQIA+ leaves no room to represent indigenous queerness. My people are vakasalewalewa. There is no V in LGBTQIA+. Indigenous identities are rendered invisible by the +. Its very insistence on universality erases indigenous queer identities. Indigenous queer identities are shoe-horned into an acronym that privileges Western queer identities. The process of forcing indigenous queer identities into Western frameworks of queerness is the neo-colonial erasure of indigenous sexualities and genders.

I arrived in Aotearoa in 2014, a year after Parliament passed a law to allow same-sex marriage. I moved into a place of privilege. My family settled in Ōtāhuhu, into a big Pacific community there, so there wasn't much culture shock, at least in South Auckland. I started at Otahuhu College. The students were predominantly Pacific, but the entire leadership team was made of white people. There wasn't much understanding of Pacific culture.

It was clear that Pacific cultures weren't as important or valid as things that were associated with whiteness. While I was given an extension of my assignments to attend a meeting at the Ministry of Education, other students were refused extensions if they had attended a Pacific funeral. As a young Pacific person in the education system, I was being taught to dissociate myself from my culture.

The Pacific was once a welcoming home for queer people. It has now become a hostile host.

Many students thought their freedom of religion was absolute. Although Otahuhu College was supposed to be a secular state school, it definitely wasn't. Anything which didn't align with conservative

Christian religious beliefs was met with aggression. In Year 11, a Christian boy threw a chair at me for refusing to accept that homosexuality was a sin. He was scared of being challenged and he expressed his fear through violence. His violence filled me with enough anger to fuel a rocket.

The Pacific was once a welcoming home for queer people. It has now become a hostile host. The unholy marriage of Christianity and colonialism destroyed our place in our homes. The Bible was weaponised against indigenous people to control them and replace their traditional knowledge and wisdom. Religion was a colonising force. Our ancestors would be ashamed of how way we treat mahu, vakasalewa, palopa, fa'afafine, akava'ine, fakaleiti and fakafifine. I am my ancestors' wildest dreams and the colonisers' worst nightmare.

I'd never heard the words 'homosexual' or 'trans' before moving to Aotearoa. All I knew were the derogatory terms. I never saw a happy queer adult. I learnt very early in my life that society did not welcome my effeminate expressions. I convinced myself I had to change to be happy. The life of a queer person was full of shame, ridicule and bullying.

All I could see was the pain and suffering of queer people. How could I want that for myself? I could not imagine a reality in which I could be free as a queer person, so I tried to hide. Young queer children deserve stories of happy queer adults. It gives us hope to continue when we have every reason not to. It allows us to believe that there is a reality in which we can be free, happy and queer.

In a transphobic world, trans people are often treated as nothing more than fetishes. Men who desire trans people are afraid of the societal consequences of pursuing a relationship with us, so our relationships are hidden behind closed doors. Accepting I am trans-non-binary has been the most liberating feeling in the world. I am asked all the time if I am a boy or a girl. I am not a boy or girl; I am the moment. Being visible isn't safe, but it is necessary. Authentic representation of trans people changes our life. It transforms how society treats us. The era of portraying trans people as imposters, something to be feared and undeserving of love and humanity, needs to come to an end.

In the summer of 2017, I was volunteering at the Middlemore Hospital's reception when a church leader walked up to me and offered to pray my gay away. I said, 'Good luck.' No, I refused to pray, so he looked at me and said, 'It's hot, but do you know what's hotter? Hell!' At 17, the idea of going to hell scared me. At 21, going to hell is my greatest fantasy. Let's be real. If all the queers are going to hell, that's where I want to be. I am ready to take over the reins when I arrive.

I couldn't believe that conversion therapy was still legal in Aotearoa. Conversion therapy isn't therapy at all. It is torture. When I was appointed the Youth MP for Jenny Salesa in Manukau East, I got up in Parliament and demanded that members of Parliament end conversion therapy. There was very little political will in government to act. I founded the Conversion Therapy Action Group and told myself that I must end conversion therapy.

Conversion therapy is not about praying the gay away or fixing the trans. It is about psychologically and physically torturing the most vulnerable people. The Labour Party would not commit to banning conversion therapy. During the 2020 election, we created a social media storm and forced the Labour Party into submission. In 2021, we hit them with a petition of over 150,000 signatures. We gave the government no choice but to ban conversion therapy.

The fear of failing to ban conversion therapy was debilitating. The select committee process was a daunting and lonely journey. The responsibility of getting the submissions in favour of banning conversion therapy fell on my shoulders. Having never done it before, I was learning the process as I was teaching others. Multiple churches started spreading misinformation in their efforts to scaremonger Christians into opposing a ban on conversion therapy. I knew I had to debunk their false claims. Those who preach love were the quickest to send me death threats. At 21, I suddenly found myself orchestrating one of the most significant movements for queer rights. I was filled with anxiety but I had no choice but to keep calm. The movement was tearing my wellbeing apart but I had no one to hand all my responsibilities to. I hope I did my best.

On 9 July 2021 New Zealand marked 35 years since Parliament passed a law decriminalising homosexuality. That law did not free me as a queer person because it did not free all queer Pacific people. I cannot be free until all my people are free. My people throughout the Moana are still criminals for being queer. New Zealand bears responsibility for that, especially in the Cook Islands, a New Zealand protectorate, and Sāmoa, a former New Zealand colony. The Pacific Islands are shamed by Pākehā New Zealanders for not accepting queer people, but they must understand that it was their colonising ancestors who brought queerphobic laws to our lands. They received the advantages of colonisation, while all my people received was trauma. Indigenous peoples have always loved queer people; colonisation has stolen that from us.

I made the mistake of entering Mr Gay New Zealand in 2020. The morning after the contestants were announced, a group of white gay men and trans women created a Facebook group called 'Shaneel Lal sucks'. They demanded the government to deport me. White gay men have given themselves a pass for racism. Queerness does not erase white privilege. Queer people need to be mindful that queer people of colour fall to the bottom of the queer social hierarchy. I do not believe that having privilege is anyone's fault, but I do believe it is our duty to use our privileges to end systems that gave us those privileges in the first place. The best way to use your privilege is to put yourself in a position to lose it. Ally is a verb and allyship is a fall from grace. I did not win the title of

Mr Gay New Zealand, but I won the public vote and the most challenges in the competition. I won the people's hearts.

Queer people need to be mindful that queer people of colour fall to the bottom of the queer social hierarchy.

As a kid, I was made to feel that there was something wrong with me. I get told that the younger generation is getting weirder. That's not true. There aren't many old people like me because they are dead. Maybe it was the AIDS pandemic, or that homosexuality was punishable by death or conversion therapy that increased suicide rates to sky-high. A generation of queer people is growing up making dangerous mistakes because the state's negligence killed our role models. We are not creating new identities; we are reclaiming what was lost to colonisation.

As queer people and people of colour, we have to fight to be treated like humans. I was born a fighter. Stonewall was a riot. Black trans women and trans people of colour fought to free queer people. We must continue their legacy. The first room to catch fire at the Stonewall was the coatroom. That night they burnt the closet so we would never have to hide again.

Two years ago, on the International Day Against Transphobia, a body of a trans woman was found lying in a pool of blood in the capital of Fiji. A year before that, a gay couple was attacked and left to bleed. I was afraid growing up in Fiji. When I moved to Aotearoa, I escaped a country ready to kill me and a government ready to justify it. But people close to my heart at home don't have that luxury of being who they are safely. I cannot be free until all my people are free.

Studying law at the University of Auckland is giving me the tools to fight institutions of oppression. We must fight for everything in the islands that we have already achieved in Aotearoa. After winning the battle to end conversion therapy in Aotearoa, I will return to the islands to overturn the homophobic and transphobic laws left behind by the British imperialists.

I am no longer asking for my rights; I am taking them. I fight to be liberated. My queerness is older than this settler state. I made a promise to my ancestors to free my people. I must, I can, and I will liberate queer indigenous people from the shackles of colonialism.

Tom Sainsbury

Tom Sainsbury is an actor and comedian who tours regularly throughout New Zealand. He is the author of *New Zealanders: The field guide*.

I grew up on a dairy farm in Matamata. It's a small town known for racehorse breeding, if it's known at all. Dad is allergic to horses, though, so we were the only ones who didn't have them. I was always friends with the animals. I don't eat animals now because I've had friendships with so many of them. I know others who profess to be animal lovers but still eat them; that's quite an odd concept to me. Dairy farming didn't suit me, but I don't judge my family for running one.

I anthropomorphised the vegetable garden as a kid, always making up stories in my head about animals and vegetables, like a mix of Smurfs and the Munch Bunch, but adapted to our farm. For cultural experiences beyond the vegetable garden, there were family trips to the bright lights of Hamilton or Tauranga. Those were our big cities. We'd go to see new movies and have a look at the bookshops. I'm not sure if my parents suspected I was gay, but they certainly took me to some eye-opening films like *Priscilla, Queen of the Desert* and *Philadelphia*, the one where Tom Hanks dies of AIDS.

I do often write queer characters into my plays; that probably reflects my own circle but also exploring that diversity on stage is interesting. *Wigging Out* was about two hyper-competitive and successful drag queen frenemies called Ann Xiety and Dee Pression. The story was that, years earlier, in their prime, they blazed a glittering trail through Auckland's nightlife scene, but I show them in the current day: they're 20 years older, the glitz and shine have worn off, and basically they're on the bones of their arse.

They accidently meet again in a WINZ office, where they're both applying for the benefit. It's all cringingly awkward, which is a bit of a specialty of mine I suppose. There's a lot of humour to be found in that embarrassing chasm between aspiration and reality; it's quite a Kiwi thing — some of our most well-known actors and musicians have needed to work in hospo or take out loans and apply for benefits, so a cold dose of reality is never far away in the New Zealand creative world.

I revel in the low-budget aesthetic — honestly, if someone gave me a huge bunch of cash to produce a show, I'd probably just pay the actors and crew more. Right now I'm a doing a monster show with a character from *Creature from the Black Lagoon*, an old black and white horror movie. I spent hours trying to make something but finally just bought the monster costumes from America. They cost $150, which is a massive outlay for me, but they're the perfect slime-green colour and came with some creepy clawed gloves.

I have a constant desire to challenge convention, but I'm also desperate to be liked and not get in trouble. Sometimes I've done things that have pushed the wrong buttons and upset people. I wrote a gender queer character once, painting them as being consciously controversial and attention-seeking, but really, it's much easier to make a joke at the expense of someone of high status or power; transgender people are already marginalised and usually have less power so it's hard to make them the target of a joke.

I also ask myself if I'm the right person to tell their stories when I'm writing characters. It's walking the knife edge between laughing at and laughing with the characters. It requires a careful touch, especially with minorities, and I don't always get it right. That reminds me of a transgender doctor we had in Matamata. He started transitioning when I was a kid; how brave to rock the frock in Matamata. Everyone seemed to take it in their stride, which was amazing for a little dairy town.

I kept a low profile at Matamata High School. I didn't want to attract attention but I did a lot of observing social cliques from the periphery. My experience at high school wasn't traumatic but it was clear that being gay was, socially, the worst thing you could be. There were two boys who were rumoured to have had sex at a party; they were completely ostracised, which was a stark warning. I learnt by that example to stay out of focus. There were a couple of out-there flamboyant guys, and they seemed to be more accepted than boys who were just shy and not very masculine. Perhaps in New Zealand culture, if you're different but confident about it, then people leave you alone, but if you show any weakness, the mob jumps on it.

I came out as gay at Auckland University. I was kind of in denial about it till then, unfortunately. I wish I could say I was confident about who I was from the get-go and I just owned it — I really admire people who can do that. I studied English literature, devoured books and plays and started hanging out in Auckland's theatre scene. I suppose I was finding my tribe, and germinating ideas.

My parents are fairly conservative but practical, so there was no commotion about being gay. They're people who just get on with things. They read and travel a lot so understand the concept that people lead different lives, although some of the questions they ask people are just like 'please shut up!' Once, Mum was backstage at a drag show helping me put my wig and bra on. She must have wondered how the hell she'd ended up behind a curtain at the back of a theatre, putting a bra on her son. I don't consider myself a drag queen, though. I'm just an actor playing a variety of characters, many of whom are women. I'm not into the fierceness or heightened femininity and glamour of drag.

People often describe me as prolific, but it's a misconception, because I actually spend a lot of time just wandering around the house beating myself up about not working. Theatre can be depressing because of the constant need to produce, then, when no one's watching, it's disappeared; it doesn't exist. One advantage is that if you create something that's not as good as you wanted, it's soon gone, whereas a terrible video or TV piece can follow you around. Theatre is a beautiful metaphor for life in that nothing lasts forever and we're all going to die. It's a reminder of mortality.

That's a bit bleak, isn't it? Don't worry, it's not all gloom. There's a camaraderie and an acceptance of difference in theatre and comedy. It's a lifestyle where we get to express ourselves, try new things with different people and ease the pressure of life. I was doing some shows at Gay Ski Week in Queenstown and those guys just let loose; they were a crazed bunch of people who only get one week a year to go completely nuts and prance around in their glitter costumes. I can do that every day, so maybe my job does have some mental health benefits after all.

I suppose we're a kind of queer double team, the WHAM! of New Zealand comedy, perhaps.

I sometimes write and act with Chris Parker. Usually those pieces end up being a hysterical farce of some kind. I suppose we're a kind of queer double team, the WHAM! of New Zealand comedy, perhaps. I'll be George Michael. We have different physicality and styles, which is good for doing different characters, parodies, travesties or whatever you want to call them. 'Parker and Sainsbury are putting the anal in banal this Comedy Festival': that was a memorable headline from a seventies-style show in 2018. It was a web series about two cops running an unsuccessful stakeout business from their Toyota Starlet.

I did a gameshow called *Drop Your Load*, as in viral load, for an HIV prevention charity. I dressed up as a cross between Steve Parr from *Sale of the Century*, if you remember the nineties, and Elton John, gold bedazzled jacket and mullet wig. It was such a good cause and was actually a gift to me as I had been so ignorant about HIV. I'd do my test, sigh with relief when it was negative and that was it, but through the gameshow I realised I was very sheltered; here I was in my mid-thirties and had never met any HIV-positive people. I learnt about these people's lives, their reactions to finding out they were positive, and they've become friends of mine now. Then I rest easy thinking I've done something noble for the year.

Stand-up is the most revealing format because there's no character to hide behind. My parents have been to some outrageous R18 shows delving into sexual encounters and financial disasters. I usually forget they're in the audience until about halfway through, when I remember and have a jolting shock moment of clarity. It's horrendously embarrassing.

Are gays just funnier? That's an interesting question.

I think if you're non-heterosexual you're an outsider and become more observant of how people conduct themselves, more aware of body language and social dynamics. That heightened sensitivity seems to lead to character ideas for me, so yes, perhaps creativity is correlated somehow to queerness and the empathy gained from being a minority. Are gays just funnier? That's an interesting question. Perhaps life on the margins gives us more material to work with, but, no, gays aren't inherently more funny, well, apart from my mates Chris Parker and Madeleine Sami.

Here's a surprise: my real love is actually thrillers and straight drama, straight as in non-comedy, not as in hetero. The problem is, I'm hardwired to find the joke in any situation. If a joke can be had I think it's a tragedy not to make it, so everything I write has comedy in it. I think about being funny all the time.

I'm not passionate about politics, or about anything at all really. Those Snapchat videos I made were just to fill the void of political satire in an election year — it was just about the jokes for me. People loved the absurdity of Paula Bennett running over Jacinda's cat Paddles while driving through Point Chevalier with Maggie Barry, Nikki Kaye and Amy Adams. The buzz from all of that is great for my live shows. Auckland people are notorious for last-minute ticket buying, so putting on a show is nerve-wracking. Sometimes I've only sold five tickets and I'm in the dressing room praying and sweating for people to come. Luckily, I haven't had to worry about that for a while, which is a relief.

People will always want to laugh. That will never change. We need comedy to alleviate pressure, to feel less alone, to survive as human beings in this absurd world. My characters all have their foibles and troubles, whether it's the prime minister or Bob next door. When people see that all of us are ridiculous in our own unique ways, I might just have helped lighten their load.

Six

Six is a journalist in Tāmaki Makaurau Auckland. She is best known for her work on *K Road Chronicles*, a web series that investigates what it is like to be homeless on the streets of inner-city Auckland.

I was a curious kid, gathering crumbs of information about sex and gender from TV, magazines and people in my neighbourhood. I've always felt more feminine than masculine. At kindergarten, the boys were separated from the girls, the girls would do crafts and painting while the boys would be sent to play with trucks and hit blocks, and I was torn between wanting to do crafts and talk with the girls and the teachers' expectations. We grew up watching James Bond and The Fonz on *Happy Days* — macho alpha males. The message was, screw as many women as you can, that's how to be cool; treating women with respect wouldn't do your reputation any good at all.

A trans woman lived on our street; she was very hostile but she did fascinate me. I remember an episode of *M*A*S*H* where a doctor helped Corporal Klinger transition to a woman, and I thought that was something I could do. So, I was aware of transgender people and the possibility of transitioning, although the details were still mysterious.

I nearly came out as transgender when I was 13 years old. I'd just seen *The Rocky Horror Picture Show* for the first time and was spellbound — that fierce, outrageous, theatrical breaking of gender conventions was a real awakening; when I found out that the person who wrote it, Richard

O'Brien, had grown up in Hamilton, my hometown, I was so proud. My hormones were kicking in then, so it was a time of sexual awakening — of course, my parents were horrified that I loved *Rocky Horror*. I decided not to come out then because it felt too risky and unsafe. Also, the AIDS epidemic was all over the news, which caused a nasty backlash against the queer community. I remember guys would boast about going out to beat up gay guys. I hardly knew what gay meant but clearly being different was dangerous. I was only young and had no support network, so I pushed it all out of my mind and distanced myself from my queer and trans identity.

I grew up in an aggressive, angry household in the working-class suburbs of Hamilton. My father was a career criminal, but not a good one — he was just a petty thief and conman who spent more time in jail than out. If you're going to be in the crime business, at least be good at it. From that environment I learnt to separate mind from body as a coping mechanism to deal with problems at home, to avoid dealing with trans issues or physical pain. I'd take my consciousness elsewhere, out of my body, away from my problems.

Mum remarried, and my stepfather was a better man, a welder who built truck-trailer units. Some of my fondest memories are of hanging out with him at his workshop. He let me try welding but I gave it up after burning my hand; no one had heard of health and safety back then. I was much more fascinated by the storeroom and how perfectly ordered all the screws and hammers and gloves and masks were; I couldn't understand how they kept track of it all.

A 10-minute bike ride from our state-house street was a more rural, horsey area with fancy houses on big blocks of land. That's where my older sister could always be found; her best friend was anyone who had a pony. She was good at insinuating herself into those circles. Mum stayed at home, she had her work cut out looking after my younger sister who was ill with diabetes and epilepsy. At school I was a loner, doing the basics and coasting along; my sisters were my friends, really. I liked softball and singing. Most kids on my street were pretty rough so we didn't play with them 'cause they'd either beat us up or try to steal something. We never had any money in the family, so I had to buy my own bike — I did a paper run for years, getting up at five in the morning to deliver the *Herald*.

Even with all Mum's help, my little sister died young; she had an epileptic seizure and suffocated in her sleep. Soon after, my grandmother died of Alzheimer's. Two close family members gone so suddenly was a terrible shock, one dying young and one without a memory anymore. It was the heart-breaking realisation that life is delicate and fleeting that pushed me towards writing and photography; it created an urge to try to capture life in words or pictures so as not to forget. I started writing about things I was interested in. I had an article about herbal ecstasy published by *Pavement* magazine and a piece about hang-gliding in another magazine.

I bought a camera and became good at portraits so I did wedding photos and events for a while. I drifted from different jobs, cleaning cars and working in a print shop, until I got a job at Baycorp, earning good money. I had my own house and nice car, but the work was immoral, pursuing people for debts and interest payments of thousands of dollars for computers and TVs worth a few hundred. After a few years my conscience won out over the money and I quit; the finance industry is designed to trap vulnerable people in poverty.

I'd been in a relationship with a woman through those years, and we had a beautiful daughter. She's 15 now and wants to start a fashion label. I tell her that's a great idea, but the rest of the family discourage it — why do that to a young person's dreams? The biggest fear I had about coming out as trans was how my daughter would react. Let me read the Christmas card she sent me after I told the family: 'Dear Dad, I wish you were here this year for Christmas. It doesn't matter what happens, you'll always be my dad and I'll always love you.' Now we get our nails done together and go out looking at clothes, or we go into Tiffany's and drool over the diamonds. I love having a daughter.

People had their different reactions to me coming out as trans, but the world didn't end, the sun still came up. When you come out, yes, you might lose a few friends but you realise they were arseholes anyway; the ones who take their place are beautiful and real. A funny thing about coming out is seeing all the other people who think they're well hidden in the closet, they think that no one knows, except *everyone* knows. For me, coming out felt like an emotional dam had burst and honesty flooded out. Living in the closet, you second-guess everything, your words, mannerisms, clothes, it's exhausting; throwing out all that useless baggage was empowering and cathartic. Having the courage to be who I am allows me to continue to develop and grow as a human.

> Living in the closet, you second-guess everything, your words, mannerisms, clothes, it's exhausting; throwing out all that useless baggage was empowering and cathartic.

When I told my mum I was trans and wanted to live more honestly and openly, she took it badly, saying, 'I feel like you're dead, the person I knew isn't here anymore.' In a sense she was right, but that person was never going to be happy or reach their full potential; that person was never going to be honest with anyone else because they weren't being honest with themselves. Mum's perception of a transgendered person was the archetypal street hooker that's really a creation of Hollywood movies. The fact is, transgendered people are all around, in all walks of life and you wouldn't even know. Now Mum says she's really proud of me and we have a close relationship; it's a relief that she's come round. My stepdad took it all in his stride, he just said, 'Well, I suppose we'll start calling him "her" now.' He's a pragmatic kind of guy.

I started transitioning without hormones, experimenting with different looks, trying makeup and women's clothing. It was gradual, a bit of eyeliner first, then more feminine shoes. I don't really have the figure for a dress, but I tried some anyway. The first time I went out wearing eyeliner I was so self-conscious, I thought everyone was staring; any little laugh I heard, I worried it was directed at me. When I realised people were fine about it, I tried ballet slippers, gradually becoming more daring.

But that growing confidence was precarious and easily shattered. I went through phases of getting a whole wardrobe of outfits, wigs and makeup, heading out to town all liberated and fearless, then someone would throw me a funny look and I'd instantly become incredibly self-conscious, go home and throw out all the clothes and wigs, certain I'd never do it again. The next week I'd think, damn, I wish I'd kept a few of those dresses. I didn't want to dress to the stereotype of transgender where they're either a prostitute or a 65-year-old in a miniskirt and tank-top.

It does take a certain amount of courage to be my authentic self, that's why Karangahape Road is so beautiful because difference is celebrated, not just tolerated. That person I used to be before transitioning now feels like a twin brother who's gone away.

When I went to the doctor to talk about transition options, I never expected to be on the cover of *Vogue*, I just wanted to become more feminine. The doctor and endocrinologists were lovely, supportive people so I decided to start hormone therapy right away. Hormones are incredibly powerful, sometimes in unexpected ways. For example, walking through a park soon after starting treatment I could see the shades of green and the brightness of the flowers in much more lucid detail. The endocrinologist explained that oestrogen causes a thinner attachment of eye retina to proteins than a male, which means eyesight can become sharper and colours more vivid.

> It does take a certain amount of courage to be my authentic self, that's why Karangahape Road is so beautiful because difference is celebrated, not just tolerated.

The hormones also boosted my social energy. If I went to a bar, instead of sitting in the corner, I'd be chatting to everyone and making friends. I blamed the hormone treatment when I found myself staring into the wardrobe taking forever to decide what to wear; that had never happened before. I'd spend hours putting on makeup, only to have a confidence crisis, suddenly certain I looked like the joker, and I'd wash it all off, crying, and start again. That's the oestrogen roller coaster for you.

They say if you change your perception of the world, the world changes its perception of you. Hormones definitely changed my interactions with the world for the better. It gave me the confidence to draw a line between the old and new me, and to say, from now on my name is Six. I chose the name Six because it's androgynous, it's a noun, it's unique and it represented a clean slate. I used to struggle with my place in the world but now I feel fortunate; it's a special gift to have experience and insight of both male and female worlds. My previous name was Paul, but if I renamed myself Paula, it would carry old baggage and assumptions; also, people don't forget the name Six.

In my family, going to university wasn't in the realm of possibility, it was just something rich kids did to avoid going to work. However, my cousin was enrolling at university to do computer science, and I thought, if she can do it, anyone can, so I signed up for a writing diploma at Waikato University. I fell in love with learning the craft and philosophy of writing. After the diploma, I moved into a hostel in Hamilton and started applying for jobs but I wasn't getting much interest and money was running out. I remember the first time I went to an ATM and the screen said I had no money. It was a foreign concept, I just stood there staring at the machine.

B ecoming homeless was a gradual slide. Outside of the medical system, I didn't have any support, I had hardly any money and my living situation was precarious, my family weren't helpful, and I was too proud to keep going back to live in a garage and be looked down upon. I shifted from spare rooms to couches to night shelters — where the communal showers were difficult because I'd started to develop breasts. I ended up at the Albert Street Lodge — great accommodation if you enjoy lice, bedbugs, and sharing facilities with alcoholics and paedophiles. In these lodges and halfway houses, there's cockroaches everywhere, people get beaten up in the hallways, hookers jump in the window at all hours. I'd come home and the first thing I'd do was scan the room to see what had been burgled that day. It was such a horrible environment, I decided I'd be better off on the streets and also have a bit of extra money. It was supposed to be a short-term solution but I ended up living on them for six years.

When I was first on the street, people would come up and offer twenty dollars for something to eat, and I'd say, 'No thanks, I'm alright.' I didn't need their charity. After a while I came to see that I was denying that person the chance to help and do something positive, so then I always accepted graciously; if they gave me a burger when I wasn't hungry, I'd accept it and pass it on to someone who needed it. It was too demoralising to beg; it's a matter of pride and principle. I was always willing to work but the work wasn't there. I had a post-grad qualification and a portfolio of quality published stories; if *I* couldn't get a job, how is someone on the streets who's barely literate supposed to get one?

It's easy for people to say 'just get a job'. So, tell me, where are all these jobs they're handing out to homeless people who are exhausted, with no address, no transport, with mental illness and addiction problems? I took my journalism portfolio to *Stuff* and Fairfax media; they told me they don't employ handicaps. I went around all the supermarkets and shops and factories to apply for jobs, but when they saw a trans woman with journalism qualifications they got confused and didn't want to know. WINZ told me to lie and say I had no qualifications. How's that for professional advice?

Transitioning while sleeping rough was miserable. I had my hormones, one outfit and some sleeping gear — it was no time to worry about looking beautiful, it was about survival. I had a suit from my office days that I wore every day. I thought, if I'm going to be on the street, I'll wear my fanciest clothes. It was a wool suit so was quite warm. I got friendly with transgender sex workers; they were lovely women who gave me courage and support. A guy named Roger noticed me struggling and took me under his wing, sharing his sleeping place with me, which was a forgotten cavity under a building, just a dirt floor with graffiti-covered walls, but it was shelter and it was dry. Roger shared his food and gave me a blanket, he looked after me and taught me how to get by. He took me to the Greys Avenue apartment building that was like a supermarket for everything illicit. The leader of the King Cobras lived there, a real staunch tough guy. He's dead now so I can tell you about it.

Roger had found a PayWave card and bought a load of alcohol he wanted to trade for crack, so we went up to the chief's apartment at the top of the building. Big Chiefy was there having his nails painted by his boyfriend. He knew he was safe with us but if anyone else had seen him like that, you wouldn't want to be anywhere near the fallout. Downstairs was a flat full of squatters huffing petrol and smoking cigarettes, in the same room. There was a different flat for every drug, one for stolen goods and one for food. Roger taught me where to go, who to trust and who to stay away from. The tragedy was that when he finally got accommodation, he was so terrified that Housing New Zealand would drug-test his flat and put him back on the streets or in prison, he hung himself.

A day on the streets starts early. I'd usually sleep outside the Newton Pharmacy so I had to be up and gone before people started marching past on their way to work. Sleeping in your clothes saves time getting dressed, I'd just pack up my sleeping gear and go in search of caffeine. Occasionally someone would buy me a coffee, which was lovely, otherwise I'd head to the City Mission. From there I might go to the library or up to Pigeon Park with a book or just sit on K Road to use the wi-fi. People often ask why homeless people sit around on the streets; well, you have to sit somewhere and that's where the facilities are.

To dine at the City Mission, you go down at four in the afternoon to get a meal ticket as there are a limited number. At six o'clock, you take your ticket back and get served in the order of your number. The food used to be revolting, mystery slop or old pies that tasted like cardboard. These days I sometimes go back to eat when money is tight and to see old friends. The food has improved a lot, sometimes it's café quality. The premises have been cleaned up too, which has meant people are better behaved. If you treat people with respect, they behave respectfully.

When I came out as trans, I was sure my sex life was over, I thought no one's going to sleep with me now, but hanging out with the trans sex workers on the streets, guys would often ask if I was working. I wasn't interested but I saw how that desire is an approval of who you are, and can be flattering; I think a lot of of those girls are addicted to the attention. That was the danger on the street, it would have been easy to become a hooker or slide into hard drugs.

People would kick me, spit on me, call me a loser. I found that wrapping myself in the New Zealand flag at night meant I'd be pissed on less often.

The best thing that came from being on the streets was learning resilience, learning that I don't need much; all I had was my backpack but I was free, and I felt I had enough to survive. People would ask for my help in violent situations because I was good at calming things down without too much blood being spilt. I was respected and became part of the street whānau; Karangahape Road became my spiritual home. There wasn't much respect from the public, though, just a lot of blind ignorance. People would kick me, spit on me, call me a loser. I found that wrapping myself in the New Zealand flag at night meant I'd be pissed on less often. Those people didn't know anything about me. I was on the street getting spat on when Auckland University Press had named me one of New Zealand's best non-fiction writers. It made me so angry.

I thought if no one will give me a break, I'll create my own. I took the energy from that frustration and anger and channelled it into starting my own publication, *The K Road Chronicles*. It's a newspaper for the K Road community, for the people, not for profit. The *Chronicle* gives our whānau something valuable to sell instead of begging for spare change, but, most importantly, it gives them back their mana. It's for sale by koha, five dollars is common but we've had fifty dollars before. The stories are honest slices of life, people sharing their truths. We have profiles of streeties, information about dodgy batches of drugs, where to get a meal, a section for lost dogs, obituaries for streeties no longer with us. *The New Zealand Herald* called the *Chronicle* 'one of the 20 best things of Auckland life'.

A few months after the paper launched, a film director approached me about turning it into a series. We made eight episodes, each focusing on a different person living on K Road, and now hundreds of thousands of people have seen them. We had t-shirts made for the streeties who distribute the paper; people started asking where they could get one, so now we sell them. I've also launched a *K Road Chronicles* podcast.

I can't walk 20 metres down K Road without someone stopping me for a chat. I might get on with lots of people but I don't connect with them on a deep level. Even as a kid I didn't have many friends. I did have one friend who ran a record shop in Samoa House, the building that looks like a fale; we used to talk about music together. I was sleeping outside the entrance to his shop when he turned up early one morning. He asked, 'Are you homeless, Six? Is there anything I can do?' He let me leave my backpack in his shop during the day because dragging your belongings around and watching out for them all day is exhausting. He even came and brought me dinner one night when I'd broken my shoulder, but then we drifted apart.

Today's generation of kids don't seem to care if people are queer or gay — that's a reason for optimism.

For people on the street, trauma is the common factor, so don't be so quick to judge; every window has two views, no one really knows what people are going through. There's a mental health crisis across New Zealand, not just for street people, and suicide doesn't discriminate along social divides. We're all on this planet for a short time, so let's treat each other with kindness while we're here. Trying to conform in this society is a major cause of depression, but we don't have to conform. We don't have to live up to other people's expectations. Today's generation of kids don't seem to care if people are queer or gay — that's a reason for optimism.

If I get reincarnated, in the next life I want to take it really easy, maybe being a hippo would be nice, lolling around in the water. After years of struggling on the streets, I now have a small flat. It's across from Western Springs and I can play my music, do my writing, I can walk to K Road, the rent is low and the park is beautiful. I love it. And if I get financially stable, I will move on and give someone else the opportunity to be here. I think that's the right thing to do.

Robbie Manson

Robbie Manson is one of this country's most successful rowers. He holds the world record for single sculls and won gold at the 2017 World Rowing Cup. He retired from rowing in 2020.

I live in Cambridge, in a house that my mother helped me buy a few years ago after I'd retired from rowing. I'd actually moved here when I was 19 because this is where the New Zealand rowing facilities are, at Lake Karāpiro. Cambridge is a calm, laid-back place. Whenever I was away at competitions around the world I couldn't wait to get back here. The garden was originally completely bare so I've landscaped it with trees and flowers. Rowing for New Zealand in two Olympic Games meant being totally focused on training — other interests never had a chance — so discovering this love of gardening has been surprisingly satisfying. I'm a homebody, really.

I grew up in Blenheim, the middle of three brothers. There's only 18 months between us so we've always been close; close but competitive. Mum and Dad met through rowing — they both won national titles — so the sport is really in the blood. Dad was a welder and Mum coaches rowing and manages the family vineyard in Blenheim. It's a beautiful place to visit. My parents split when I was 14, and I still see them both, but I'm closer with Mum.

I really wanted to be good at sports, always dreaming of going to the Olympics, but for a long time I wasn't good at anything. Like most rowers,

I'm a bit uncoordinated. I was no good at running, kicking, throwing or catching but I did ride horses with my older brother, Cory, so I thought perhaps I could go to the Olympics in equestrian. However, it's incredibly expensive to keep horses and transport them around the world, so that wasn't realistic.

At school I was a painfully shy, quiet kid. I was more rowdy at home with my brothers, but at school I was teased for never saying anything, which made me even more self-conscious. I went to Marlborough Boys' College, where I always had a feeling of not fitting in. I was the weird kid who rode horses. Deep down, even before high school, I knew I was attracted to guys, but I pushed those feelings right down and felt like I could never even admit it to myself. People would say homophobic things at school that weren't directed at me, but at that age we're so sensitive about everything that I'd go red and have to quickly get away. In my mind, I had a picture that being gay would mean a mountain of negativity, that I'd never be accepted and that no one would want to know me anymore. I was so shy and insecure I couldn't handle that.

Halfway through high school Karl, my younger brother, started rowing. Kids naturally want to do the opposite of what their parents do, so I'd always cringed at the thought of having anything to do with rowing. I only started because I didn't want my brother to be better than me at anything; also, I had visions of getting really fit and having abs for summer. After being no good at all those other sports, rowing a boat was something I was surprisingly good at, and I started regularly beating the other kids.

The calm, focused feeling of being out on the water and the camaraderie of the team were addictive. I loved the simplicity of rowing, where training harder meant going faster — equestrian wasn't like that, the horse could always be unpredictable. Rowing appealed to me because it was about power and strength. At school I was associated with horse riding, a sport with a high number of gay guys, so I thought rowing would make me seem more masculine and straight, and proving myself to be better than someone else physically was important, probably because of my low self-esteem.

In my last year of college, I moved to Saint Andrew's, a private school in Christchurch that had recruited me for their rowing team. After years of being the weird horsey kid, I was suddenly the shiny new imported rowing star. Being treated with respect by other students was a pleasant new experience. I joined the New Zealand rowing team after high school and moved to Cambridge. Training was rigorous: six days a week on the water and in the gym.

Dark, foggy winter mornings weren't much fun, but with a coach and team mates relying on you, you just get up and do it. Doubles rowing is great because when the dynamic is right, the physical and mental capabilities of two people merge into one finely balanced machine. But even so, two people are never perfectly matched; one is always slightly faster than the other. Singles rowing is different. I saw it as a sport where I could rise or fall on my own merits. My world record is for singles so I can say that's something I did myself, no one was pulling me down the track.

The social life of a New Zealand rower is unusual: my friends were mainly other rowers, and we'd never go out and have big drinking or clubbing nights because it would interfere with our performance on the water. I've always been very focused, tackling one task at a time, so all my energy went into rowing. I tried to do some study alongside, but I found it a distraction. I bought a guitar 10 years ago and hardly touched it. Looking back, perhaps I was too intense, but that's what helped me be as successful as I was.

My sexuality started to weigh on my mind when I was about 19. It was becoming harder to ignore and I'd get quite depressed about it. Some days I was sure I was gay, then other days I thought maybe not. I didn't want to tell anyone until I was completely sure because it felt like something that couldn't be put back in the box. Success in rowing had helped me grow in confidence, and probably helped me slowly come to terms with my sexuality and start to accept it.

My older brother, Cory, had come out to me two years earlier. I was surprised yet it made sense. I'd been so worried about me I'd never considered my own brother could be going through the same thing. He said of all the family I was the one he was most afraid to tell, thinking I'd be the homophobic, judgemental one. I think when you're trying to hide something, you naturally radiate a negativity towards it. I was supportive of him but I wasn't ready to come to terms with myself; however, when I was, it was Cory I told first.

I was very emotional and made a big deal out of it, but he was full of kindness and understanding. A year later I told Mum, just before Christmas. Thinking I wouldn't be able to start the conversation in person, I called ahead to say there was something I wanted to tell her. Driving home from the airport, I made her guess because I was too emotional to say it. Of course, she was fully supportive and comforting.

I phoned Dad to tell him before he found out from someone else. Before I started rowing I didn't have much in common with Dad. Sometimes it seemed like all he wanted to talk about was rowing. So, as usual, that's how the conversation began, but I interrupted to tell him I was gay and had a boyfriend. He just said 'OK' and went straight back to talking about rowing. There may have been some homophobia in his early life which seeped into the family when I was younger, but now he's fully supportive and I'm open with him about everything. Having that cornerstone of family support made me stronger; I felt that any negative reaction I might encounter in the world had much less power.

There was a guy in Cambridge who I liked a lot, but I'd never been brave enough to ask him out. Soon after coming out to my family I plucked up the courage and he said yes. I was so nervous on our first date I was almost shaking. We went out for dinner in Hamilton instead of Cambridge because I was so worried people would see us. I gradually relaxed and enjoyed the evening. We were together for a while, but it didn't work out. I'm grateful for that first relationship.

I'd been obsessively dreaming of going to the Olympics since I was kid. The week of the London 2012 team announcement I didn't sleep all week with the pressure I'd put on myself. When the New Zealand Olympic Committee read out my name it was a massive relief, then I had to try on the Kiwi Olympic kit for press photos and the media interviews. With all the emotions and cameras, I was completely strung out but it was very special and I'll never forget it.

I'd always watched the whole Olympics from start to finish on TV, but when I made it there as an athlete I was so laser-focused on competing I didn't see much until our event was over. We were based at the Eton rowing lake, near Windsor Castle, which is away from the central Olympic village. With rowing one of the first sports to compete, we weren't at the glitzy opening ceremony with the Spice Girls and the Queen. The team had an amazing result, with three gold and two bronze medals. When our event was over we moved into the athletes' village and experienced the full Olympic atmosphere.

People ask me what it's like in there, with everyone walking around in peak physical condition, and of course they are the world's best athletes and look incredible, but what I remember is the vastly different body types to match their sport, such as lean marathon runners, huge weightlifters and towering basketball players. The village atmosphere gets louder as the event goes on. Towards the end, there were athletes preparing for their Olympic final, having breakfast in the dining hall with others who were just getting back from a night on the town in London.

Of the 11,000 athletes at London 2012, only three were out gay men, including gold-medallist Matthew Mitcham, the Australian diver. By then, I was out to my family and team but not to the public. I'd watched Mitcham win his gold at Beijing four years earlier and admired his courage. I arranged to have a coffee with him, and we talked about our experiences. He was very generous and friendly. Having someone I could relate to who was living openly and successfully as gay gave me confidence that I'd be OK. So after the London Olympics I came out publicly and received nothing but kind support. None of the old fears I'd harboured were realised. I was happier and more relaxed; I could be myself without hiding that part of me from the media.

Four years later I was selected for the Rio Olympics. Rio was a chaotic event, but the silver lining was that I'd made lots of friends from London, and so once the rowing competition was over, we had a lot of fun out at the Ipanema Beach bars and clubs and around the Olympic village pool where everyone socialised. I met Tom Daley and other gay athletes; there were more out athletes in Rio than London. I had a disappointing result in Rio but it motivated me to train harder, and the next year I was in Poland for the 2017 World Rowing Cup. The build-up had been smooth, and I was feeling strong and rowing fast on the lake in New Zealand.

On the final race day, conditions on the course were good, the lake was calm with a light tailwind. When the starting gun fired, my only focus was to go as fast as possible. I won, and while being the new World Cup champion was sinking in, I looked up at the race times. It had felt a fast race but next to my name were the words 'world record'. My time was three seconds faster than the previous record, more than a boat length! Disbelief turned to elation. Thousands of messages flooded in from around the world — I got carried away for a while. A week later I came crashing back down to earth with a rib fracture that forced me to realise how physically and mentally draining it is to compete at that level.

I've retired from rowing now, but I still make a point of pushing myself. When I was asked to take part in a series around New Zealand high schools talking about homophobia in sport, the idea of speaking in front of hundreds of students and teachers was terrifying, so I agreed to do it. I was nervous the first few times, but now I relax and my speech notes usually stay in my pocket. The charity that runs the school talks is called WaterBoy, and I usually go with a straight ally, and at the end there's an opportunity for a Q&A. Some of the kids remind me of myself when I was their age.

Usually there's a few who don't say much during the event but hang around and talk to us quietly afterwards. They'll ask about how to talk to their parents or deal with bullies. I feel I'm not qualified to deal with some of those difficult issues, but I relate to them and share my own experiences and show them there are people who care. Our teenage years are turbulent for most of us, but it's true that it gets better when you leave school. No one came to talk to us about bullying and homophobia when I was at school, so things are changing, and I'm happy to help keep it moving in the right direction.

Now, athletes confide in me about their struggles with sexuality the way I did with Matthew Mitcham years ago, and over time they've been able to come out and live authentically. I have some close gay rowing friends. I think having two such fundamental things in common has meant we've built strong bonds.

The gay dating culture has been hard to navigate. I've found a lot of vanity, and people segregate into narrow little groups based on age or body type or ethnicity. Most queer people have similar experiences of hiding a part of themselves, of experiencing shame and discovering themselves fully in their twenties or thirties, so we should be more inclusive and kinder to each other, given the common struggles we share. Cambridge is quite restrictive for dating, and I do want to meet someone eventually, which does bring to mind thoughts of moving to a bigger city. I've had a few relationships, not long ones, but because the intensity of rowing didn't make it easy, I'm thinking about it a bit more now that I've retired.

Transgender people in sport is a controversial issue right now. Sport is for everyone and being transgender shouldn't be a barrier. The best part is simply participating — winning or losing are less important. I know that the Olympic Committee is working on how to include trans people; they're not shutting the door on them. Hopefully having a good example of inclusion at the highest level of sporting achievement will help.

Retiring from my first career is like leaving school again. I'm lucky to have travelled so much; 12 trips to Europe, and many to America, Japan and South America, and I have many brilliant memories and proud achievements, but not much in the bank. Rowing is not a sport with big-money sponsorship. For now, I'm enjoying being at home, reflecting on what I want to do when I grow up — at 31 years of age. I like helping people, so I'm using my experience and am studying personal training so I can create programmes for rowers around the world and for anyone who wants to get in shape. There's also the possibility of getting into coaching at one of the rowing universities like Harvard or Oxford.

I don't see myself as an activist; I'm not doing anything special, just living my life openly and talking about my experience when asked. The best part of my rowing career is realising that my achievements didn't end on the water. They're gifts I can keep sharing with others, at schools, or in interviews, and when people confide in me I can give them encouragement. If kids know that the fastest rower in the world also happens to be gay, hopefully they'll see that being gay is no barrier to following their dreams, whatever those dreams may be.

Charlotte Goodyear

Charlotte Goodyear is a model and designer from Ōtepoti Dunedin. She was the first openly transgender model to walk in the iD International Emerging Designer Show, in 2018.

I never dreamt modelling was something I could do. That was a
glamorous, distant world, not for someone nerdy and awkward
like me. It was my dad who encouraged me. He heard a story on
the radio about transgender models in New York City, looked it up online
and told me all about it, said I should look into it, so I did. There were
already some very successful trans models, which was inspiring. The
local agency, Aart Model Management, sent me on a short course in
posture and walking, and I soon got my first modelling job at the fashion
graduates' show at my design school in Dunedin.

I was worried it would be awkward in the backstage changing room,
but models have to be so quick to switch outfits that no one has time
to look around and gossip. My body looked no different from the other
girls anyway. I found fashion and modelling to be such an accepting
environment, and to realise there were spaces where I could fit in and be
accepted was such a breakthrough for my confidence.

I built up a portfolio and secured a job modelling at iD, the big fashion
event in Dunedin; it was exciting and completely nerve-wracking. Before,
I'd always hidden myself away. I never did drama at school and avoided
anything to do with a stage or being the focus of attention; I would have

loved to do those things but growing up I was just too self-conscious.

Some people assume modelling is simple — they should try the iD runway, in stilettos! It wound its way through the Town Hall, sloping up and down the aisles, then upstairs to the mezzanine. As we traversed the ramps and stairs we couldn't look down at our feet but had to keep stealthily checking the other girls' positions so the choreographed stops and starts were all synchronised. Leading up to the show I practised for months, walking everywhere in heels.

There's a thrilling, electric silence backstage before the show starts, then when your turn comes, it's a deep breath to focus the energy and out you walk into the glaring lights. TVNZ was filming a piece on me about being the first trans model at iD Fashion Week, as well as all the usual media there. With that much pressure, it was a relief to not mess it up. In the weeks after the show, I couldn't walk through Dunedin without someone stopping me to say hello. I'm proud of that achievement. It changed how I see myself and opened my eyes to what's possible.

Perhaps it opened up other people's minds as well. Honestly, how I convinced myself to see a modelling agency and then get on a catwalk is still a mystery to me — I think I needed a hard challenge to prove I could break out of being timid and do something bold. Bowie, Gaga and Prince and others who don't easily fit into normal society are powerful sources of courage for me. They help when I struggle with confidence or feel like an outsider and have got me into music as well. I've been playing electric guitar for a year and I'm really into the synthesiser sounds from the eighties.

At design school we learn to make different products, furniture, fashion accessories, using 3D-modelling software, and we study how things actually get manufactured and the philosophy of design innovation. I've always loved making things. I did a lot of woodwork as a teenager and I made a whole rowboat out of wood once. I met most of my friends at design school. One of my close friends, Charly, is a trans guy. We bonded over music and after we became friends we figured out that we started hormone therapy on exactly the same day, even though we didn't know each other at the time.

Trans health doesn't get taught in medical schools in New Zealand, so it's not surprising that I have found the health system to be frustrating and alienating. Because I live in Dunedin, where many of our doctors are trained, I became part of an Otago University project to raise awareness in the medical community about trans healthcare issues. A group of us did a series of panel interviews with a med-school lecturer and told our stories about what it's like to experience the New Zealand health system as trans people. We didn't just exchange facts, we also shared our personal experiences, and that had a big effect. We found that med students are really interested to learn about trans health if they get the chance. It felt gratifying to be able to do this, although telling all those intimate details about my medical history was emotionally draining. I hope it makes some difference. At least we've started the conversation at Otago Uni and perhaps created some more understanding.

From my earliest memories I felt different. I always identified in a deep sense with girls and, looking back, there were so many ways it must have been obvious I wasn't like other boys. In my mind I've always been a girl — my thoughts, imagination and dreams were a girl's. I thought that was normal for a while; when I found out it wasn't, I learnt to hide it. If I ever expressed feminine feelings or actions I was treated badly, especially by other boys, so from an early age I built a shell and lived a lie, constantly being careful to keep the mask in place.

When I hit puberty, I got really depressed. I just had no clue what was going on. I stopped seeing friends, cut out hobbies and escaped into computer games and the internet. I only discovered the concept of transitioning when I was 16. Otago Boys' High was a very sporty, conservative place. There was a boy in my class with beautiful long hair who was into fantasy books and he was bullied so badly. I tried to stay hidden. I didn't know that I was trans at that stage, but I knew being different was dangerous. After one term, I broke down and refused to go to school. I couldn't articulate why at the time, but it was the stress and constant worry of being in an environment which was so hostile to anyone who wasn't a macho sporty boy. My parents let me change to an artsy co-ed school, which was much better, but I still struggled with mental health, and even getting out of bed. Mum helped me feel OK; I'm so grateful for her.

It takes a lot of mental energy to maintain the pretence of being someone you're not, constantly acting out mannerisms just to fit in. It's exhausting. Researching gender and sexuality on the internet made me wonder if I was bisexual, or maybe a cross-dresser. Gradually I read more and came to an understanding that I was transgender and I saw from other people's experiences that it was possible to have a good life as a trans person. I kept learning more until I was 18 and that's when I decided that fully transitioning was what I needed to do. I was doing all that reading and research in secret but I did tell my partner at the time. She was accepting and so kind when I told her about these feelings I had.

I found the courage to go and ask a doctor about transitioning. He didn't know anything about it but wrote down some information about a psychologist I could talk to. I paid them for an expensive session only to find out they couldn't help either. I saw a different doctor who referred me to a psychiatrist, who thankfully did understand what I was experiencing. After seeing him for six months, he had no doubt that transitioning was the right step for me. He knew about the process and medical community, and wrote me an approval letter for hormone therapy, the start of a long, tough process.

I then told Mum and my oldest sister. My sister was quite open to it, but Mum was afraid. It was all new to her and she worried it could be the wrong thing for me to do. She did a lot of learning about it before she could understand why I needed to, and she became my biggest supporter. Dad lives in Invercargill. I told him a while later, and it was a hard conversation because he had no awareness of trans people at all and so he was really confused. He made a big effort to understand and learn what the transition process would be, and now he's amazing, so kind and compassionate. I couldn't ask for better parents.

I thought I'd never fit into normal society. People were always staring at me on the street and I worried that I'd squander any chance of having a good life. But even so, I was prepared to take the risk because I felt so strongly that transitioning was for me. In the trans community, it can be frowned upon when others say they grieve for the person they knew before they transitioned. But I think grief can be totally appropriate. Friends and family deserve time to absorb it, learn about it and grieve if they need to; grief and loss can apply to many of life's twists and turns.

Mum and my stepdad have a funeral business in Dunedin so they're very knowledgeable about grief. I'm doing a project for them looking at different ways of designing cremation urns, which for now are quite similar and conservative in style. Learning about the funeral industry has reminded me that everyone has upheavals in life, and when someone passes away, that can be such a huge transition for those left behind.

After taking hormones for a while, I saw my body begin to change and I became closer to what felt comfortable, and any remaining doubt about transitioning was swept away. But it still took a long time until I was ready for gender reassignment surgery. My family said they would support me, and I saw trans women living life and doing normal stuff as women, but getting mentally ready for the operation and long recovery took time. My family and the local community in Dunedin, lecturers, friends, other trans people all came together to support me so I wasn't on my own.

When I was ready for the surgery, I flew to Thailand for a month-long stay. I knew it was going to be tough in the hospital system of a foreign country, so Mum came with me for the first half and Dad flew over for the second half. It would have been so hard without their support. I underwent gender reassignment surgery and a laryngeal shave, a procedure that lasted seven hours. The medical system in Thailand is very advanced for trans people, and the nurses and surgeons are very experienced. The problem is after the surgery, because we have no experts in New Zealand in the procedure or the aftercare.

Back in Dunedin, I spent the whole summer at home recovering and following an intense after-care programme designed by the Thai surgeons. During this time, I'd often worry about things, which turned out to be quite normal, but without any medical support I could only rely on advice from a friend who'd had the same surgery. Through those months I hardly saw anybody, it was hard to leave the house, and I couldn't go to work so I had no money. My mood dropped a lot. The GP put me on antidepressants but the side effects were horrible. They made me even more depressed and even suicidal sometimes; I ended up in hospital for a week to get off them.

It's crazy that the waiting list for gender reassignment surgery is over 30 years in New Zealand.

I don't want people to think it was a bad decision or something went wrong that caused those mental health issues — that's totally not the case. But it was a lot to go through, and the lack of medical assistance in New Zealand is a real issue. That's why I went to speak to the Otago med students, to try to get some awareness at the grass roots. It's crazy that the waiting list for gender reassignment surgery is over 30 years in New Zealand.

Now that my body has repaired itself and I've restarted life, I'm very happy with the results. I feel so settled and comfortable in my body that I hardly even remember I've had surgery — that's how right it feels. Thinking back on my old self is like remembering somebody I used to know who isn't here anymore. When I see old photos of that person, it feels like looking at a twin or an old friend.

The effect of hormones isn't just physical. A new palette of emotions emerged, and feelings became more vivid and expansive, with more shades of awareness about the world — that must be what it's like for a biological teenage girl hitting puberty. Everyone goes through the process of trying to figure out who they are, how to present themselves and express their identity to the world, but that turmoil of body image and self-esteem happens in the teens for most people. With hormones, I've gone through many of those same challenges, but I'm doing it in my early twenties. Of course, my body changed as well. Now I have proper hips and softer skin, the shape of my face has changed, my cheekbones are more defined and my nose is more feminine.

At first, I felt a lot of pressure to look a certain way as a girl. I had massive insecurity about being seen as masculine, so I tried to present as extra feminine. I'm trying to quash that now and be confident about my own style, and embrace the way *I* want to look, not how I think I should look to everyone else. It was a process of sliding along the scale of gender presentation to somewhere that felt right — and this place on the spectrum can change; it's not static. I still like an androgynous style which mixes gender norms. I love space-age stuff — Bowie is still such a big influence, so fearless and inspiring. I went to the exhibition in Melbourne after he passed away to see all his iconic costumes and outfits. It was a deeply meaningful experience. Lady Gaga is also amazing. I have a little Gaga tattoo. People notice it and want to come and talk; I've made some friends through this tattoo.

In becoming Charlotte fulltime, I had to decide how to present myself, and ask what's appropriate, what's comfortable, what looks good? Learning to use makeup took a long time. Most women have years to get that right, and many of those first experiments with clothes and makeup I cringe at now, but everyone goes through an outfit-fail period, I suppose.

To choose a new name I looked at lists of baby names from the year I was born so it would naturally match my generation. Charlotte was on the list. I didn't know anyone by this name, but my grandmother had always said if she'd had another daughter she would have called her Charlotte; Grandma was amazingly supportive with my surgery and transition, so it felt right for me to become Charlotte. My twenty-first birthday was the day I became Charlotte. It was such a special day. I went clothes shopping with Mum and my sister and later at the party all my family was there, and everyone acknowledged that from then on I would be Charlotte. It was a bit different to drinking a yard glass and getting one of those big wooden keys!

Training my voice wasn't easy; that's one thing that hormones can't change. I started with quite a deep voice, and having a breathing tube stuck down my throat for the seven-hour operation damaged my vocal chords, so it took a while before I could speak at all after that. I tried singing techniques that use different vocal muscles to help raise my pitch and resonance. When I'd learnt how to use those new muscles, I read books out loud for months to practise maintaining the sound. Eventually it became easier and now I don't have to think about it. It's my new natural voice, an androgynous middle sort of range that I'm ok with.

When I get asked if transitioning was worth it, I say yes, for sure it was worth it — more than anything else I've ever done. I still deal with mental health issues, but they come and go, like they do for many people. My life is good. I'm happy, I've graduated and have some exciting design projects to work on, and my friends and family are wonderful.

Meagan Goodman

Meagan Goodman lives in Whakatū Nelson and is pursuing a master's in psychology. They are also a roller derby player and hope to make the team for the next Roller Derby World Cup.

I'm a queer, polyamorous, relationship-anarchist single parent. In Nelson there's no group you can join for that, so I don't know anyone else like me, but I wouldn't change who I am, and Nelson is a beautiful place to live.

Autumn is my favourite season. It's the best time to go foraging, which reminds me of my childhood. We lived on Vashon Island, a 45-minute ferry ride to Seattle. Dad would take me out into the forests searching for berries and fungi. Fungi are little bursts of magic in the real world and foraging for them is a treasure hunt. Some are edible and delicious, some are psychedelic, and some are poisonous but still beautiful and delicate. Around Nelson each landscape has its own fungi species. I go for walks in the bush, head down in the micro-world around my feet.

I'm a bit of a lone wolf, finding my own path through life. I was 14 when my grandmother passed away and left me enough money for a plane ticket and an adventure. I went to France and joined a language school. The classes were very loose, and most afternoons I'd be hanging out on the beach swimming and drinking wine — it felt like being in a movie. France changed me. Despite everything I'd been told, I could see that America was far from being the greatest country in the world.

I understood that there are so many places and ways of living, and I wanted to see them. American children have constant nationalist propaganda hammered into them that the US is the best in every way. I'm glad my kids don't have any of that pushed on them in New Zealand. I would never go back to the States to live; I've drifted so far from that culture now.

I moved from Vashon Island to North Carolina for university. It's a deep-red Republican state, but my school was in a town called Asheville, which was a bit like Wellington. It was a little liberal oasis in the conservative Deep South. I studied psychology and environmental science and those two passions came together perfectly with my first job after graduating. I joined a wilderness therapy school in the Appalachian Mountains for adolescent boys with substance abuse issues.

The boys would come up into the mountains for two months to learn practical survival skills like making fire and shelter, and we'd take them hiking and let the natural beauty both calm them and challenge them. Those boys had a tough exterior, but they were so soft and vulnerable inside. There was a lot of crying. Our culture doesn't afford boys and men much space for tenderness and vulnerability. Later, when I moved to New Zealand, I worked with young people for the Department of Conservation, instilling conservation values and a connection to the environment in young Kiwi kids.

My path to New Zealand started in Australia, where I went to research how Aboriginal identity is tied to the natural environment. While I was there I met a Kiwi man and we hit it off. He invited me to New Zealand, which I loved, and once I'd finished my Australian studies I moved permanently to Nelson to be with him. We got married and he is the father of my two children. I'd always been firm in my mind that I didn't want to have children because the planet is already overpopulated, but I suppose biology kicked in and I found that I really did want kids.

When I meet new people I don't say, 'Hi, my name's Meagan, I'm a polyamorous relationship anarchist', but I like to talk about it when it comes up. Try this thought experiment: Imagine if, like a cicada, you could shed the dry, restrictive husk of cultural expectations that dictate how to 'do relationships'. Remove the psychological wall of separation between partner and friend groups so that each person you meet is the blank canvas of a new relationship. Consider your human connections with the questions: What could my relationship with this person be? What would we like it to be? That's how I approach relationships in my life, by removing the barriers to being authentic and honest.

> Queer people, perhaps especially women, live life to such a heteronormative script that it can take a long time to untangle from that and emerge to discover who we really are.

I was 27 when I had my second child, and soon after it dawned on me quite suddenly that I'd had the wrong perception of myself. I realised I was gay. I had dated a woman at uni, but I thought of that as a separate thing that people do at uni — I didn't equate it with me being gay. It seems so odd to think about that now. My older brother is gay and my younger sister is trans. My family is very open and accepting, and so it's so curious that it never hit me earlier than that. Queer people, perhaps especially women, live life to such a heteronormative script that it can take a long time to untangle from that and emerge to discover who we really are.

Polyamory has always interested me. I met some polyamorous people and read about it because it felt important to explore, and it really fit for me. I no longer felt comfortable with monogamy, and certainly not in a monogamous heterosexual marriage. It was difficult for my husband. When we tried to transition to a more open marriage there was a morass of shame and stigma to wade through for him. It takes strength to be different, to refuse to do what everyone else does, and it wasn't what he wanted.

Although we've gone our separate ways romantically, on the spectrum of marriage break-ups we've done alright. There were no lawyers or courts involved and we certainly don't hate each other. We share the care of our children and we both want what's best for them.

Polyamory is all about transparency and honesty. It needs open communication, clear boundaries and self-awareness. The discrimination against us is outrageous; the culture we live in is much more accepting of cheating in relationships. The assumption is that polyamorous people are sleeping with everyone in town, but most of my relationships would be traditionally described as friendships. My friendships keep space open to become something more if that's desired. I'm very far from being a nymphomaniac; in fact, I'm demi-sexual. I need to develop an emotional bond with someone before I have sex with them. I'm privileged to have many close deep connections in my life, but polyamory isn't really about sex at all.

I'm from a blended family of five kids. My older brother came out at the dinner table when I was 10 years old. I remember him being really nervous. Mum and Dad were very comforting. They said, 'Don't worry about it, we expected it and it's fine.' I was one of my half-sister's main caregivers from a newborn to five years old. When she came out as trans, we all were happy that she was moving towards her more authentic self.

I didn't have a coming out. It feels like that's happening less these days. I told my family I was separating from my husband, and they know I've dated women since then. They hardly blinked — I feel very lucky to be from a family like mine. I've heard so many horrific stories about queer people being mistreated by their families.

Dad commuted from our little island into Seattle every day for his accounting job. He was bored by it and when I was 17 he quit to start a microbrewery. He's happily run that ever since, and now it has a pub attached. It's so cool that he's found his passion. He's the most laid-back guy I know; he's so calm he almost sleeps through life. I don't remember him yelling at me once. Mum runs a coffee magazine. Coffee culture is huge around the Seattle area and she's well known in the caffeine world.

The next confronting morality debate on the horizon is polyamorous relationships. We face a lot of discrimination, especially non-monogamous parents. Under the law, committed relationships can be only two people. Living outside that legally privileged scenario creates problems with housing, immigration, child access and other fundamental aspects of life. It's a wider issue than polyamory: it affects non-traditional and blended family structures, which is a weighty issue for many queer families.

Before my daughter goes to sleep, she likes to say the names of all the people she loves and who love her. There are so many amazing people consistently in her life who nurture her in different ways; it's like a big extended family. I don't think it would be like that for us if I followed the conventional approach to a relationship.

Nelson is a small town, and choosing to be open about my relationship values has led to some judgement, although Kiwis are averse to conflict so I think most of it is not verbalised. I definitely feel uncomfortable in some spaces, which is common for queer people. At school events and around the school gates for pick-ups and drop-offs I sometimes feel uneasy among the other parents.

Sometimes the discrimination can be hilarious. I had a wonderful therapist who I went to originally for massage when I was nervous about childbirth. As I got to know her we'd chat away while she was working, and the subject of queerness came up. I mentioned that I was queer and she said that being a Christian she didn't believe in that. I sensed her edging towards delivering me a sermon, so I beat her to it by asking if she thought I was doomed for hell. 'Yes,' she said, 'but don't worry, I also do exorcisms.' To her credit she is an incredibly talented vagina physio — or pelvic floor therapist, she might prefer to call herself. I thanked her for the exorcism offer but said I'd prefer to keep my demons. After that awkwardness I asked her if she could help with a facial scar I had from a motorcycle accident. As she was working on the scar tissue she said, 'Wow, it's really intimate, touching people's faces.'

Nelson has a pride meet-up group with about 300 members. I try to join the monthly event, there's usually about 20 people at that. Then there's a lesbian group, mainly of older women, but if you're queer and dating, Nelson is a desert. I was on Tinder for a while and it was mostly tumbleweed, but I believe there are awesome people everywhere — you just have to find them.

'Violent Femme' is my roller derby alter ego, and I like to think I live up to that name on the track. A roller derby game is called a bout, and I saw my first bout in Nelson with a crowd of 2000 watching all these super-fast, hard-hitting, bad-ass women on roller skates, fighting it out. I immediately thought, yes! I'm signing up for this right now. There are 50 roller derby leagues in

New Zealand, and it's one of the fastest growing sports in the world. It's very inclusive and queer-embracing.

The Nelson league is an eclectic group, mostly women, and a lot of mums who don't have many opportunities to let rip with the competitive, aggressive side of their personalities. We've played many men's teams, but my most brutal hits have been delivered by female-bodied people. Even though it's fierce and the sport involves smashing the shit out of each other, there's always hugs at the end. I've never seen fights or bad behaviour. I've felt a sense of community in roller derby that I've never had before.

> ## Juggling parenting with my studies and roller derby is a busy gig, but I'll continue to smash heteronormativity when I get the chance.

My kids and I have deep roots in Nelson now, so we'll happily be staying. I'll be a registered psychologist in 2023. I'm going to work in private-practice therapy, focusing on queer youth and non-monogamous people; there aren't many psychologists specialising in that area. Another ambition is to make the Aotearoa Roller Derby team for the next World Cup. I've been training with the national team so I'm in the running to be selected if I work hard. Juggling parenting with my studies and roller derby is a busy gig, but I'll continue to smash heteronormativity when I get the chance. We are so steeped in outdated gender roles and expectations, but youth are more switched on about these socially constructed rules and they're beginning to push back. Just look at all the new Netflix shows with queer characters. We need more space for open minds, more passion, more freedom from bland conformity, so that every person has the chance to blossom and live a beautiful life.

It took me a while to figure out my identity. Although it happened gradually, the more I realised that I was queer, the better I felt. My queerness still feels new to me, and definitely precious. There isn't a day that goes by that I don't feel joy at being more aligned with my identity and life choices. I encourage people to hang in there even if it's rough — it is worth it to be your most authentic self.

Edward Cowley

Lealailepule Edward Cowley is involved in a range of Pacific health initiatives. He is also the drag queen Buckwheat, and has worked as an entertainer for over 35 years.

I was the sixth of eight kids and the youngest boy. We had a small family house in Kingsland until my father got lucky and won big on the horses. Mum took the money off him immediately and bought a bigger house in Te Atatū, which was mostly rural farmland at the time. We were one of the first families to settle out there, and being the 1960s, definitely one of the first Pacific families. I was brought up in a strict Christian home with strong Christian values. I was in the church youth group and was a Sunday School teacher. Our whole social circle was built around the church and religious-based activities.

My parents were firm but fair, and with so many kids and being busy with the church, the only way to keep some kind of order was with military-style rules. Despite this, I started sneaking out to clubs in town when I was 14; you had to be 21 to get into bars in those days, so I'm not sure how I got away with it. I saw my English teacher from Rutherford High there one night, and he was great about it. He said, 'I always knew I'd see you here one day.' If I was ever questioned about why I wasn't at home, I'd say I was out with youth group friends and people believed me.

I always knew I was gay, and as I got older the teachings of the church clashed with my identity. I really struggled with that. I'd get home from the gay clubs at five in the morning and climb in the window to get a few hours' sleep before I had to get up for Sunday School. I'd present myself at church like a good Christian boy, but really I was out having a great time at the gay bars every weekend. I felt tortured and torn between the church's teachings on sexuality and my own sexual thoughts about boys and men.

All my life I'd heard that being gay was wrong and so I kept up a secret life in the city, meeting beautiful gay boys and seeing how they were living. They did interesting things and had nothing to do with churches; being around those guys, I realised there was no way I was staying in West Auckland, or going to Sunday School and being a good Christian boy any longer.

I was 17 when I told Dad I was gay. I explained to him that the teachings of the church didn't sit well with me because I kept hearing I was going to hell and I didn't think that was true. Dad said he knew I was gay, and if I didn't want to go to church that was between me and God, so it went quite well. I suddenly had so much time on my hands, and so to make myself useful, I cooked lunch for when the family returned home from church events. When Dad became ill, and as his sickness worsened, he told my brothers to keep an eye on me and make sure I was looked after because I was different to everyone else. My brothers told me about that after he passed — it was so lovely to hear he had that special care for me. I'm still very close with my family now.

After high school I lived in Sydney and London for nine years and worked doing drag. I felt as if I had to keep my distance from my family. I was nervous about dealing with the issues of being gay with my siblings, and so I told myself I was shielding them from being upset, but really I was just nervous and afraid of hard conversations and bad reactions. In the end they were all fine about it. Anyway, I needed to go and see the world — Auckland was so small in the mid-eighties, like a village.

AIDS killed a lot of my friends. Almost my whole circle died. At this age now and to have lived this life, I don't know how I'm still here. Why was I the lucky one? I was always slightly reluctant to completely throw caution to the wind with the partying — I preferred to stay on the periphery of things — but I wish I had been a bit wilder at times. Maybe that's why I'm here today and most of my friends are not.

When I was growing up, my aunties referred to me as fa'afafine, an effeminate boy; the literal Samoan meaning is 'in the manner of a woman'. I first went to Sāmoa when I was 18 and found that I wasn't like the fa'afafine I met there; they were presenting as girls or women, which was completely accepted in Sāmoa, but definitely not in 1970s New Zealand. Wearing women's clothing and presenting as a girl just wasn't an option for me in Auckland back then; I'm not sure I would have wanted that anyway. So, I absolutely identify as fa'afafine, but in my own way. The concept of fa'afafine has evolved as Samoans have moved around the world and blended into other cultures, and there's no single right way of being fa'afafine.

Samoans first landed in Auckland with the big Pacific migration of the 1960s. The fa'afafine who arrived found that the streets that were supposedly paved with gold were also very conservative. They were told to put away their female clothes and mannerisms to avoid trouble, and so rather than endure persecution they lived inauthentic lives. That's changing now. Even in Christchurch I've seen fa'afafine wandering about being themselves with not a care in the world. I couldn't have done that in Te Atatū in the seventies. The role of fa'afafine has definitely shifted. Traditionally we would support the family domestically as nurturers — fa'afafine often have a natural affinity with children — but they can also do the masculine roles. As more of us have had higher education you can now find us working as teachers, lawyers and in government in Sāmoa and New Zealand.

Being fa'afafine is great. I can cook up amazing food in the kitchen then go out to mow the lawns and fix the roof; if you've got a fa'afafine in your family you know things are going to run smoothly. They can provide a natural stability in a family because the other kids will go off and get married, while the fa'afafine is a constant anchor and often looks after the parents in later life. It really depends on the family. Sometimes we're revered and valued, but other families are embarrassed by us.

Fortunately, I didn't have any problems at all; my dad never worried about how it reflected on him. Samoan culture doesn't really have a concept of coming out. The Samoan way is about not creating a fuss. Gay people are usually left alone if they keep to themselves and don't start waving rainbow flags and getting vocal about equal rights. Is that right or wrong? I don't know, but it's existed without question for many years and has resulted in a fairly harmonious society.

If you've got a fa'afafine in your family you know things are going to run smoothly.

I see drag and being fa'afafine as quite separate: one is performance art, the other is an intrinsic identity and way of life. Both drag and fa'afafine have become part of the landscape in New Zealand now. The queer arts collective Fafswag is the latest in an evolution of Pacific people pushing queer culture in new directions in New Zealand. They're fiercely confident about who they are, and now they're an influential export; from Pacific South Auckland they've performed around the world, and it's lovely when they acknowledge that us drag artists paved the way for them in the early queer and drag scene of the eighties.

The eighties were also a time of fiery debate about homosexual law reform. Anytime the media wanted a comment they'd come to drag queen events and put a microphone or camera in my face. Lots of gay men didn't think a drag queen should be speaking for them — get a grip, I say, we're all in it together fighting the same fight; I never asked to be a spokesperson. Drag in those times was a non-threatening way for straight people to encounter gay people.

There was still a small-town mentality across New Zealand, and people were afraid of what they didn't know. I'd get them laughing and having a good time, and they'd go off and tell their friends they'd met a gay person and had fun. That's how hearts and minds get changed. It wasn't the same little village when I returned in the nineties; it was more open to the world with a lot more going on.

There was another role for drag in those illegal days and sometimes still today: people can be nervous about walking past a gay club, let alone going inside. The poor things walk up and down, passing the door and glancing around, full of anxiety. It's quite obvious. But if there's a big, welcoming drag queen outside the door, nervous people feel more safe because the attention is on someone else, and they stop worrying that everyone is looking at them. Then there's the entertainment. Life is stressful for a lot of people, and when they come to a show my role is to make sure they have a great time — I try to create some joy and lift them up.

I learnt to deal with trouble in the early days by performing at RSAs and rugby clubs — in those days I'd go anywhere for a booking. There would usually be a drunk loudmouth shouting 'show us your cock'. When it got too much I would challenge them to an arm wrestle, and I've never lost an arm wrestle. Still, it's thanks to those idiots that I have these audience skills today. Rugby crowds were also great because I had a chance to change the way they felt about people like us. I'd find out the recent rugby scores, which would create a connection, and they'd be eating out of my hand. On the way home, driving in feathers and sequins at 5 a.m., I'd often be pulled over by the cops. They'd be wondering who the hell just drove past, but I was never drinking so they always let me go with a bewildered smile.

There have been some truly thrilling experiences in my performing career — being lowered out of a helicopter onto Eden Park as Tina Turner singing 'Simply the Best' was a high point, literally. The early Hero gay parties were on a scale that we rarely see in Auckland now. I've got three garages full of costumes and wigs — does that sound like a lot? Well, they're all absolutely essential pieces, and happily they've all more than paid their way over the years. I've worked in Berlin, New York and Bangkok doing corporate events with epic budgets, and there were six summers in Ibiza swinging on a trapeze through lasers and disco balls. Thinking back on those times now, I'm amazed it all happened; it's a long way from the Waitematā Rugby Club to Ibiza.

Being a drag queen made dating difficult. People would like either Edward or Buckwheat, but not both of us. In the early days they were completely different entities — Buckwheat was crazy and wild, totally outrageous, while Edward was much calmer. I thought I was never going to find someone who appreciated both sides of my character. As soon as I gave up and decided I was quite happy by myself, I met someone wonderful who did appreciate both. There was a phase when Buckwheat became all-consuming. She drew all the attention and pushed Edward into the background. I had to consciously work on Edward and get Buckwheat to take more of a back seat. The psychology of drag is complex. There can be a tug-of-war between the performing character and the real self. Buckwheat has changed over time; she's mellowed now and has become closer to Edward, and the two have found a balance somewhere in the middle.

Family has always been so important to me, so when some good friends asked my partner Peter and me if we would help them have a child, we decided yes. All four of us went to a counsellor together to talk about how it would work and make sure everything had been considered. We'd heard some horror stories where these things haven't turned out well, and we didn't want anyone to get hurt. We tried for eight years with the women but it didn't happen, so we gave it all away, but then the other partner tried and she immediately fell pregnant. Everything worked out well with the first beautiful child, our maternal and paternal instincts kicked in, and now we have two.

The psychology of drag is complex. There can be a tug-of-war between the performing character and the real self.

We all went away on holiday to Europe together the year before Covid hit. There's a lot of good sharing that goes on — I don't know how two people do it by themselves, let alone a solo parent. When the mums get tired, they give us a call and say it's the dads' turn. It's difficult not to spoil the kids, having two sets of parents and four sets of grandparents, but we're careful not to. My family were supportive about my fatherhood, although Mum was a bit unsure, but now she's seen how it all works, she's so pleased. Peter and I are in our fifties now, so the kids keep us young. Most of our other friends are already grandparents, and the children have brought great joy for everyone.

It's a different landscape for young queer kids today. In some ways it's better, but I know it can still be tough.

If you are going through hard times and it seems like there's nothing else ahead, just know that many of us have felt like this, and if you hold on, you'll find your people. There's others like you out there, and you'll find that you're not alone. I've known a few young people who have taken their own lives. If only they'd waited a bit, it might have got better. If you're in an unhealthy circle of friends, find another group — you can absolutely break out of your circle and create your own life and make it how you want it to be.

I feel so lucky to be here; many of my friends didn't make it. Life's certainly had its challenges, being Pasifika and being fa'afafine, but it's all led to where I am today — happy with my place in the world.

Ross and John Palethorpe

Ross Simpson and John Palethorpe immigrated to New Zealand from the United Kingdom. They settled in Auckland, where Ross works as a guidance counsellor and John is a primary school teacher. They are the parents of four-year-old Finn.

Ross: My father called me 'son' for as long as I can remember. I think he wanted a boy. We went hiking together, and I helped out in the garage with engines and tools. He wanted someone to share those things with, it was the way he showed his affection. Mum went to university and then became a teacher. Dad was a nuclear engineer, working on power stations. Scottish men are not known for being in touch with their emotions so I've rarely had heart-to-heart conversations with my dad. But our family was close, and because we travelled we learnt a lot about history and science on our family holidays.

I grew up in Glasgow in the 1980s and 1990s. When I was five years old, the conservative Thatcher government introduced Section 28 of the Local Government Act, a law banning the 'promotion' of homosexuality. It caused many queer support groups to close down or self-censor, setting the fight for LGBTQIA+ rights in Britain back decades. It's so nasty to have the leader of your country stand up and say children should *not* be taught that it's OK to be gay. That law was a dark cloud hanging over my entire time at school. It meant I grew up with no concept of being queer or of gay life. I never saw gay families or trans people out in the world living their lives doing normal jobs.

If you can't see it, it doesn't seem possible, and so as a young person I had a sense of hopelessness. Now as an older queer person I understand the simple power of being visible. The only fragments of queer life that reached my world were related to AIDS or George Michael being arrested for 'lewd behaviour'. It was always negative and I had no role models. There's a huge void when you don't even have words to describe who you are.

Now as an older queer person I understand the simple power of being visible.

Growing up, I was a pretty masculine person. I enjoyed getting muddy and being outside but found the strict gender roles at school very difficult to manage. I knew I was different, but had no way to access information about being LGBTQIA+ so didn't know what that difference was. The bullies at school were horrible, they seemed to figure out I was a male long before I did, and the torment was relentless. Homophobia should have been addressed by the school, but because of Section 28, homosexuality couldn't even be named.

In Scotland, gender roles were tightly nailed down and policed by everyone, with insults and violence for non-conformists. Young men should not show empathy or gentleness, young women must be extremely feminine — those were the rules. My sister has never followed those rules, either. She's married to a man, and runs a saddlery business and spends a lot of time sword fighting.

I went to the University of Glasgow to study marine and fresh-water biology. I was swiftly disabused of my visions of Jacques Cousteau-style trips to Antarctica researching seals and whales when I realised the rigorous academic application that would be required. University was better than school because I wasn't bullied but I felt awkward and adrift and was drinking far too much, sometimes to the point of blackout. Those were the years where I could survive on pies, beer and two hours' sleep a night. I joined a group of hard-drinking, pool-playing lads who basically lived in pubs and bars, and I went through a series of terrible relationships with both men and women. I look back and feel like I missed out on a lot of opportunities because of my struggles with my identity. I knew I was part of the queer community in some way. At first I described myself as bisexual, which was a homeless sort of identity because gay people didn't believe me, and straight people assumed I must want a threesome.

I look back and feel like I missed out on a lot of opportunities because of my struggles with my identity.

Miraculously, I scraped through the degree and graduated in 2003, but rather than working on research ships sailing to exotic locations, my first jobs were in generic London offices where the expectation of how a woman should look came into sharp focus. Ever since I'd finished with a school uniform, I'd worn jeans and t-shirts every day. Suddenly I was being told to dress more appropriately, be more feminine, but wearing a skirt felt alien to me, like I was in drag.

It also seemed that there was an expectation for women to have low self-esteem, as if we were expected to hate our bodies. The magazines and culture were all shouting, if you're not slim and pretty you're a fat failure. Body positivity wasn't a mainstream concept back then, which made it difficult to understand my gender dysphoria. I read a lot about transgender people but I didn't feel like I met the very specific criteria; it felt as though there was a high bar to cross to be trans 'enough'.

I got involved in an activist left-wing politics group, and that's where I first met John. We were both members of an early internet forum called Urban75, which organised anti-war protests and underground dance parties. At weekends I'd escape office life to talk earnestly about socialism and dance to techno till the sun came up. Gender and sexuality politics weren't our group's objectives then, instead it was anti-Bush and Blair's Iraq war and pro-drug reform. I remember feeling like we were on the cusp of big changes, but in the end the war happened, and the drug laws still haven't changed.

There was a shortage of teachers in the UK and so, with a government grant, I retrained. At age 25 and after a few years in UK schools, I decided it was time to explore the world. I'd been on holiday to New Zealand before and liked it, so in 2009 I arrived and got a job in a South Auckland high school, teaching biology and science.

John: Portsmouth, where I come from in the UK, is a navy city. It's at the opposite end of Britain to Glasgow, but there are similarities. They're both rough, conservative places. Dad was an engineer in the navy and for the first years of my life he was away at sea fixing battleships; in fact, I was christened on the HMS *Manchester*, a British destroyer. I was raised to respect all kinds of people, but I never saw that respect extended to gay people. Homophobia was everywhere in the UK and my whole upbringing was soaked in it. If a rugby player fell over and showed they were hurt, they were 'gay', if a boy was interested in art or dancing he was 'a pansy'.

I was a strange-looking, uncoordinated kid with bad acne. Our family's British military history stretches in an unbroken line from Iraq and Afghanistan back to both world wars. I remember telling Dad that I wanted to join the navy, but he said I didn't have to be a copy of him and to follow my own path. He did that with sport, too; Dad loved rugby but he never pushed me into it. I decided to go to university, but before that, I'd endured a traditional, stuffy boys' school, steeped in homophobia — all ties and starched collars worn with blazers that we could never take off. I just kept my head down and got through it.

University was a relief. I could finally relax, smoke a joint and collect my thoughts. I did a degree in American history and had some unfulfilling, sexually awkward hetero relationships. It still hadn't entered my mind I could be gay or bisexual. The only queer representation I knew was of camp, limp-wristed queens, and so I thought, of course I'm straight. In my last year of university, a friend had the TV series *Queer as Folk*, which is about young gay men living in Manchester, on DVD. It was ground-breaking at the time. I was already aware of Canal Street in Manchester and Soho in London as being England's very gay places, to be avoided lest you immediately turn gay, but I'd never considered that those rainbow flags could be waving for me until I watched those DVDs. 'Well, maybe that is me,' I said to myself. One night I went to an LGBT society drinks at a gay pub to find out more, and a guy I was talking to told of the angry abuse he'd received while walking down Portsmouth's main street holding his boyfriend's hand. It frightened me to think that's how my life could be.

A few nights later, I was at a rock music pub and noticed a Gothic-looking guy with eyeliner and black clothes. I thought, damn, he's hot. After a couple of strong drinks to calm my nerves, I went over to talk to him. I must have said the right things because he let me take him home to see what would happen. Well, a lot of stuff happened that night. I never saw him again but my first time with a guy felt right. It was a relief. I began to think of myself as bisexual, but I was still afraid of being out, so after that epiphany and pivotal experience, I went back to hiding away and ignoring it. I had other girlfriends. I feel sorry for the people I dated when I was still grappling with my identity.

In a curious parallel with Ross's life, after university I became a teacher and moved to London to escape my suffocating hometown. I'd stayed in touch with Ross through anarchist left-wing politics websites and emails over the years and I knew he was coming back from New Zealand to spend Christmas in Glasgow so I invited him to a club night in London, saying, 'It'll be just like the old days, you can stay on the sofa.' Ross called me to pick him up from King's Cross Station. We did go to the club night, but he didn't stay on the sofa. That's how we finally got together, after years of being friends. There was an intense spark between us. It felt like a very English version of a Hollywood film: before we first kissed, I made him a cup of tea.

Ross: After that fairytale weekend in London with John, I flew back to my family in Glasgow. I'd only had a few days with John, but it felt fateful; something had shifted. My family wasn't pleased that I'd come all the way from New Zealand for Christmas and was spending most of my time in London. 'I have something to figure out,' I told them. I went to meet John's family. His dad was a bit awkward, and then his sister arrived with her hand in an ice pack. She had just caught her boyfriend with another woman and had knocked him out cold. She saw me looking alarmed and told me not to worry — she'd left him in the recovery position.

John: Time was of the essence: we only had a few weeks in each other's company so there was no drawn-out courtship. We had robust, honest conversations about our lives and what we wanted, and we were open about our sexual identities and our previous relationships with men and women. I agreed to visit Ross in New Zealand. If the visit went well the plan was for me to move there. My first New Zealand experience wasn't seeing the majesty of the South Island or the white sand beaches of Coromandel; I spent most it in Ōtāhuhu, and I loved it, I felt happy.

There was an adjustment at being in a straight-passing relationship, although we never tried to hide the fact that we were both queer. After I returned to the UK, Ross and I had regular morning and evening video calls. Hanging up on those calls was always tough, and I knew we couldn't keep doing this. I packed my life into a few suitcases and headed for Heathrow Airport to get on a flight back to New Zealand. In the arrivals area of Auckland Airport, I proposed and, luckily, Ross said yes.

Ross: Exactly a year after John and I were in London, we were married at a friend's bach at Mathesons Bay, north of Auckland, but this meant facing all the expectations of what a bride should look like: a flowing white gown with lace and silk, hair shaped into gentle ringlets. I was always uncomfortable being seen as feminine, and having to dress up as a bride magnified this struggle. The more I felt uncomfortable, the more I tried to lean into being feminine but it didn't make it any easier. If anything, these very prescribed gender roles of marriage and then pregnancy was what eventually made me decide to affirm my correct gender. I finally settled on a dress that, in retrospect, looks like what your Nan might wear to bingo, and my hair was a short shock of cherry red. We plan to get some updated 'wedding' photos done this summer where we're both looking like ourselves.

Before we got together we didn't talk about gender or the possibility that I might transition. I hadn't reached that understanding yet. I'd read the memoirs of lots of trans people and I defended transgender rights in a way that felt personal, but I was suffering from a kind of impostor syndrome where I still didn't feel trans enough to own that identity. We had talked about kids before getting married and a year after our wedding I got pregnant. Pregnancy was the most difficult experience. If getting married was a distressing display of expected femininity, then being pregnant was a new level of awful.

> I defended transgender rights in a way that felt personal, but I was suffering from a kind of impostor syndrome where I still didn't feel trans enough to own that identity.

It's hard to be told that pregnancy should be a magical time of flourishing fully into your femininity, wafting around in flowing gowns on the beach like a Greek goddess, at one with nature, when actually I spent half the time feeling sick and throwing up, hating how my body changed and how people reacted to me being a pregnant woman. I wanted to be a parent more than anything, and I love our boy Finn so much, but the process was dreadful. I was literally counting the hours to my due date.

By this time, the transgender conversation had become more nuanced, and the language of gender fluidity was replacing delineated categories, so I felt less excluded from the possibility of being trans. As my body recovered from pregnancy and birth, I knew I was still uncomfortable with the whole concept of 'motherhood'. A couple of months after Finn was born, I told John I wanted to explore my gender identity. I reassured him that transitioning wasn't a reaction to the pregnancy; it was something that had been within me for a long time and was finally ready to unfurl. We were very honest with each other and had similar fears about what this step might mean for our family. We were both afraid of being abandoned by the other and having Finn taken away.

My family have taken a while to adjust to my identity, something that's been made harder by the Covid travel ban and being unable to have those key conversations face to face, however, they now accept and support me. Some of the first steps were buying my first chest binder and going shopping for men's clothes with John, and once it was time to fully embrace my identity, I went to see my GP for a referral for medical transition, and started to socially transition too.

John: When Ross told me he wanted to transition, I hadn't slept properly for weeks and I was in that dazed, disoriented state parents find themselves in when a newborn arrives. After the momentous event of giving birth, I worried that it was too soon for a huge life decision. I said I would love and support him no matter what, but I wondered if post-natal depression or the recovery from pregnancy could be having an effect. But it also reframed a lot of what had happened in the past, for example, the struggle for him finding and wearing a wedding dress.

In a sense, the whole family transitioned. Ross has become the happy, whole person he was meant to be; it radiates out of him like sunshine. Finn is four now, he's a little rocket. My parents' only concerns were that we'd stay together and that Finn would be cared for. They live in a little village in Devon now, where everyone knows everyone's business. Mum wears rainbow accessories and fields all manner of inappropriate questions about her son and son-in-law who live in New Zealand. Mum and Dad were so good about it that I wish I'd told them more about myself from a younger age. When Finn was born my parents came over to help.

Dad was holding Finn one day when he looked at me and said something so touching: 'Don't make the same mistake I did. Be as close as you can with him, especially in the first few years.'

In a sense, the whole family transitioned. Ross has become the happy, whole person he was meant to be.

I work at Fairburn Primary in Ōtāhuhu, a school of 500 children who are predominantly Pasifika, Indian, Māori and Asian. I'm the only male on a staff of 40, except for the groundskeeper. The only time I've had an issue being a male teacher was when I'd taken over a class mid-year from a woman who had been fired when empty liquor bottles were found in her cupboards. Some parents went to the principal to ask why a man was now teaching their children, with the implication that a man must have sinister motives. The principal apparently put them in their place immediately.

Since Ross transitioned, I now refer to him as 'my partner' rather than 'my wife'; there have been a few curious questions but my teaching colleagues are very supportive.

Ross: I've noticed that now people listen to me differently when I speak, and take what I say more seriously. I've gone from being perceived as a quirky woman, who was perhaps a bit too brash and forthright, to Ross, confident guy who has some great ideas.

Finn is a very affectionate kid who likes to crawl all over us. We have socially transitioned to becoming a gay couple. Before transition we held hands without thinking about it; now there's a little edge of anxiety about it. We haven't come across anyone nasty and malicious, but we get a lot of confused looks and inappropriate questions. We're open and unapologetic about who we are, and we never hesitate to let people know when they've overstepped the line in their curiosity about our lives if it extends to what we do in the bedroom or personal details about transition.

> ## We're open and unapologetic about who we are, and we never hesitate to let people know when they've overstepped the line in their curiosity.

We have a firm parenting philosophy: don't hide anything from kids, tell them things at the appropriate level which matches their ability to understand. Finn knows he's got two dads, and that one of his dads used to be a girl but is now a boy, and that bodies come in all shapes and sizes. We feel that's enough information for a four-year-old. Some days he's told us he's a girl, other days he's told us he's a dinosaur. We know in the future he may have to deal with issues from other people, especially from other boys, because their attitudes are modelled on the narrow definitions of masculinity that they grow up around. We already see it: as well as dinosaurs and trucks, Finn likes *Frozen* and pompoms and sometimes he wears a dress. Other three- and four-year-olds tell him those are only for girls — that's how early the conditioning can start.

I had fears about what I'd be putting Finn through, but I know that having a parent who wasn't their authentic self would be much harder for him. The teenagers I work with have no idea why adults have such a hard time with gender and sexuality. Homophobia still gets passed down from conservative older generations, but their cultural grip on New Zealand is loosening, and as their influence wanes and our society becomes more progressive, we can all be free to be ourselves in ways I never could in my younger years.

Ross and John: There's been a massive shift since we were both at school. Finn is growing up in a world where his classroom is supportive, encourages curiosity, acknowledges that queer people exist and explores ways to help them feel comfortable. We have the love and support of our friends and whānau, and this is just the beginning of the story for our family.

Ramon Te Wake

(Te Rarawa, Ngāti Whātua)

Ramon Te Wake
is a New Zealand
documentarian, singer-
songwriter and television
presenter. She has been
a presenter and director
for the Māori Television
show *Takatāpui*, the
first ever indigenous
LGBTQIA+ series.

I 'm a curious girl who's trail blazed her way into a life of creativity, music and storytelling. From a young age I felt a sense of empowerment through creative expression, and for some beautiful reason, I've been able to carve out a life doing that on stage, television and through music. I have an inquisitive nature and a bizarre imagination that have me constantly intrigued about new ideas for stories or shows. I want to keep learning and discovering new ways to see the world and present them through art to engage and inspire others. I feel grounded in my identity as a Māori trans woman, anchored by my family, community and sisterhood. Family is massive for me and that means both my blood family and chosen family; I love hard, those who are important in my life are left in no doubt about it.

My television career started with presenting *Takatāpui*, the world's first indigenous queer TV show. It was a great break, but I soon got bored with being in front of the camera and I began to wonder about my potential. I was interested in writing and directing, but when I tried to discuss doing so I was laughed at by the production people. They thought a trans woman was OK in front of the camera but nothing more. Television was a masculine, straight world. As a trans woman, there was a lot of prejudice to navigate and I had to constantly push against being pigeonholed and underestimated.

This was 2004, and Māori TV was quite fresh; fortunately, attitudes have moved on a bit since then. I ignored the people who said I should stay in my place, and learnt to write and direct by watching other people, absorbing their techniques and styles. I never thought too much about other people's reasons for limiting me. I'm not a girl who sits crying in the corner. Now, I'm a trans woman director with nearly 20 years' experience, telling honest, accurate stories of trans people's experiences. Finally, it seems the world is ready for that.

> As a trans woman, there was a lot of prejudice to navigate and I had to constantly push against being pigeonholed and underestimated.

I use writing, music, artistic expression and my own life to empower queer and trans people, to show that we deserve opportunity and that we're complex and multi-layered, as are all human beings. The perception of a trans woman is usually that we're sexual objects, aggressive hot heads, the butt of jokes, good for a laugh . . . all those mocking caricatures. That's what people learn through films and TV, and so that's how we've been treated. There's beauty and contrast in all aspects of humanity, and I try to show that in my work.

When Carmen Rupe, New Zealand's transgender icon, was celebrating her seventieth birthday in 2006, I went to Australia to film a documentary about the event. She lived the last years of her life in Sydney and we wove sections of her daily life through the film. I've met famous people before but Carmen was more than royalty — she literally delighted all my senses. Just being in her magnetic presence made me aware of all the life she'd lived, and she loved to share the stories of her life in vivid detail. When she walked down the streets, she'd turn every head. With tropical flowers in her hair, flowing scarves and beads, and a cleavage-popping dress, she was a whirlwind of colour and drama.

Carmen is admired for being a fearless trailblazer for trans people, but making the documentary I learnt what a lonely life it was for her to stand up and be the first. She put herself out there to push society forward, and in conservative 1960s and 1970s New Zealand, she did it alone.

In Australia and New Zealand, she was mostly revered and respected, but walking around Sydney with her, we still saw people hurl abuse at her. Groups of men shouted 'faggot' and other nasty stuff. The crew and I were so angry but Carmen was perfectly serene — it was just water off a duck's back. The quiet dignity of this elderly woman in the face of such cruel ignorance was beautiful and empowering to see, but it was also sad that, after all she'd been through, she still had to endure people shouting at her in the streets.

Her poise and resilience have stayed with me to this day; when people are nasty to me, I remember Carmen and she helps me to be brave and peaceful within myself. After the documentary, we kept in touch. Carmen wasn't really an email girl but she loved talking on the phone and she sent me letters with beautiful handwriting and carefully cut-out pictures, which I've kept and treasure. She died five years later.

I was born in Dargaville, but luckily I only stayed there for 18 months before we moved south to Porirua. Nana and Papa stayed in Dargaville, so we would go back for Christmas holidays. I always said, 'Gross, not Dargaville', but my older brother and I would get thrown in the Cortina for the long drive north. We'd fight in the car, and I'd cry and get him in trouble, just like normal siblings.

Papa was an intimidating man for us kids, like a towering kauri tree. He made us get up at dawn to collect wood, dig potatoes, clean sheds — all that farm stuff. It was never a holiday. We'd get so pissed off when our cousins would come up for Christmas Day and swan around playing when we'd been working every day to get everything ready. I have to admit it did teach me a work ethic, and perhaps the grit to finish things I start.

Dad was the club captain of the local rugby team so he was well known in Porirua. It was a masculine sort of household. I struggled through three years of rugby to make him happy. I was a decent player, and I even won a few trophies, but sport was never my jam; I preferred to hang out with my girlfriends creating dance routines to Prince songs. When I finally broke down in tears begging Dad to let me quit rugby, he let me stop immediately. That was a huge relief. I was only about 11 and I thought I was going to have to play rugby forever.

At school I learnt quickly how to use my personality to avoid getting beaten up. Acting confident and entertaining to get a laugh gave me a power that could distract and deflect bullies, but it didn't always work. I was a camp kid so just being myself was interpreted as too girly and I'd get whacked in the head. It was horrible. For all of primary school, I was constantly worrying about being beaten up. As I got older I realised what a formidable weapon humour can be, but at the time I was just surviving. Most bullies are weak. They're thin-skinned and self-conscious — if they're afraid you might embarrass them they usually keep their nastiness to themselves.

Aotea College, a state school for the northern suburbs of Porirua, was a bit better because my older brother was there. If anyone messed with me, he and his boys jumped on them. I was friends with a tough group of girls so we had strength in numbers. We called ourselves the Pink Ladies. One of those sisters, Erina, is still my best friend after all these years. Another was Raphael. We always had the best time, and later in the nineties we joined a dance group called Pure Funk and did drag shows together in Wellington. We called them drag shows for simplicity, even though we were trans women. Coca-Cola hired us to be go-go-girl backing dancers for The Exponents in a TV ad in 1996. It was a big-budget campaign with hundreds of extras and we were probably the first trans girls in a Coke ad, but at the time it was just, 'That was fun, can we have our fifty bucks now?' We never thought about being the first to do anything; we were just a bunch of girls trying to get by.

When we were 16, Raphael and I made a pact to tell our parents we were trans, and we planned to do so on the same night. That night came and Raphael told her parents and it was no problem for them at all. I admired her balls. When it came to my turn, I didn't have the courage; I didn't have the words to say what I needed to say. It was another five years before I could explain my world to them. I wrote a letter instead, explaining, in brutal honesty, everything that had been building up since I was 16. It said, 'If you don't accept me and love me, I can't be your daughter, our relationship is over.'

I was prepared to give up my family. It seems extreme now but at the time I felt hurt and worthless, and hurt people can be driven to extremes. My parents called me straightaway, then drove up to Auckland. We sat face to face and acknowledged that we didn't want to lose each other, and from then on, I knew I was going to be OK. We needed that difficult time of honesty to reach the beautiful relationship we have now, which is completely solid and built on real understanding. After this, I could get on with living. Everything was said, and nothing was secret. I could move on with a fresh sense of freedom and lightness to figure out what I wanted to do and be.

I prefer the term takatāpui or trans woman to describe myself; 'transition' is a word which doesn't feel right for me. Transition implies moving from one fixed place to another, but that's not what my journey is like. My essence has always been feminine and that of a girl. 'Evolution' feels like a better word than transition. After I'd been on hormones for 20 years, something shifted, and I started embracing my masculinity a lot more. I stopped taking the hormones for a few days, and then a few days became weeks and then months. I was having fun and it was sexually liberating to explore my masculine side for the first time in many years. I felt I was moving back into balance with my duality at that time, riding a wave of empowerment and harmony.

This *is* the real world and we will not be pushed into little boxes to make others comfortable.

The growing awareness of trans people is beautiful. Any way we can be visible and celebrated is a wonderful thing, although that visibility has brought new attacks on trans people. Some people feel challenged when their safe, tidy view of the world is disrupted, but this *is* the real world and we will not be pushed into little boxes to make others comfortable. The murder rate of trans people is extremely high and they often go unreported and uninvestigated. Around the world politicians use us as pawns in their games, appealing to fear and prejudice to get votes. They deny our human rights, our access to healthcare and even our basic right to be a peaceful member of society, and then there's the ridiculous raving about which toilets people should use.

A new generation of queer heroes is blossoming and creating

platforms to have their voices heard. It's an interesting time to be living in New Zealand, where I feel that most people do want to try to understand and learn about the lives of others. Trans people have always been seen as controversial — even others in the queer community see us as loud troublemakers. Some gays would love us to just sit down and be quiet so they can collect their dogs from the pet-groomer and enjoy their coffee from the Grey Lynn market. It's wonderful so many Kiwi queer people have a life free from worries about safety, money or discrimination, but others are still oppressed and so the fight continues — we need to be heard.

I love men and I consider myself straight. Every trans woman will tell you it's hard to build authentic relationships. Men seem to be becoming more OK with their attraction to trans women, but society tells them it's shameful, so they react to their relationship with fear and secrecy, like a fetish or something to be kept in the shadows. I used to be hard on these guys and think they're arseholes but now I understand that it's hard for men to live their truth within the narrow limitations of what society allows masculinity to be. I know it's possible to have a good relationship, though, because I have some trans sisters in loving relationships with men who adore them; sometimes I do wonder, God, how did they do that?

I have a decent dating life. I've figured out how to approach it: if I meet a man, one of the first things I say is that I'm a trans woman. My twenties were a risky time, and I used to put myself in dangerous situations, taking men home without telling them my full story. Back then it was always about the gratification of the man and I'd immediately relinquish any control, but now I enter these situations as a sexual being with my own empowerment. After 40-something years of life, I've found that doing things that nourish my soul creates a more grounded and authentic version of myself, which leads to more confidence. It's like a peaceful aura of calm that lets in positivity and shields me from negativity.

People seem to come to me when they have issues in their life and I always try to be a source of support, but I'm not a fucking guru or anything. Actually I worry that I'm not a good mentor. I use my intuition and experience to guide me. Often when people are hurting they just want someone to listen to them. We all have our struggles and demons. I wade through occasional bouts of depression, days when there's a dark cloud over everything. Many people in my life have similar issues, and so it's good that we've become more comfortable saying the words 'depression' and 'anxiety' out loud. Some people don't make it, though. Friends have killed themselves when the struggle with their identity and place in the world was too overwhelming, and that's so terribly tragic and I'm left questioning myself: Could I have done more? Sometimes the honest answer is no.

I've lived on K Road for years. It is more gentrified now, and art galleries and tapas bars are replacing sex shops and strip clubs, so it's maybe not as queer as it was, but it's still queer enough. I think 'queer' itself has evolved. I've evolved but I'm still queer enough. The traditional K Road gay places where worlds collide are still here — the business guy, the sex worker, the club kids all sharing the street, drinking in the same bars. It's still the only place I can imagine living. When I die I'm planning a procession down K Road so my ashes will be scattered. But not all my ashes: obviously they'll need to be shared around due to high demand.

My parents are getting older now, and the idea of looking after them when the time comes fills me with so much joy. My career has become a benevolent monster with a life of its own, so I'll keep feeding it and riding it. I'd like to direct a feature film, write a book, do the things I haven't done yet. I want to get better as a human, and shed more insecurities. I don't really mind about having a boyfriend or getting married. Looking to the future I just want to do more of what I love, like laughing with friends — the simple, soulful stuff.

Victor Rodger

Victor Rodger ONZM is an award-winning playwright of Samoan and Scottish descent. He is best known for his critically acclaimed play *Black Faggot*, which was published in the anthology *Black Faggot and Other Plays* in 2017.

I wasn't like the other kids in Christchurch. I was really into reading movie magazines and couldn't wait for church to be over so I could go to the movies. My mum was still at high school when she had me and my dad was absent, so I spent a lot of time with my grandmother, who loved all the old film stars like Gloria Swanson. And I remember Grandad taking me to a Greta Garbo movie.

I was a spoilt little shit. I never really wanted for anything because Mum was driven to give me everything she could. When she became pregnant with me, Nan pushed her to finish doing her School Certificate and then train as a shorthand typist. Ever since I was born, Mum has either worked or studied. I have so much admiration for her. I haven't inherited Mum's extraordinary work ethic. Spoilt kids who have everything done for them sometimes face a battle against ingrained entitlement when they finally enter the real world. Stepping into my humility and spurring myself to action takes conscious effort. I think that fight will continue until I die. Getting my ONZM in 2021 at the Governor-General's house with my mum watching on was a really proud and emotional moment. Any success I have is truly a reflection of her love and support.

My father and I had no more than a week together over our whole lives, a few hours here and there, separated by years. Mum never disparaged him, though; she never wanted to endanger any chance of me having a relationship with him.

Charlton Heston was my first crush, when I was about five. After I saw him in *Planet of the Apes*, I even researched how to change my name by deed poll so I could become Charlton Heston Rodger. I have a vivid memory when I was six of watching a boy at school being mean to a girl, and having this really clear thought that when we got older he would get with girls, but I wouldn't. I didn't attach it to my sexuality back then, but I did know in that moment that my path was going to be different and not like most of the other boys. By high school, my crush was all about Tom Selleck.

Mum and I went to Faith Family Fellowship, a church which was full of Māori and Pasifika members. Scribe and Ladi6 were there, too. I went until I was 12. Mum is still a Christian and my father became a pastor in Brisbane, but Christianity made me very conflicted about my homosexuality. It took a long time for me to not feel guilty about being gay.

Linwood College was a real mix of working-class kids and rich kids from Redcliffs, Sumner and Mount Pleasant; today it skews much more towards working class and brown. I played the flute in the school orchestra, but because I was a big boy, the rugby coach wanted me for my size and I eventually joined the First XV, even though I'd never played before. *Dynasty* was my favourite TV show at the time and I would trot down to rugby practice with pictures of Joan Collins in a pink negligee on my school folder. I might as well have had a neon sign on my forehead saying 'GAY'. I was a terrible rugby player. I was fat and unfit, and I was always being told to fake injuries so I could come off the field early. I never even understood all the rules.

Kids at school suspected I was gay so I got teased a fair bit. I still have my old diaries from back then; they're full of yearning to be like everyone else but plastered with pictures of hot men. And because I couldn't even admit to myself that I was gay, I told myself that these men I fantasised about sleeping with were just examples of the physique I wanted to attain. The first person I came out to was my best friend when I was about 17; it didn't seem like much of a surprise to her. My friends were all straight back then so I didn't go to the Christchurch gay bars because I didn't have the courage to go by myself.

In the past I'd called myself Afakasi, meaning half-caste, but now I just say I'm Samoan. There is some irony that I've chosen to embrace the culture of my father whom I never lived with. At school I always hung out with white kids and was comfortable in that world. I never considered myself to be any different — until one specific moment in my last year of high school when someone made a Samoan joke; I didn't understand it or think it was funny. The white kids rounded on me, saying I should be able to laugh at myself, and where was my sense of humour. In that instant, I consciously thought for the first time: they are white, and I am not. It was a defining moment where I began to embrace my Samoan heritage.

I flew to Paris just before I turned 21. That was the beginning of my OE. In London, I dipped my toe into gay clubs while often living hand to mouth and sometimes working tedious office jobs, like licking envelopes. Sometimes I'd recite Sylvia Plath's poem 'Daddy' in my head to stay sane. It was a bit of humble pie after working on a Christchurch newspaper as a cadet reporter after I'd left school. I was rubbish at hard news, so they'd made me the film critic and entertainment writer, which felt much more my style.

Returning to New Zealand from London, I wrote stories for *Ears*, the kids' programme on Radio New Zealand. The first piece I sold was called 'Pig in the Bedroom'. It was inspired by a holiday I'd had once with my grandparents in Timaru, where I'd woken up one night and thought there was a pig in the bedroom. It turned out to be the sound of my grandmother snoring.

As a kid, I'd felt destined for a career in acting until I read an interview with Kirk Douglas after he'd done a nude scene, at age 60, and he was quoted as saying, 'There are no roles for fat leading men.' That really impacted me as a tubby kid so I turned my sights more towards writing. But I didn't want to be 50 years old and look back with regret that I'd never given it a go, so, at 25, I auditioned for Toi Whakaari New Zealand Drama School. My audition pieces were both written by me — a monologue about being a Samoan supermodel and a poem titled 'I Hate You Daddy'; I didn't know how to learn other people's words yet. I was accepted, formed some profound relationships, both personal and professional, fell in love for the first time and started to become comfortable in my own skin.

It was around this time that I came out to my mother, having put it off for a long time because I was afraid she would blame herself and question what she'd done wrong to 'make' me gay. However, she was completely supportive of me although terrified that I'd go to hell. She still is. It took a long time before I came out to my father because I was afraid he'd somehow think it reflected badly on Mum's upbringing. I expected him to throw the Bible at me but all he said was, 'It's a choice.' I asked him, 'Who would choose this?' We agreed to disagree and move on. It wasn't the dramatic scene I expected at all.

In 2000, I got a job writing for *Shortland Street*. The thing I've always liked about *Shorty* is that, like it or loathe it, it's a chance to hear our own accents and see our own faces after years of being fed stuff from America, the UK and Aussie. It took a lot longer before we saw two men kissing on *Shorty* rather than just two women, but *Shortland Street* has put gay characters into people's living rooms, and recently trans characters as well. Sometimes it has portrayed an idealised view of New Zealand society — I'm not sure how many hospitals have Māori CEOs, but it was powerful to see Dr Victor Kahu in the swivelly chair for a while.

A quote that cuts to the heart of my artistic sensibility is, 'Art should comfort the disturbed and disturb the comfortable.' Traditionally, theatre audiences are a comfortable bunch, so if I send them home without having shaken their beliefs and assumptions about the world in some way, what is the point?

Black Faggot is my most successful play so far. The thing that really drove me to write *Black Faggot* was a Destiny Church march against the Civil Union Bill, where I saw fathers marching with sons. Watching them, I was thinking, at least one of those kids will be gay and feeling wretched about themselves; plus, I wanted to broaden the spectrum of gay Samoan male acting roles because up until that point they were generally super camp and normally an object of mirth. The title comes from me being called this as a term of endearment by friends, and also as an insult by others trying to hurt me. It was originally a series of individual and unrelated monologues, until director Roy Ward encouraged me to thread them into a narrative and give it a heart.

> I wanted to broaden the spectrum of gay Samoan male acting roles because up until that point they were generally super camp and normally an object of mirth.

I thought I'd really pushed it with *Black Faggot*. I mean, the language is explicit, there's sex in just about every position you can imagine, cum on the wallpaper, all of it. One night, I saw a bunch of my Samoan cousins in the audience and thought, awesome — until I saw their very Catholic mother there with them. I was like, shiiiiiiit! But the funny thing is that she laughed along with everyone else. The only thing she didn't like was that I'd used a particular Samoan swear word. It reminded me that we sometimes put our elders in a box and forget that they've been around the block. However, recently after a performance, a Tongan woman told me about her nephew who had been outed. His family chose to engage a religious elder to 'fix the problem', so progress doesn't improve evenly for everyone.

Mum doesn't often come to see my plays. She doesn't like all the swearing and is always worried people think it's a reflection of my upbringing — which it isn't!

Not everyone likes my work, some people hate it, and that's alright: the important thing is that I stand behind it as an artist. Writing can be torturous. Some days I dream of running away to join the circus, but I always come back to it.

Sometimes, still, I feel like an outsider in the Samoan community, but I think I feel like an outsider in most of the communities that I'm tied to: the gay world, the theatre world, the uni world. I've learnt that there's a freedom to being on the margins — but also an occasional sadness. I'm a Gemini so I accept that there are two sides to all of these aspects and how I navigate the world.

It's been a journey with its slings and arrows, but I know who I am and where I come from.

Loughlan Prior

Loughlan Prior is a multi-award-winning choreographer with the Royal New Zealand Ballet. His works have been presented in New Zealand, Australia, Germany, the United States, Denmark and Canada.

I 'm six years old and sitting with my parents in the audience at *Jesus Christ Superstar* at a packed Rod Laver Arena in Melbourne. John Farnham is playing the lead role. I'm utterly captivated by the music and transported into another world. I remember watching the lights, costumes and dancing with such wide-eyed wonder. This musical was my first introduction to the world of theatre, the first stage show I ever saw. It changed my life forever. That powerful love of the stage has stayed with me ever since, and I don't think I've lost a drop of the excitement I felt as a kid in that first mind-blowing moment. Now, two decades on, as the Choreographer in Residence at the Royal New Zealand Ballet, I have the privilege of entertaining, seducing and captivating audiences with my own stage creations.

I was born in Melbourne, the eldest of four children. I have two sisters and a brother. My family are all very active people, with physical jobs, though none are in the arts. They are teachers and sports fanatics. My life in dance began with my parents trying to channel my energies away from getting in trouble. I was a hyperactive kid, a bit mischievous. Dad took me to join an Aussie Rules football team. He was a good football player, and I suppose he hoped I would be too. I didn't enjoy it at all and spent most of the time crying instead of playing the game. I'd always had a strong connection to music, singing and dancing around the house, so Mum decided to send me to try ballet instead.

I started with ballet and jazz, and was later introduced to tap when we could afford the tap shoes. I think at first Dad must have been apprehensive about his son doing ballet — there's that ingrained idea of what's acceptable for a boy to do — but when he saw that I loved it and had a talent, he was proud. I'm incredibly lucky because I know if I'd been forced to play football I would have been incredibly unhappy. I wouldn't have had the artistic and creatively fulfilling life I've had.

Dad was in and out of hospital for years with an autoimmune disease. He passed away when I was eight, leaving Mum to raise four kids alone on a low income. My grandparents stepped in to help us. They were very generous and their support softened the blow to the family. We were all devastated. Looking back I feel for my brother. I was never going to be the son to follow traditionally masculine pursuits, and that's where he really missed Dad's influence. The concept of mortality is one that most people make peace with gradually through their lives, and having it forced on me at an early age taught me how precious life is. The effect of that shock has rippled through the years. I'm only now understanding that it gifted me an instinctive drive to do what I love and to use my time on this earth for good.

Throughout my early school years I trained hard. I auditioned at the Victorian College of the Arts, a high school for talented artistic kids, and I was accepted. We did the key academic subjects but the reason for going there was to develop skills in our creative disciplines. I was a dancer, but there were also musicians, painters, gymnasts and kids across all areas of the arts. To spend those formative years having my young mind exposed to such fertile and diverse artistic worlds was thrilling; I absorbed as much as I could.

I was still a shy and reclusive student in those days, and I wasn't comfortable with myself. That's probably why I wasn't out. I threw myself so completely into ballet training that I would almost say I identified as being asexual. I was using dance as a distraction from thinking about my sexuality and identity. Queer people often feel they have to be the best to compensate for this perceived flaw in their character. That's how I felt; I always had to achieve perfection.

I look back with some regret on those days. I wish I had been more open. Since graduating I've reconnected with some of my male class-mates and discovered that nearly all of them are gay, out and proud. They were going through a similar thing to me, but at the time we never talked about it. It feels like a missed opportunity to have had a supportive honest time as teenage gay guys, which is rare in those anxious high school years. I've learnt from those experiences and am a very different person now.

My coming out story is entwined with the story of how I came to live in New Zealand. After graduating from high school I auditioned abroad and was thrilled to be accepted into the New Zealand School of Dance in Wellington. The night before I departed for New Zealand I had a sleepover with my two best friends. We've known each other since primary school. As cheesy and clichéd as this sounds, the sleepover movie 'coincidentally' happened to be *Brokeback Mountain*. At the end of the film I said, 'Hey, I'm gay,' and a huge weight was lifted. They were the first people I told, and of course they were great about it. A few years later both of those friends came out as queer, and now they're both engaged. It's funny how life unfolds. When we are children our friends are people we instinctively know are kindred spirits, and for me they've often turned out to be queer. I think we subconsciously drift into the orbit of people like us — there's a subliminal connection.

Arriving in Wellington gave me a fresh start with a new group of people. I left any closeted anxieties behind in Australia, and there was a freedom to be honest and present myself as who I was from the beginning.

It was really lovely and helped me come out to my family soon after. I told my mother when we were on summer holidays together. We talked a lot that summer. I never had to say the words 'I am gay'; instead our conversation naturally flowed to a place where we reached a calm honest understanding about my sexuality. She was amazing and said all the right things, and that she would love me no matter what. My family experience was very happy. I know not everyone is so fortunate; hopefully, one day soon, coming out won't even be necessary.

After a wonderful few years at the New Zealand School of Dance I graduated in 2009 and following a series of auditions I joined the Royal New Zealand Ballet. It was a huge achievement. Only one or two graduates a year are accepted into the RNZB, but really that was only the beginning. A day in the life of a professional ballet dancer might start with Pilates and conditioning exercises followed by a workout at the gym, then we do a ballet class and the rest of the day is devoted to rehearsals. When we're learning new choreography the rehearsals can be fairly relaxed, then leading up to a show they become much more demanding. Practising choreography is intensely physical and requires acute mental focus. Losing concentration can be dangerous.

Surprisingly I never got very nervous as a dancer. I had an ability to calm my mind and become the character. When the costume goes on I leave Loughlan behind. A large number of international ballet companies are based in one place and don't really travel outside their cities, but the RNZB tours its productions all over the country. It's been so heartening to spread our art form into charming small-town theatres and I've been able to see so much of beautiful Aotearoa. Melbourne and Wellington are my two homes now. I'm constantly energised by the creative culture that these cities produce, and they both hold a special place in my heart because of my incredible friends and family who live there.

There are only a handful of dance companies in New Zealand so the competition is fierce; gruelling training is required to get through an audition. At times it can feel like being in the military. Ballet dancers need resilience to handle the competition, take rejection and get up and keep going. I think it's even more demanding than what Olympic athletes experience because we don't have any off season; we perform constantly throughout the year.

Ballet is like an iceberg — the audience only sees the very tip sitting statuesque above the water. They only see the finished product on the stage. What they don't see is the huge bulk hidden below the surface; the countless years of discipline, rehearsals and training in the studio, and the intense, emotional and ephemeral experience of being a performer. In many ways I wish we could flip the iceberg so most of our time was spent performing on stage rather than in the studio. Our time on stage is so precious in relatively short careers that can be plagued by injury. The performing is what you do it for. You really need to make the most of every precious minute on that stage.

I was lucky to have a relatively fast metabolism when I was dancing, and I ate what I wanted. There was a period in my early twenties, when I'd just joined the RNZB, where I became a little obsessive. I would get up at 5.30 a.m., hit the gym for two hours and then go for a run at lunchtime — all on top of ballet classes, rehearsals and not eating very much. My body looked great but it wasn't healthy and deep down I knew it wasn't the right way to sustain a long dance career. I eventually switched to a more balanced training and diet regime and rose to the rank of soloist. Now that I've retired from dance and moved into choreography, I've let myself go a bit, by a dancer's standards anyway.

I've always had a spiritual affinity for music. I'm lucky to have been surrounded by it most of my life. When I hear the sounds of an orchestra or piano I often see shapes in my mind, and if I close my eyes and listen I see bodies moving and steps being formed — a kind of synesthesia. It felt like a natural progression from dance to begin exploring choreography. I have always been a creative person (I call it creative compulsion) and expressing myself through making art is the way I have come to deal with my place in the world. I was fortunate enough to have had some success, winning choreographic awards in 2015 and 2016 and travelling to Toronto to stage one of my works. I retired from full-time performance in 2019 to become Choreographer in Residence with the Royal New Zealand Ballet.

My first full-length ballet with the RNBZ was *Hansel & Gretel*, a dark and quirky fairytale for children. My artistic partner in crime, composer Claire Cowan, and I turned the witch into a shape-shifting, gender-fluid character with a Kylie Minoguesque showgirl persona who first appears riding a steampunk bicycle made of tuba parts before transforming into an ominous child catcher, luring victims into the forest with ice creams.

My next big project was in 2021, when I choreographed *The Firebird*, a ballet which premiered in 1910 in Paris. It was cutting-edge at the time and over a hundred years later it's a work that people are still entranced by. My production with the RNZB re-imagined *The Firebird*, making the phoenix an allegory for our natural world which is being damaged by humanity's greed and desire for possession. The production blended multimedia digital projections to create a dystopian future of floods and fire. I wanted to use Stravinsky's beautifully luscious and devastating score to explore the urgent climate crisis which is affecting us right now.

When I create dance I start with nothing but the music. As I listen, possible steps are conceived in my mind, and I experiment on my own body to see if they are physically possible before transposing them onto other dancers. I collaborate directly with the dancers, creating dynamic movements and interesting shapes together; trust between dancer and choreographer is crucial. In contemporary ballet, which is the style I would most identify my work with, the steps are created from a place of expression and innovation in the form. The movements are often uncodifiable and so vigorous that rehearsal is required to enable the choreography to soak into the muscle memory of the dancer.

RNZB has some wonderful programmes to bring young audiences from schools around the country to see us perform. The tickets and transport are sponsored, and it's so fun to see the excited kids arrive at the theatre. They remind me of myself at their age. Visiting schools around the country, I meet the young dancers coming up. Since the *Billy Elliot* film and dancing competitions on TV there's been an increase in male dancers, which is encouraging. I still encounter the lazy assumption that boys do rugby and girls do ballet. It's such a limiting and unnecessary division, but I do see it changing very slowly and gradually. Ballet is often perceived as an elitist art form, so I strive to make inclusive, engaging work which speaks to a broad audience because ballet belongs to everyone. I think Kiwis can be fans of the All Blacks *and* the ballet. They have more in common than you might think; they both provide exciting, athletic and uplifting entertainment.

The audience's love of ballet springs from many sources. Some are drawn to traditional classical ballet with its graceful, elegant movements. I will always love classical ballet, however my real passion is for the visceral, primal, athletic side of dance and human connection. Choreography and dance-making for me means seeing the body as a moving sculpture, the instrument which brings the dance to life, the architecture and geometry of the human form in space.

Traditional ballet is extensively heteronormative; crafted to suit the strengths and movements of a woman coupled with a man. Over the past few years I have become more and more interested with disrupting this binary and exploring greater representation across the spectrum of relationships and dance partnerships in my work. In a dance with two people of the same gender, the art form is challenged and extended because partners of equal physicality (body type and strength) require new ways of thinking when it comes to technique, counterbalance and symmetry in partnership.

I'm pushing for greater LGBTQIA+ representation in my work. It's time to see serious, nuanced roles for queer people. While the dance world is very welcoming of queer people, the traditional side of classical ballet remains a bastion of straight romantic storylines, where serious queer stories struggle to break through. 'Gay' characters are portrayed as clichéd camp parodies or *grand dame* men in drag, and although those characters are fun and very enjoyable to portray (I have played several in my career), I would love to see the sensitive side of queer and non-binary characters explored; a love story which features their experience at the heart of the narrative. There is a long way still to go, particularly with trans representation in ballet.

I'm heartened and excited for the future of queer performance in Aotearoa. It's incredible to see the surge in LGBTQIA+ representation in theatre, music and film, with every small part helping to break down old ideas. I feel a certain responsibility to use my position as a creative artist to push through the remaining conservative barriers, and I think the audience is ready. Ballet is an incredible way of expressing yourself. I encourage everyone to try it.

As a queer person, inhabiting different skins on stage helped me become comfortable in my own. I was a shy person, but dance gave my inner extrovert permission to take flight and allowed me to share the emotional, intimate side of myself with courage and confidence.

Ann Shelton

Ann Shelton is one of New Zealand's leading photographic artists. Now based in Te Whanganui-a-Tara Wellington, her work is exhibited both nationally and internationally, and a major survey exhibition — *Ann Shelton: Dark Matter* — showed at Auckland Art Gallery Toi o Tāmaki and Christchurch Art Gallery Te Puna o Waiwhetū from 2016 to 2018.

Photography is so compelling to me: the way images are transformed by the person who views them, the future they have that cannot be predicted, and the way that events can unfold to alter our perception of them. Photography can mask the truth or reveal it; despite the fact we often use images as evidence, they are incredibly 'slippery' objects.

Over the course of my career, I've sought to create images that examine the edges of culture, and of knowledge, and to redefine or complicate those edges. I've explored issues around power and agency, layers of gender and queerness, the relationship between the viewer and the viewed. Many feminist themes have emerged in my work as I confront the boundaries of acceptability regarding the idea of what a woman 'should be' or, to take that a bit further, how the idea of 'woman' has been constructed.

Mine was a working-class New Zealand childhood in Timaru. My parents were extremely hard-working, and Mum, retired now, was a secondhand dealer and renovated houses. She had a shop called Bargain Basement, full of curiosities. I'd hang out there looking for treasures that she might let me take home. Dad was a car dealer, and I have three younger brothers, so it was a bit of a 'gasoline alley' upbringing; they'd always be in the garage fixing cars and motorbikes. I liked riding motorbikes, but I wasn't interested in fixing them. We spent our school holidays travelling around the country in a little 1950s caravan. I don't know how Mum and Dad managed to fit us all into it. Both of my grandmothers had baches, or cribs as they're known in the South Island. The grandmother on my mother's side, Hilda Downs, had a crib on the Ōpihi River in South Canterbury, where she lived fulltime. She'd go down to the river with my brothers and haul out huge slimy eels, which she smoked and we ate.

When I became a teen my paternal grandmother pushed for me to go to Craighead Diocesan, a private girls' school in Tīmaru, thinking it would offer some advantage to get ahead in the world. Craighead was the girls' school where the professional classes and land owners of this community sent their children; I ended up there a bit of a fish out of water. I was immediately aware that I was different to the other girls, but at that point I was not sure why. It was clear that they thought they were better than me, and I guess, reflecting back, they'd learnt at home that it was acceptable to judge and divide people by class and social status. I was subject to the covert hostilities of exclusion, but I didn't let it render me helpless. I had other friends and I worked hard at school and did well. Art and sewing captivated me the most, and I considered becoming a fashion designer.

My high-school experience was a microcosm of Tīmaru really. Like all New Zealand towns, Tīmaru grew out of colonial suppression of Māori. Its white settler culture, of which I am part, lived, and some prospered, through its wealthy farming community and its activities as a service town and port.

My mother had me when she was 17, and my feeling was she didn't want me to be in the same position. I always had the sense that in subtle ways she was encouraging me to spread my wings further. Some of my friends and all my brothers happily stayed in Tīmaru, but I never felt like my life was going to be there. Mum and my maternal grandmother instilled in me that I could do anything I wanted, and a few days after I turned 18 I left Tīmaru with the intention of exploring the world.

With a budget of about three US dollars a day in Europe, it wasn't a glamorous expedition. I made a wonderful American friend, also called Ann. We were both on our own so we travelled around Italy together in the summer of 1986. If we couldn't find a good cheap place to stay, we made a camp on a little piece of grass away from the road or on a beach. One evening near Pompeii, we were happily setting up our camp when a local Italian family passing by came and said, 'You can't sleep there, come with us.' They took us to their home, made us a beautiful meal and let us camp in their lovely orchard. Travels in Europe left me a more thoughtful person, understanding the world as a collection of diverse perspectives.

On the way back to Aotearoa I stopped in India, where I travelled for some months, and in Kolkata I volunteered at Mother Teresa's hospital. Her mission was to provide a safe place for people to spend their last days as they died from diseases like tuberculosis, diseases that are virtually eliminated in the Western world. The hospital was full of people, rickshaw drivers, children, people with no family and no alternatives. I helped out with making people as comfortable as possible, until some of the nuns found out that I could sew and gave me a job making clothes for the children.

Mother Teresa's philosophy was to pass very sick people into what she believed was 'Christ's arms' without intervening, meaning no medical drugs were administered. I visited a British doctor, Jack Preger, who took a different approach. He set up a totally secular stall on a street corner and gave medical care to try to cure the conditions which Mother Teresa's institution simply left to run their course. After witnessing people die, I of course felt this was a much more effective way to work, and I would have moved on to volunteer with Jack were it not that I was getting sick myself by then. I left Kolkata soon after for Mumbai. These experiences did change me.

After nearly three years away, I arrived back in Aotearoa and took a job at Tīmaru's Bluebird potato chip factory. It was a workplace full of fabulous characters. Some of the older ladies kept their half-smoked 'fags' in their smock pockets; occasionally one would escape from the vibration and fall onto the conveyor belt and we ended up with a cigarette in a packet of chips. The whole production line would get shut down, and all the chip packets had to be opened until it was found. We would get in big trouble for that. My favorite position on the conveyer belt was throwing potatoes over a blade to get them to a manageable size before they vibrated on down the line to the next machine.

Before I went away, my parents had bought me a camera, and while travelling I had developed an interest in making images. I'd heard of a one-year qualification at the Christchurch Photographic Training Centre. I enrolled there and learnt about the technical aspects of photography, studio-based work and documentary practice.

It was the late 1980s when I finished the course, and newspapers and print media were still thriving. I asked around to see if I could find a job as a press photographer. The *Otago Daily Times* told me they'd just hired the *Oamaru Mail*'s photographer, so I went to Ōamaru and got hired as their replacement. I was the only photographer at the *Mail*, covering all the 'big' events: ribbon cuttings, cheque signings, flower competitions . . . Actually I loved the flower shows — all the carefully nurtured, exotic dahlias and huge wispy chrysanthemums. The paper needed about eight pictures a day, so when we were short on news I'd drive up and down the Waitaki Valley and all over town to find what they called a 'human-interest' photo, like someone taking their horse for a ride, or a sweet old lady's eightieth birthday lunch at the local retirement home.

Then the *Dominion* and the *Dominion-Sunday Times* advertised for a new photographer. They wanted several years' experience and I only had one, but I applied for it anyway and, incredibly, I got the job. I was their second-ever female photojournalist, joining a team of about five male photographers. Next door was the *Evening Post* office, where there was another team of six male photographers. After I'd been working there about a year one of the *Dominion* photographers told me that my portfolio was so good he thought it must have been taken by my boyfriend.

Initially, being a woman, I was given the 'soft' news stories to cover, but over time I was sent to cover a broader range of stories like the Gulf War protests and the ordination of the first woman bishop in Dunedin. I travelled a bit but mostly we'd whip all over the city in a little red Honda and the writer would interview people while I took the photographs to go with the story.

But after a while aspects of working in the press began to weigh on me. Part of the job was to capture horrible life events where people were in pain and distress, like car accidents and fires; chasing ambulances was no fun. At the same time, with the advent of colour photos in the newspaper, the development and selection of pictures was taken out of our hands and given to the picture editor. Part of the job I had loved was getting back from a day of shooting, heading downstairs to the darkroom to develop my images, seeing which shots best fitted the story, and then printing them and bringing my selection up to the picture editor.

In response to some of these concerns I'd become interested in long-form photographic projects, which I began developing on my weekends. My first was a series of images of street kids, as they prefer to be called; the project was about street life in Wellington.

Around that time, through photographing gallery openings and other events, I'd met and become friends with Giovanni Intra, who was then an intern at the Wellington City Art Gallery. Giovanni and I got on very well. We went to art shows together and became good friends; he was my 'gateway drug' into the art world. We discussed the creative restrictions of newspapers and he encouraged me to consider how as an artist I would be able to edit and present my work in my own way. Some people thought I was mad to leave my well-paid job at the *Dominion* but after a few years there, having gained a strong technical grounding, I quit and moved to Auckland to study photography at Elam School of Fine Art.

There was an incredible creative energy in Auckland in the early and mid-nineties, and through Giovanni, who had also moved back there and with whom I'd now started a relationship, I was introduced to an energising group of creative people. Giovanni and his friends had just opened New Zealand's first artist-run space on Vulcan Lane called Teststrip. A collective of eight artists, including Denise Kum and Kirsty Cameron, founded and funded it through shared contributions, showing their own and other artists' work.

These artists took their careers into their own hands, exhibiting work which wasn't being shown in mainstream galleries at that time. Back then Karangahape Road was still full of empty warehouses and other spaces, surplus from the downturn of the 1970s and 1980s, and artists could afford to live in huge spaces above the shops. I moved into one such space above a butcher. There was a real community feeling. Verona Café was at the centre of it and was like our 'lounge', the place where some of the distinct scenes and 'subcultures' on K Road converged.

In my second year at Elam, the Films, Videos, and Publications Act was being revised. Spurred on by this incoming legislation, my friends Kirsty Cameron and Paul Booth and I became involved in co-curating an exhibition called *150 Ways of Loving*, with a film screening, performance night, and one-day conference. We wanted a new, inclusive Act which recognised and supported broader expressions of sexual desire and didn't discriminate against non-heteronormative material. The Chief Censor at the time was Jane Wrightson, New Zealand's first woman in the role, and we invited her to speak at our event. I felt she understood that the legislation needed to cater to a wider range of expression and it was significant that she attended.

At this point my own desire to explore my sexuality had been emerging for a few years. It felt increasingly important and reached the point where it couldn't be ignored. Giovanni and I had discussed it. He was bisexual himself and so was understanding, but it did bring our romantic relationship to an end. We stayed close, always friends, and he remained a very important person in my life.

Meanwhile, I began photographing Auckland's burgeoning fetish party scene at club nights like Cheap Sex, Hell for Leather, and the fetish balls. I would set up photo booths for people to come in, mid-party, to be photographed if they wanted. It was an incredibly creative scene, a bit underground, a bit exciting and, most importantly, together the people who made that scene created an open context that accommodated all sorts of ways of being in the world. The vibe was loving, tolerant and captivating.

People planned what they would wear for weeks. I remember one person I photographed had a locker where they kept their secret outfits. Their attendance was a well-planned, covert operation ending with D Day — party night. I also did a series of images of people's feet around that time called *From the waist down*. They were made at the Cheap Sex parties and exhibited at George Fraser Gallery. I made one of my first handmade book maquettes of these images; it's falling apart now but has that much-loved look.

A t one of the early Gay Pride Parades, I spotted Fiona Amundsen looking dapper and dressed in a suit. She was also working and taking photographs. Through our common interest in photography we bonded, became close, and started what was my first relationship with a woman. If you'd asked me around that time, and as our relationship developed, I would probably have said I was a lesbian, but with the passing of time I've come to understand that for me sexuality moves across a spectrum, and now I identify as bisexual.

I've been lucky to not confront much negativity about my sexuality from my family or in the art world. My mother was accepting of my evolving sexuality and having girlfriends. Dad likely found it a bit more difficult to process but never said anything. My brothers and I have never spoken about it directly but it's never been a problem. My art friends are very open-minded; ironically, I felt most of the prejudice against my sexual orientation at queer bars or lesbian clubs.

> # Biphobia is a thing still; perhaps the prejudice against bisexual people in the queer and straight community comes from fear.

One evening, when a woman approached me in one of these bars and asked about my sexuality, I told her that I was bisexual; she moved on pretty quickly. Biphobia is a thing still; perhaps the prejudice against bisexual people in the queer and straight community comes from fear — fear of stereotypes about bisexuality, the main one being that bisexuals just can't decide what they want. A friend recently told me that the Lesbian and Gay Archive at the Turnbull Library in Wellington still doesn't hold any bisexual material, so the bisexual is still an outsider.

Susan Sontag's writing on photography was influential during my early years at Elam. She wrote about the voyeuristic capturing of the 'other' that photography so enjoyed, and the power dynamics between the subject and the person holding the camera. Her critique of this approach to photographic practice shifted my thinking about the subject as an active participant in image creation, and I became interested in the effect of direct eye contact between the viewer and the lens. I decided to turn the camera inward, and I started to photograph my friends, their artworks, galleries, and our world, an approach that was then sometimes called 'new documentary photography'.

My friends and I got dressed up all the time, in drag or in costumes, or just for the sake of it. Photographing my social milieu was my examination of identity as a fluid concept, of gender outside the limitations of 'him' and 'her'. My photographs captured the pulse of the mid-nineties art and club culture on K Road. The creation of those images formed the basis of what became the book *Redeye*. For a while there, friends would try to tempt me out for a drink, but I was so focused on seeing *Redeye* published that my connection with Dewi Lewis, my publisher on the other side of the world, became my focus, while the rest of the house partied.

Redeye was published in 1997. I was 30 years old, and it was a major goal achieved. I was completely elated to see it out in the world. You can see that in TV3's *Nightline* coverage of the launch, where I was interviewed by the fabulous Dylan Taite. I came across this clip again recently while researching something; it was set to Darcy Clay's 'Jesus I Was Evil'.

Around 1996 I had moved along K Road to number 295, opposite Artspace, first to the third floor and later upstairs to the two-storey penthouse with my girlfriend Melissa Anderson, Bob Buck and Lisa Reihana. The penthouse had been built a few decades before by a wealthy entrepreneur for his mistress. We completely re-painted it and fitted it out with our various artwork and retro collections. By this time I was lecturing in photography at the Manukau Institite of Technology in South Auckland, which I loved. We had huge parties. There was a grille on our lift which you had to unlock to let guests in, and sometimes people got stuck there for ages, waiting to get into the party. We had a blow-up pool on the back deck and would get home late in summer from parties or gigs and cool off with a glass of bubbles while viewing all the antics below us on K Road.

It was a pretty magic time. I absolutely thrived there on K Road. The friendships, the creativity, the places I lived, the innovative and diverse communities, both queer and multicultural, and the doing — we all did so much, we made things and put them into the world. I'd be working on my artist book at one end of the house and the Pacific Sisters would be having a fundraiser at the other. I found my place there, as it were, in amongst all that amazing productivity, and I chronicled it with my camera. And it's all still here, in in my largely untapped archive. I have carried it around from flat to flat, and now to Wellington. I've taken care of it because I understand its value in all kinds of ways.

A few years after graduating from Elam, Vancouver emerged on the horizon and I arranged to take two years' unpaid leave from my job at MIT. Vancouver is known as the home of conceptual photography, and Giovanni, with whom I was still in regular contact, recommended the University of British Columbia's master's in fine art. So once again I departed Aotearoa, to begin post-graduate study there.

By then Giovanni had moved to Los Angeles and was building a mini cult-hero empire in the art world, helping revive the rundown Chinatown neighbourhood and making it the locus of a contemporary art scene. He had co-founded a gallery called China Art Objects, which became a new focus point for contemporary art, much like Teststrip had years before in Auckland. Artists congregated in Chinatown and other small galleries started to pop up. I'd go down from Vancouver to LA and spend time there, seeing shows, soaking up the amazing art scene and hanging out with Giovanni and my good friend Joyce Campbell, who also lived there then. Devastatingly for me and for our community, Giovanni died unexpectedly in 2002.

I met Duncan Munro in 2006, and he is the amazing gentle, supportive person who has been my partner ever since. I told him about my sexuality from the very start, but he never found that challenging and has always supported my articulation of this part of myself. In late 2006 I was offered a lectureship in photography at Massey University in Wellington. Duncan lived in Auckland, but we soon found a way to move his work here, and in Wellington we remain.

A lot of my work over the last 10 years has been focused on plants. The *jane says* series used still-life style portraits of flowers, herbs and seeds. The plants I photographed have histories of being utilised in ways that we're mostly unaware of now, to control women's fertility or induce abortion. The peaceful domestic rituals of arranging flowers collide with this history of plant knowledge and the political context around the controls society attempts to impose upon women's* bodies.

The co-director of Denny Dimin Gallery in New York, Elizabeth Denny, read a review of these works that were presented as part of my survey exhibition *Dark Matter*, curated by Zara Stanhope for Auckland Art Gallery Toi o Tāmaki, in an international art magazine. She invited me to join a group show in New York. That show went well, and the

---

* 'Women', when used throughout this text, is intended to be inclusive of people on the trans or gender-queer spectrum.

gallery, which is in Tribeca, now represents my work throughout the United States. Having representation with a New York gallery has been a real high point for me; I'm still excited about it now.

I left my job as associate professor at Massey University in 2019 to pursue being a fulltime artist. Academic life is at once rewarding and very demanding, and of course my attention was being pulled in different directions. In a parallel with leaving my job at the *Dominion Post* years earlier, I once again said goodbye to a secure, well-paid job and directed my energies into making art, into taking risks and creating a future that holds integrity for me. A friend of mine, Mark Adams, once said when he was talking about my upbringing in Tīmaru, 'Tīmaru is a fucking weird place, and weird places are the best places to come from, because they give you the petrol.' I'm so grateful for Tīmaru and even for the hard and confronting times: they make us who we are. I wouldn't go back and do it any differently.

Bisexuality is where I've found my resting spot on the sexuality spectrum. That's who I am and it's still important to me. Understanding this and being in that liminal space has made my life rich, and I am in a place now where that diversity continues to inform my world. I may look like a straight old lady to a young 20-year-old, but I am not. That's the trouble with veneers, they hide so much.

My friendships extend far and wide and I love the conversations I have with my younger queer and trans friends about our lives, and where we've arrived at now, politically speaking, in terms of LGBTQIA+ identity, and where they will take us in the future as they carve out the next political breakthrough on this continuum. Occasionally a student would discover *Redeye* in the university library, and I must confess it always made me smile a little when they came into class looking confused, asking, 'Ann — is this you?'

Further reading

This selection of excellent non-fiction books is a useful and inspirational resource.

James Allan, ed. *Growing up Gay: New Zealand men tell their stories*. Auckland: Godwit, 1996.

Mark Beehre. *A Queer Existence: The lives of young gay men in Aotearoa New Zealand*. Auckland: Massey University Press, 2021.

——. *Men Alone—Men Together*. Wellington: Steele Roberts Aotearoa, 2010.

Chris Brickell. *Mates & Lovers: A history of gay New Zealand*. Auckland: Godwit, 2008.

Brent Coutts. *Crossing the Lines: The story of three homosexual New Zealand soldiers in World War II*. Dunedin: Otago University Press, 2020.

Joanne Drayton: *Hudson & Halls: The food of love*. Dunedin: Otago University Press, 2018.

Evan Hazenberg and Miriam Meyerhoff, eds. *Representing Trans: Linguistic, legal and everyday perspectives*. Wellington: Victoria University Press, 2017.

Jessica Hutchings and Clive Aspin, eds. *Sexuality and the Stories of Indigenous People*. Wellington: Huia, 2007.

Witi Ihimaera. *Native Son: The writer's memoir*. Auckland: Penguin Random House, 2019.

Kyle Mewburn. *Faking It: My life in transition*. Auckland: Penguin Random House, 2021.

Lil O'Brien. *Not That I'd Kiss a Girl: A Kiwi girl's tale of coming out and coming of age*. Auckland: Allen & Unwin, 2020.

Liz Roberts and Alison Mau. *First Lady: From boyhood to womanhood*. Auckland: Upstart Press, 2015.

Carmen Rupe and Paul Martin. *Carmen: My life*. Auckland: Benton Ross, 1988.

Peter Wells. *Long Loop Home: A memoir*. Auckland: Penguin, 2012.

A guide to the many outstanding volumes of fiction and poetry by queer New Zealand writers can be found at www.anzliterature.com/feature/why-arent-you-reading-queer

About the author

Matt McEvoy completed a Bachelor of Music degree between Auckland and Otago Universities. Later, a holiday job at an Auckland tech company turned into 10 years of working in communications technology around Europe and finally Qatar, where he joined a small team creating the first outpost of Vodafone in the Middle East. Returning to Auckland, Matt now spreads his time between teaching piano, managing property interests, accepting the occasional local technology contract and writing, with a particular interest in social history and the diverse stories of extraordinary people who are seldom given a voice in New Zealand culture. His first book, *The Grey Lynn Book*, was published in 2018.

MASSEY
UNIVERSITY
PRESS

First published in 2022 by Massey University Press
Private Bag 102904, North Shore Mail Centre
Auckland 0745, New Zealand
www.masseypress.ac.nz

Text design by Kate Barraclough
Cover design by Jo Bailey and Michael Kelly

A catalogue record for this book is available from the National Library of New Zealand

Printed and bound in Singapore by Markono Print Media

ISBN: 978-0-9951229-2-5
eISBN: 978-1-99-901616-4